INTRODUCTION TO
HEALTH CARE LAW

DELMAR CENGAGE Learning

Options.
Over 300 products in every area of the law: textbooks, online courses, CD-ROMs, reference books, companion websites, and more – helping you succeed in the classroom and on the job.

Support.
We offer unparalleled, practical support: robust instructor and student supplements to ensure the best learning experience, custom publishing to meet your unique needs, and other benefits such as Delmar Cengage Learning's Student Achievement Award. And our sales representatives are always ready to provide you with dependable service.

Feedback.
As always, we want to hear from you! Your feedback is our best resource for improving the quality of our products. Contact your sales representative or write us at the address below if you have any comments about our materials or if you have a product proposal.

Accounting and Financials for the Law Office • Administrative Law • Alternative Dispute Resolution • Bankruptcy Business Organizations/Corporations • Careers and Employment • Civil Litigation and Procedure • CLA Exam Preparation • Computer Applications in the Law Office • Constitutional Law • Contract Law • Court Reporting Criminal Law and Procedure • Document Preparation • Elder Law • Employment Law • Environmental Law • Ethics Evidence Law • Family Law • Health Care Law • Immigration Law • Intellectual Property • Internships Interviewing and Investigation • Introduction to Law • Introduction to Paralegalism • Juvenile Law • Law Office Management • Law Office Procedures • Legal Nurse Consulting • Legal Research, Writing, and Analysis • Legal Terminology • Legal Transcription • Media and Entertainment Law • Medical Malpractice Law Product Liability • Real Estate Law • Reference Materials • Social Security • Sports Law • Torts and Personal Injury Law • Wills, Trusts, and Estate Administration • Workers' Compensation Law

---

DELMAR CENGAGE Learning
5 Maxwell Drive
Clifton Park, New York 12065-2919

For additional information, find us online at:
www.delmar.cengage.com

INTRODUCTION TO
HEALTH CARE LAW

JANICE KAZMIER

DELMAR
CENGAGE Learning

Australia • Brazil • Japan • Korea • Mexico • Singapore • Spain • United Kingdom • United States

Health Care Law, First Edition
Janice Kazmier

Vice President, Career and Professional
    Editorial: Dave Garza

Director of Learning Solutions: Sandy Clark

Acquisitions Editor: Shelley Esposito

Managing Editor: Larry Main

Product Manager: Robert Serenka

Editorial Assistant: Lyss Zaza

Vice President, Career and Professional
    Marketing: Jennifer McAvey

Marketing Director: Debbie Yarnell

Marketing Coordinator: Jonathan Sheehan

Production Director: Wendy Troeger

Production Manager: Mark Bernard

Content Project Manager: Steven Couse

Art Director: Joy Kocsis

Technology Project Manager: Tom Smith

Production Technology Analyst: Thomas
    Stover

For product information and technology assistance, contact us at
Professional & Career Group Customer Support, 1-800-648-7450

For permission to use material from this text or product,
submit all requests online at **cengage.com/permissions**.
Further permissions questions can be e-mailed to
permissionrequest@cengage.com.

Library of Congress Control Number: 2008922257

ISBN-13: 978-1-4180-1110-9

ISBN-10: 1-4180-1110-X

Delmar
5 Maxwell Drive
Clifton Park, NY 12065-2919
USA

Cengage Learning products are represented in Canada by Nelson Education, Ltd.

For your lifelong learning solutions, visit **delmar.cengage.com**

Visit our corporate website at **cengage.com.**

Notice to the Reader

Publisher does not warrant or guarantee any of the products described herein or perform any independent analysis in connection with any of the product information contained herein. Publisher does not assume, and expressly disclaims, any obligation to obtain and include information other than that provided to it by the manufacturer. The reader is expressly warned to consider and adopt all safety precautions that might be indicated by the activities described herein and to avoid all potential hazards. By following the instructions contained herein, the reader willingly assumes all risks in connection with such instructions. The reader is notified that this text is an educational tool, not a practice book. Since the law in constant change, no rule or statement of law in this book should be relied upon for any service to any client. The reader should always refer to standard legal sources for the current rule or law. If legal advice or other expert assistance is required, the services of the appropriate professional should be sought. The publisher makes no representations or warranties of any kind, including but not limited to, the warranties of fitness for particular purpose or merchantability, nor are any such representations implied with respect to the material set forth herein, and the publisher takes no responsibility with respect to such material. The publisher shall not be liable for any special, consequential, or exemplary damages resulting, in whole or part, from the readers' use of, or reliance u~ ~~ ~~ ~material.

Printed in the United States of America
1 2 3 4 5 6 7 12 11 10 09 08

For my students—teaching has illuminated my career

CONTENTS

PREFACE

Why should paralegals take a class in health law? A health law survey course can be daunting because students must integrate several traditional subjects of the law—contracts, corporations, torts, and ethics—along with specialized areas such as regulatory compliance, antitrust, and tax law. A health law course conveys a sense of the political, social, economic, and cultural context of health care delivery in the United States today. It allows students to relate to the material in ways that other paralegal classes may not. Who has not had problems with their health insurance? Who has not visited a doctor or a hospital emergency room? Who has not watched news accounts of health-related legal issues such as the right to die?

The health care industry is fertile ground and offers many employment opportunities for paralegals wishing to assist attorneys in traditional law firms, as well as in government, corporate, and academic offices. Numerous statistical studies have projected continued job growth in the health care sector. The complexities of health care regulations and the industry's expansion have created options for educational institutions to offer new courses to students to address the diverse needs of health care organizations.

This text focuses on the major areas of health law that a paralegal is likely to encounter. Many of the subject areas have significant regulatory compliance issues. As with all textbooks, it is not possible to cover all matters. Medical malpractice, antitrust, and tax are outside the scope of this volume. However, the text offers a variety of other timely topics that should be of interest both to students and to teachers.

I would like to extend my thanks to the staffs of Delmar Learning and Tulane University School of Continuing Studies for their enthusiasm for this project. I am also grateful to the faculty and my fellow students in the Health Care Management program at the University of New Orleans. Lastly, I am indebted to family, friends, and colleagues for their patience and support.

New Orleans, LA and Chicago, IL
August 2007   *Janice L. Kazmier*

ACKNOWLEDGMENTS

I would like to acknowledge the reviewers who provided valuable comments and suggestions. They include:

Leonard H. Friedman, PhD, MPH

Associate Professor and Coordinator
Health Management and Policy Programs
Department of Public Health
Oregon State University
Corvallis, Oregon

Hope I. Haywood, MBA, BA

Institute for Law & Public Policy
California University of Pennsylvania
Pittsburgh, Pennsylvania

Eva Irwin, CMA

Ivy Tech State College

Jennifer Jenkins

South College
Knoxville, Tennessee

Mary Marks, MSN, RN, BC, Pbt (ASCP)

Program Coordinator
Medical Assisting and Related Allied Health Programs
Mitchell Community College—Mooresville Center
Mooresville, North Carolina

Michael R. Meacham, JD, MPH

Associate Professor
Department of Health Policy and Administration
Executive Director
Master of Health Administration Program
The Pennsylvania State University
University Park, Pennsylvania

George Moseley

Diane Pevar, JD

Chairperson, Business Division and Director, Legal Studies
Manor College
Jenkintown, Pennsylvania

Jill Bush Raines, JD

University of Oklahoma Health Sciences Center
Oklahoma City, Oklahoma

Arnold J. Rosoff, JD

The Wharton School
University of Pennsylvania
Philadelphia, Pennsylvania

Scott Silvis, Esq.

Business and Information Technologies Chair
Paralegal Studies Program Coordinator
Griffin Technical College
Griffin, Georgia

William I. Weston, JD, PhD

Dean, School of Legal Studies
Kaplan University
Fort Lauderdale, Florida

Melinda Wilkins, MEd, RHIA

Director and Associate Professor
Health Information Management Program
Arkansas Tech University
Russellville, Arkansas

Stacey F. Wilson, MT/PBT (ASCP), CMA

Cabarrus College of Health Sciences
Concord, North Carolina

Many of the definitions in the text are reprinted from *Dictionary of the Law* (3rd ed.) by Daniel Oran. Clifton Park, NY: Delmar/West Legal Studies, 2000.

TABLE OF CASES

TABLE OF CASES

CHAPTER 1

AN INTRODUCTION TO HEALTH CARE DELIVERY

OBJECTIVES

After reading this chapter, students should be able to

- Identify different types of health care organizations and providers who deliver services and items to patients.
- Define terminology used in health care delivery and its financing.
- Identify different types of business organizations used in the health care industry.
- Describe the role of insurance in health care delivery.

HEALTH CARE ORGANIZATIONS AND PROVIDERS

Forty years ago, obtaining **health care** meant going to a doctor's office for routine shots and tests or entering a hospital for an operation, delivery of a baby, or emergency treatment following a car accident. Advances in medicine, population growth, the creation of the Medicare and Medicaid programs, and economic trends have changed health care delivery dramatically. This section of the chapter examines the most common types of **health care organizations** and **health care providers** in an industry that is large, complex, and heavily regulated.

A student whose intent is to work as a paralegal in the general counsel's office of a health care organization or in a health law firm must know about the different segments of the health care industry. The wide variety of settings offers diverse opportunities to develop expertise. For example, acute care hospitals may need legal personnel who understand medical staff credentialing and patient privacy and safety. Health plan insurers may need legal specialists who are familiar with appeal of denied claims as well as state insurance laws. Teaching hospitals may need legal professionals who can comprehend and apply regulations relating to clinical research studies. A health law firm may hire paralegals to assist with administration of physician and managed care contracts. The job of the paralegal working in health care is to know where to look for industry best practices and for the laws and regulations that control different segments of the industry.

The health care industry has a language all its own, full of jargon and legalese that may be perplexing to novices. In addition to this chapter, you may also consult the glossary at the end of the book and the Acronyms list in Appendix A to familiarize yourself with health care's particular language. Appendix B shows helpful websites for health care and health law.

Hospitals

In general, hospitals can be categorized as community, governmental, part of a system, or ambulatory, outpatient services.

Community In 2005, the **American Hospital Association's (AHA)** annual survey counted 4,936 community hospitals in the United States.[1] The largest group of these is nongovernmental, not-for-profit hospitals. The AHA defines community hospitals broadly to include all nonfederal, short-term general, and specialty hospitals. "Excluded are

ACRONYM

AHA: American Hospital Association

hospitals not accessible by the general public, such as prison hospitals or college infirmaries."[2]

General hospitals are the ones most of us are familiar with. They are set up to treat a full range of medical conditions. General hospitals are not always able to offer the latest specialized treatments for every disease or disorder, but are usually equipped to treat common health care situations such as delivering babies, setting broken bones, and treating severe cases of influenza.

Teaching hospitals are also considered community hospitals but have a variety of goals besides health care delivery. In addition to treating patients, teaching hospitals are training sites for future physicians and other health care professionals. They may also engage in clinical research, often asking their patients for permission to enroll them in clinical studies on disease progression and new treatments. Teaching institutions are almost always affiliated with a medical school or with an academic medical center, which means patients have access to highly skilled specialists who teach at the school and are familiar with up-to-the-minute technology and the latest scientific data.

Specialty hospitals are included in the AHA's definition of community hospitals. These hospitals may be devoted exclusively to specific health care areas such as obstetrics and gynecology; eye, ear, nose, and throat; rehabilitation; psychiatry; cancer; and cardiac care.

SPOTLIGHT ON... SPECIALTY HOSPITALS

The Medicare Prescription Drug, Improvement, and Modernization Act of 2003[3] imposed an 18-month moratorium, from April 2003 until June 2005, on physician investment in specialty hospitals. The Centers of Medicare and Medicaid Services later extended this moratorium.[4] What the moratorium means is that physicians may not refer their patients to specialty hospitals in which they have an ownership interest.

ACRONYMS

CPG: Compliance Program Guidance

DHHS: Department of Health and Human Services

OIG: Office of Inspector General

All types of hospitals pose numerous compliance challenges, many of which we discuss in this book. The **Office of the Inspector General (OIG)** of the **Department of Health and Human Services (DHHS)** has issued a special **Compliance Program Guidance (CPG)** for the hospital segment of the health care industry to address potential risks.[5]

Governmental Governmental hospitals are local, state, and federal institutions that are supported by taxpayers. According to the 2005 AHA Annual Survey, there are 226 federal government hospitals.[6] Many states and local governments also sponsor hospital services. As of 2005, there were approximately 1,110 hospitals in this category.[7]

Governments may set eligibility criteria for patients who wish to use the hospitals. For example, all veterans of military service are potentially eligible to receive medical, surgical, and rehabilitative care at the **Veterans Health Administration (VHA)** Medical Centers, sponsored by the federal government. The VHA Medical Centers are the most easily identified type of governmental hospital.

Systems A hospital can be part of a multi-hospital system that consists of two or more hospitals that are owned, leased, sponsored, or managed by a central organization. In today's competitive health care industry, multi-hospital systems or "chains," such as Tenet Healthcare, Inc. and Hospital Corporation of America, Inc., are the norm rather than the exception. Hospital systems raise compliance issues in the areas of antitrust and fraud and abuse.

A system may also be affiliated with a network—a group of hospitals, physicians, other health care providers, and insurers that coordinate and deliver a broad spectrum of services to their community.

Ambulatory, Outpatient Services Hospitals routinely treat patients on an outpatient basis for non-acute medical problems. Outpatient clinics may be freestanding or may be housed in the hospital. For example, hospitals often have obstetrics clinics that treat pregnant women prior to labor and delivery as well as maternal and child health clinics for follow-up after birth.

For Medicare and Medicaid patients, outpatient services include three general areas: psychiatric services and partial hospitalization; observation services; and outpatient services that are linked to inpatient hospital stays. All of these areas pose compliance risks, which are discussed in Chapter 5.

Ambulatory Surgical Centers

Advances in medicine and rethinking of recovery times have lead to the use of **ambulatory surgical centers (ASCs)** for many routine operations. An ambulatory surgical center is a self-contained facility that provides outpatient surgical services. Many ambulatory surgical

ACRONYM

VHA: Veterans Health Administration

ACRONYM

ASC: ambulatory surgical centers

centers are freestanding facilities, while others are dedicated sections of existing hospitals. Hospitals face competition from independently owned ASCs and may wish to invest only in those to which they can refer patients. Investment activities may trigger compliance concerns under federal law, including anti-kickback laws,[8] which may be triggered by referrals, and the Stark regulations,[9] which govern financial relationships. These laws are discussed in Chapter 6.

Academic Medical Centers

An **academic medical center (AMC)** or academic health center educates health professionals, conducts biomedical and health services research, and delivers patient care through its schools, clinics, and teaching hospitals. The Association of Academic Health Centers has over 101 members whose organizational structure varies by institution. Some are components of public or private universities or state university systems. All centers that are members include a school of medicine, at least one other health professional school or program, and at least one affiliated teaching hospital.[10]

Because academic medical centers are engaged in a variety of enterprises, compliance risks may be high and duties may be onerous. AMCs that engage in clinical research have additional regulatory burdens that give rise to compliance-related programs such as institutional review boards and research conflict-of-interest committees. Some AMCs have divided compliance tasks into two broad areas—health care delivery and research—because the oversight duties would be too numerous for one compliance officer.

Physician Practices and Networks[11]

Two forms of physician practice organizations are the physician–hospital organization and the independent practice or physician association.

Physician Hospital Organizations The term *physician–hospital organization* **(PHO)** denotes a business arrangement entered into and/or a legal entity formed by a hospital and its medical staff. If a legal entity is created, it may be owned jointly by the hospital and its physicians. A PHO is formed primarily to establish contracts with large employers or managed care health plans. Sometimes, a PHO allows only **primary care physicians (PCP)** to be owners or partners. It then contracts with specialists and ancillary providers for services and items that the PCP does not offer.

Managed-care organizations like PHOs because a master contract with a PHO eliminates the need for multiple contracts with individual physicians. Employers like to contract with PHOs to provide benefits for employees because they offer better rates for health coverage along with a variety of services: hospitalization, primary care, and specialty referrals.

ACRONYM

IPA: independent practice or physician association

Independent Practice or Physician Associations An **independent practice or physician association (IPA)** is a group of unaffiliated doctors who join together to create an organization. This improves efficiency when contracting with managed care insurers. The doctors may be solo practitioners or members of small practices. The legal structure of an IPA may be a corporation, a limited partnership, or any other type of legal entity authorized under state law. Managed-care insurers like contracting with IPAs because they can access a large pool of doctors in different specialties, but they do not need to contract with each individual doctor. Some IPAs also perform administrative functions such as billing and collections and utilization review.

From the patient's perspective, being able to access physician services from a large group gives the patient some freedom of choice and eliminates the need to shop around for specialists. Patients often experience fewer paperwork headaches when they deal with IPAs that perform administrative functions such as claims processing. Attorneys structuring new IPAs must review antitrust laws to avoid allegations of price-fixing and monopolization. Because of the ease of referrals among doctors in an IPA, legal and health care compliance professionals must also pay attention to federal anti-kickback laws[12] and Stark regulations.[13] Besides federal health care law, any state law limitations on physician practices must also be considered.

ACRONYM

IDS: integrated delivery system

Integrated Delivery Systems[14]

Integrated delivery systems (IDS) have gained prominence in the health care industry in the last two decades. Different health care providers band together under one corporate umbrella or structure to form an IDS. Integrated delivery systems can vary; there is no one correct model.

The goal of an integrated delivery system is to provide all of the services that a particular patient may require. For example, an IDS may own a physician practice, a hospital, a home health agency, a durable medical equipment supplier, and a nursing home. A doctor in the physician practice may treat a patient and refer her or him to the hospital for an operation. Upon discharge, the patient may need in-home assistance offered by a home health agency or may need a wheelchair from the durable medical equipment supplier. Eventually, a patient may need to enter a nursing home or long-term care facility for around-the-clock care. With this model of an IDS, the patient has the benefit of "one-stop shopping" for health care services. Depending on how well the IDS is run, the patient may also benefit from this coordination of care.

Integrated delivery systems offer the parent company the usual benefits of incorporation: corporate rather than personal liability; increased profits because of standardized or centralized administration; economies of scale; and leverage to negotiate contracts with payers and vendors for favorable rates and terms. An IDS may also have a large supply of capital or other liquid assets that can provide a financial cushion for delayed reimbursement, shifts in patients and their service needs, and increased competition.

Integrated delivery systems pose interesting legal challenges. Health care attorneys advising clients who are establishing new integrated delivery systems must ensure that antitrust laws are not violated. Other areas that impact IDSs are fraud and abuse laws, such as the federal anti-kickback prohibition in the Social Security Act[15] and prohibited financial relationships that are in the Stark regulations.[16] Tax laws and state corporate and licensing laws need to be reviewed prior to the establishment of an integrated delivery system to avoid potentially negative consequences.

Other Providers

The number of health care providers sometimes seems limitless. As advances in medicine and technology are made, new providers emerge to deliver items and services to patients. Described below are a few of the most common of these, not all of which may come to mind when you think of health care.

Ambulance Companies[17] Services provided by emergency medical technicians during the course of transporting a patient to a hospital are often critical to a patient's future well-being. But abusive practices, such as mileage inflation or billing for advanced life support when only basic services have been provided, have caused the OIG to issue a special compliance program guidance[18] to these providers.

Durable Medical Equipment Suppliers[19] Companies that provide wheelchairs, oxygen tanks, prosthetics, orthotics, and some medical supplies are referred to as durable medical equipment suppliers. **Durable medical equipment (DME)** is prescribed by a doctor to serve a medical purpose. It can withstand repeated abuse and is appropriate for use in the home. Like ambulance companies, DME suppliers have been targeted by the OIG for specific compliance advice.[20] Some potential compliance risks include false physician certifications, unlicensed distribution of drugs, and excessive billing for delivery or maintenance of equipment.

Home Health Agencies[21] Home health care allows individuals to stay out of institutions such as nursing homes and receive needed medical services at their homes. These services include skilled nursing, home health aides, physical and occupational therapy, speech pathology, medical supplies (other than drugs and biologics), durable medical equipment, and medical social services.

Home health care costs less than providing services in a hospital or nursing home. The industry grew rapidly during the 1990s and fraudulent activities became a concern. In response, the federal government changed its payment system under Medicare from a cost-based one to a prospective payment system to cut down on abusive billing practices.

In 1995, the OIG issued a Special Fraud Alert regarding referral practices between physicians and home health agencies.[22] Later, the OIG issued a CPG for the home health industry.[23]

SPOTLIGHT ON...

Amedysis, Inc. was one of the home health agencies that nearly went bankrupt when Medicare changed its payment methodology. Instead, it began to acquire other agencies that were exiting the home health business, learned how to trim expenses, and became a profitable company, now traded on the NASDAQ.

Long-Term Care, Nursing Homes, and Hospice Care Long-term care refers to a continuum of health care and maintenance services, from retirement home to assisted living to nursing home and, perhaps, to hospice care. A long-term care facility may be a single building with different floors devoted to different levels of care or may be a "campus." Residents often enter long-term care facilities when they are still healthy, choosing to live independently in retirement apartments or homes. As their needs change, residents may need the assistance of home health services or the more skilled services of nursing homes or hospice care. When a long-term care facility encompasses all of these areas, residents can enjoy a continuum of care without leaving the facility.

Nursing homes are institutions for residents who need round-the-clock care. They can be either **skilled nursing facilities (SNFs)** or general nursing facilities. A SNF covers nursing home stays of limited duration, usually following a patient's discharge from the hospital. A general nursing facility serves residents who need long-term, custodial care. Nursing homes are subject to state laws in addition to Medicare and Medicaid regulations. Some of the potential risk areas that legal professionals need to be aware of are quality of care, residents' rights, billing practices, and employee screening.[24] Nursing home abuses, such as inadequate clinical care and decrepit physical facilities, prompted the OIG to issue specific compliance guidance for nursing homes.[25]

ACRONYM

SNF: skilled nursing facility

SPOTLIGHT ON...

Medicare.gov, the official government site for people with Medicare, provides data on nursing home characteristics, quality measures, inspection results, and nursing staff information for licensed nursing homes in the United States.

Hospice care often is provided in connection with or as a substitute for nursing home care when a patient's illness is terminal. Hospice care focuses on relief from pain and suffering, rather than on elimination of illness or disease. It also assists relatives and friends with acceptance of a patient's impending death. It may be difficult to believe that fraud and abuse occurs in the practice of something so sensitive. However, the OIG issued a CPG specifically for compliance issues involving hospice providers.[26]

TYPES OF BUSINESS ORGANIZATIONS

Paralegal students may already be familiar with the different kinds of legal entities that reflect ownership structure. This section provides a brief review of business organizations for those who may not be acquainted with these concepts.

Like any business, every health care organization and provider has an ownership structure. The following subsections describe the most common types of business organizations.

Proprietorships

A proprietorship is a business owned by one individual. Proprietorships are easy to form. The proprietor—for example, a physician—simply needs to begin business operations. There are few governmental regulations and no corporate income tax. Proprietorships may be subject to state or city licensing laws, however. Despite the freedom and autonomy associated with opening up one's own shop, there are disadvantages to proprietorships. All income is considered personal and is taxed on the proprietor's tax return. The life of the proprietorship is limited to the life of the proprietor; when he or she retires or dies, the business entity is finished. The proprietor is also personally liable for all torts associated with the business, though professional malpractice and errors and omissions insurance may offer some protection.

Corporations

Larger health care organizations typically form *corporations*, legal entities that are separate and distinct from their owners (shareholders) and managers. There are several advantages to forming a corporation.

First, corporations usually have perpetual existence. Corporations may stay in business indefinitely, or as long as their success allows.

Second, transferring ownership is easier than transferring ownership of other types of business organizations. Shareholders generally may sell their stock when they no longer want to be a part of the business.

Third, personal liability of each owner is limited to the amount that he or she has invested.

Lastly, corporations also have the advantage of being able to raise needed capital for operations; unincorporated businesses like proprietorships have a much more difficult time in raising or borrowing money.

Despite these benefits, corporations have disadvantages as well.

First, corporations are subject to double taxation. Corporate earnings are taxed as income of the corporation and as personal income of the owners (when paid out in the form of shareholder dividends or realized as capital gains).

Next, corporations can be costly and time consuming to set up. Drafting charters, articles of incorporation, and by-laws calls for legal expertise in transactional matters and knowledge of state corporate law. Financial expertise in bookkeeping and tax matters is also needed. Officers and board members who will serve the corporation's mission and guide the organization's management must be chosen.

Not-For-Profit As the earlier section of this chapter pointed out, most hospitals (and many other health care organizations) are established as not-for-profit entities. Not-for-profits do not issue stock, nor do they have shareholders. They rely on grants and donations for start-up costs. They are governed by a board of directors who hire and oversee management.

Not-for-profits have advantages that for-profit corporations do not possess, mainly in the area of taxation. Not-for-profits are exempt from income and property taxation if they meet the **Internal Revenue Service's (IRS's)** criteria and are engaged in a charitable purpose. The promotion of health care is considered a charitable purpose.

Not-for-profits enjoy other advantages, such as the ability to raise capital through the issuance of municipal bonds and to accept charitable donations from individuals, other corporations, and foundations.

The law poses restrictions on not-for-profits that for-profit corporations do not share. First, no profits can be used for personal gain or private inurement, although managers of not-for-profit health care organizations are paid competitive salaries and enjoy additional perks. Second, political activity is banned. Third, in the event that a not-for-profit ceases business operations or declares bankruptcy, all assets must be liquidated and used for another charitable purpose. Finally, fulfillment of its charitable mission of health care promotion must be taken seriously or the not-for-profit may fall under the scrutiny of the IRS.

Examples of not-for-profit entities include private hospitals, some health plan insurers, and faculty practice plans at academic medical centers.

ACRONYM

IRS: Internal Revenue Service

SPOTLIGHT ON... HEALTH CARE EXECUTIVES

In 2004, the IRS announced its executive compensation enforcement initiative, which focused on excessive compensation for officers and other general compliance areas. About 2,000 not-for-profit organizations were targeted, some of which were health care organizations.[27] Some state attorneys general have also pursued allegations of excessive executive compensation against not-for-profits such as Health Midwest and HealthPartners.

For Profit For-profit corporations exist to maximize the wealth of their shareholders. Shareholders get annual reports on profitability and certain shareholders have voting rights on management's major decisions.

For-profit corporations are increasing in the health care industry. Though significantly few hospitals are for-profits, these are often part of chains such as Tenet Healthcare or Hospital Corporation of America. Other for-profit health care corporations include many of the different health care organizations and providers mentioned in this chapter.

Other Types

Limited partnerships, limited liability partnerships, limited liability companies, and professional corporations are other types of entities in the health care industry. State law dictates the requirements for formation of each type.

Of these, the professional corporation is the one most commonly seen in health care. Using this structure, a doctor may incorporate his or her practice to limit personal liability.

HEALTH INSURANCE PLANS

This section examines the financing of health care costs, primarily through health plan insurance. The U.S. health care system is one of free enterprise, which, of course, comes with a price. In today's market, the price for professional medical services can be quite steep. Health care expenditures in the United States went up 88 percent from 1992 to 2002 and, at nearly $1.9 trillion in 2004, were more than two and a half times the $717 billion spent in 1990. National health care expenditures in 2004 represented approximately 16 percent of our gross domestic product, meaning that health care is a significant product in the U.S.[28]

How is the American public paying for these needed services? About 62 percent of Americans have employer-based health insurance. Nearly 18 percent are uninsured, while the rest depend on private or government insurance.[29] The poor and the elderly are disproportionately represented among the uninsured and underinsured.

Enrollment in a health insurance plan affects people's access to health care, their health status, their job decisions, and their financial security. Those without health insurance or who have limited benefit plans often find themselves "doing without" or in financial straits when they are unable to pay for the high costs of medical care. Though hospitals are required by law to provide "charity care," uncompensated care to uninsured and underinsured individuals and the public safety net of hospitals and community clinics do not fully substitute for health insurance.[30]

The "Blues"

The Great Depression of 1929 forced the U.S. to look at social welfare issues for its citizens. During this dark economic period in American history, Dr. Justin Ford Kimball, an administrator at Baylor University in Texas, had an idea that became the genesis of modern health insurance. As an administrator, Dr. Kimball noticed that many unpaid accounts receivable belonged to Dallas-area schoolteachers. Recognizing that most of these low-paid teachers would never be able to pay their bills, he initiated the not-for-profit Baylor Plan, which allowed teachers to pay 50 cents a month into a fund that guaranteed up to 21 days of hospital care at Baylor Hospital. The Baylor Plan sparked interest in hospitals and employers across the country, and they strove to set up similar plans. These eventually merged into what is now known as Blue Cross. Soon afterwards, state medical societies began offering coverage for physician services under what became known as Blue Shield.

Today, Blue Cross Blue Shield (referred to as "the Blues" in the health care industry) offers a variety of health insurance plans including traditional indemnity contracts and different types of managed care products.

Types of Insurance Plans

The Blues were only the beginnings of the health insurance industry. Today, consumers have a variety of health plans from which to choose. These generally fall into the categories of governmental, employer-provided, or private plans.

Governmental health insurance plans include Medicare, Medicaid, TRICARE, and CHAMPVA. Eligibility for participation in Medicare is generally limited to those of retirement age, but is subject to some exceptions. Medicaid is a state-run plan for participants of limited economic means. Since the federal government provides some matching funds, states must follow federal requirements. TRICARE is a federal health insurance program for military personnel, their dependents, and retirees. CHAMPVA is a federal health insurance program for disabled veterans and their dependents.

Employer-sponsored health insurance represents a large segment of the health insurance industry. Employers usually offer a variety of group health insurance plans to their employees, including traditional indemnity plans and several types of managed care policies. The same types of plans are available to private individuals, though usually at a higher cost than group health insurance plans.

Greater details about health insurance plans can be found in Chapter 2.

SUMMARY

In this chapter, we covered three basic areas of health care delivery:

- organizations and providers of health care services and items
- types of legal/business entities that these organizations form
- financing of health care services and items through different types of insurance plans

Organizations and providers are numerous and reflect different segments of the health care industry. Many are highly specialized, evidencing the scientific and technological advances in medicine. The provision of health care is costly and practically guarantees fraud and abuse. The OIG has singled out industry segments for compliance program guidance.

Business entities vary according to size and the organization's needs and purpose. Though sole proprietorships offer autonomy and ease of establishment, most organizations choose more formalized legal structures. Federal taxation and state law must be considered when forming a legal entity. Entities may be for-profit or not-for-profit. If an organization has a charitable mission, it may be organized as a not-for-profit corporation, the predominant structure in health care.

Financing of or payment for health care services and items is primarily done through different kinds of insurance products. Attention to social welfare issues led to the development of insurance plans for most segments of the U.S. population. These plans fall into the general categories of governmental insurance, employer-sponsored group plans, and individual insurance plans.

KEY TERMS

health care: Care, services, or supplies related to the health of an individual; may include diagnostic, preventative, rehabilitative, maintenance, or palliative care, and counseling, service assessment, or procedures with respect to the physical or mental condition, or functional status, of an individual, or that affect the structure or function of the body.

health care organization: A business or legal entity with a formalized structure whose primary enterprise is delivery of health care items or services. Examples include hospitals and physician networks.

health care provider: A person or organization who provides medical or health services for which payment may be billed and reimbursed. Examples include physicians and hospice facilities. Health care providers may also be health care organizations.

REVIEW QUESTIONS AND EXERCISES

1. What is the difference between a community hospital and a specialty hospital? Give characteristics of each.

2. Research the number and types of hospitals in your city. Does your city have at least one of each type that was explained in the chapter? How many of the hospitals are organized as for-profit corporations?

3. What types of supplies does a durable medical equipment company provide?

4. What advantages can you see for an integrated delivery system? Would the advantages benefit the company or the consumer? Are there any legal risks?

5. What are the advantages of a health care organization that is set up as a corporation?

6. What are the disadvantages of a not-for-profit corporation?

7. Check with the human resources department of your employer to see what types of health insurance plans are available. See if the department keeps statistics on the number of employees covered under each type of plan. Which is the most popular?

8. What are the different governmental health care programs? Who is eligible for each?

ENDNOTES

1. "Fast Facts on U.S. Hospitals," *AHA Hospital Statistics*, American Hospital Association, http://www.aha.org, accessed June 21, 2007.

2. Id.

3. 42 C.F.R. § 411, P.L. 108–173.

4. "Specialty Hospital Issues," available at http://www.cms.hhs.gov, accessed August 8, 2007.

5. OIG Compliance Program Guidance for Hospitals, 63 Fed. Reg. 8987 (Feb. 23, 1998) and Supplemental Compliance Program Guidance for Hospitals (January 27, 2005).

6. "Fast Facts on U.S. Hospitals," *AHA Hospital Statistics*, American Hospital Association, http://www.aha.org, accessed June 21, 2007.

7. Id.

8. Social Security Act § 1128B(b); 42 U.S.C. § 1320a-7b(b).

9. 42 U.S.C. § 1395nn.

10. "AHC Members," http://www.aahcdc.org/, accessed June 21, 2007.

11. See generally, Daniels, Anthea, "Healthcare Transactions and Contracting," Fundamentals of Health Law (3d ed.), American Health Lawyers Association, 2004.

12. Social Security Act § 1128B(b); 42 U.S.C. § 1320a-7b(b).

13. 42 U.S.C. § 1395nn.

14. See generally, Daniels, Anthea, "Healthcare Transactions and Contracting," Fundamentals of Health Law (3d ed.), American Health Lawyers Association, 2004.

15. Social Security Act § 1128B(b); 42 U.S.C. § 1320a-7b(b).

16. 42 U.S.C. § 1395nn.

17. See generally "Ambulance Services," Health Care Program Compliance Guide, Bureau of National Affairs, 2004.

18. OIG Compliance Program Guidance for Ambulance Suppliers, 68 Fed. Reg. 14245 (March 24, 2003).

19. See generally, "Durable Medical Equipment," <u>Health Care Program Compliance Guide</u>, Bureau of National Affairs, 2003.

20. OIG Compliance Program Guidance for the Durable Medical Equipment, Prosthetics, Orthotics and Supply Industry, 64 Fed. Reg. 36368 (July 6, 1999).

21. See generally, "Home Health Agencies," <u>Health Care Program Compliance Guide</u>, Bureau of National Affairs, 2002.

22. OIG Special Fraud Alert: Home Health Fraud, Fraud and Abuse in the Provision of Medical Supplies to Nursing Facilities, 60 Fed. Reg. 40847 (Aug. 10, 1995).

23. OIG Compliance Program Guidance for Home Health Agencies, 63 Fed. Reg. 42410 (Aug. 8, 1998).

24. See generally, "Nursing Homes," <u>Health Care Program Compliance Guide</u>, Bureau of National Affairs, 2004.

25. OIG Compliance Guidance for Nursing Facilities, 65 Fed. Reg. 14293 (March 16, 2000).

26. OIG Compliance Program Guidance for Hospices, 64 Fed. Reg. 54031 (Oct. 5, 1999).

27. IR-2004-106, August 10, 2004.

28. "Trends and Indicators in the Changing Health Care Marketplace," Healthcare Marketplace Project, Henry J. Kaiser Family Foundation, updated 2/8/06, <u>http://www.kff.org/insurance</u>, accessed June 21, 2007.

29. <u>Id.</u>

30. <u>Id.</u>

CHAPTER 2

STATE AND FEDERAL ROLES IN THE REGULATION OF HEALTH CARE

OBJECTIVES

After reading this chapter, students should be able to

- Discuss the overlapping roles of federal and state authorities in health care.
- Identify legal issues facing hospitals and insurers.
- Research regulations and laws that affect hospitals and insurers.

STATE AND FEDERAL AUTHORITY

State and federal authority over health care providers and organizations often overlaps. In this chapter, we will look at laws and regulations covering hospitals and insurance. These topics are or should be of interest to legal professionals, investors, patients, and consumers.

Health care professionals often work in hospitals, which bill insurance companies for their services. But state and federal authority over health care reaches beyond the regulation of hospitals and insurance to involve other health-care–related regulatory issues. Here are some examples:

State laws control the licensing of health care professionals such as physicians. But disciplinary procedures for the medical staff who work in hospitals are also subject to federal laws such as the Health Care Quality Improvement Act of 1996.[1]

Contracts between doctors and hospitals are subject to federal anti-fraud and anti-kickback regulations, and may also be subject to state anti-fraud and anti-kickback laws. Clinical research on human subjects that is directed by physicians at teaching hospitals must follow federal regulations, though states may have laws that offer greater protection to subjects. Payment for treatment in clinical research programs is often subject to state insurance laws on permissible and impermissible reimbursement.

Physicians who evaluate patients presenting at hospitals in emergency situations must follow the federal Emergency Medical Treatment and Labor Act and its state equivalents.

Finally, many hospitals and insurers are part of larger entities or health systems that offer a variety of health care services and products. Health systems often operate in more than one state. Competition among hospitals and insurers may be affected by the dominance of a particular health system, thus invoking federal antitrust laws.

REGULATION OF HOSPITALS

Hospital operation is a complex business. Chapter 1 describes a number of different types of hospitals, such as acute care, community, specialty, not-for-profit, and for-profit. This section focuses on the state regulatory environment and hospital accreditation.

All states regulate the operation of hospitals because of their interest in protecting the public. Since operating hospitals is expensive, most acute care hospitals participate in federal government funding programs to deflect costs. But federal government programs always come with strings attached in the form of administrative regulations. Hospitals must balance the costs of providing health care services against the expected reimbursement from federal programs and private insurers.

Obtaining a license to operate a hospital usually involves filing an application with the appropriate state authority or agency, such as a department of health. Let's take a look at Louisiana's law on hospital licensing, which mandates that applications be filed with the Department of Health and Hospitals:

A. An application for a license shall be made to the department on forms provided by it and shall contain such information as the department reasonably requires, which may include affirmative evidence of ability to comply with such reasonable standards, rules, and regulations as are lawfully prescribed hereunder and information required for health planning pursuant to R.S. 36:256(B). Additional information required by the licensing agency or for health planning shall be supplied on supplemental forms as needed.

B. As a condition of licensure, the department may require hospitals to provide certain information including but not limited to financial, demographic, and census information. The department shall promulgate rules to implement this Subsection in accordance with the Administrative Procedure Act. Such information shall be shared with the Louisiana Hospital Association, which shall be subject to the same confidentiality requirements provided for in this Subpart.[2]

The application generally involves a description of the type of hospital proposed, the extent of medical services offered, and the number of in-patient beds available. Many states require new hospitals to obtain a Certificate of Need, which is discussed later in this chapter. Hospitals must also provide proof of patient safety standards as well as systems for reporting medical errors.

Patient Safety

The Patient Safety and Quality Improvement Act[3] signifies the federal government's commitment to patient safety. It creates Patient Safety Organizations to collect, aggregate, and analyze patient safety event information that is reported confidentially by health care providers. Analysis enables providers to identify patterns of failures and address measures to eliminate patient safety risks and hazards. Patient safety event reports prepared pursuant to the Act cannot be used in medical malpractice cases or in disciplinary proceedings. The Act includes provisions for monetary penalties for violations of confidentiality or privilege protections. The Director of the Office of Civil Rights for the Department of Health and Human Services has the authority to issue subpoenas in investigations of alleged violations of the Patient Safety and Quality Improvement Act of 2005.

States, too, have an interest in protecting their citizens from harm when they receive hospital care. Typical state laws governing patient safety in hospitals focus on reducing patient infection rates and the proper use of patient physical restraints to avoid injury.

Upward trends in hospital infection rates, particularly in inner-city hospitals, have led many state regulatory bodies to pass and enforce regulations aimed at reducing those rates. These may include requirements for sterilization and cleaning of facilities and medical equipment and mandatory reporting of particular infections in hospitals (e.g., tuberculosis) to limit the spread of disease.

Physical restraints are often used on patients with mental conditions for protection of themselves and the hospital's staff. Care must be exercised when using restraints to avoid injury. Many incidents of injury and some deaths have been attributed to the type of restraint used, duration of the use of the restraint, and the manner and monitoring of the restraint's use. Therefore, state regulations may be stringent in this area.

States may also regulate other patient safety issues such as the types and modalities of treatment available and the standard of care expected from health care practitioners when administering those treatments. Occupational health and safety regulations dictate standards for physical safety on the hospital's premises. Hospitals may also be subject to other state laws governing topics such as laboratory safety, elevator equipment, and standards for food preparation.

Certificates of Need

ACRONYM

CON: Certificate of Need

How many hospitals does a community need? Several states regulate the construction of new hospitals and the acquisition of existing hospitals under **Certificate of Need (CON)** statutes. These laws were passed in conformity with federal health planning initiatives, which have now ended. Certificate of Need laws generally limit: (1) construction of new hospitals, (2) the number of beds allowed, (3) sale or transfer of ownership, and (4) the closure of existing hospitals without state approval.

An examination of state CON criteria can be found in *St Dominic-Jackson Memorial Hospital v. Mississippi State Department of Health*.[4] The text of this case can be found in the Online Companion that accompanies this text.

The Mississippi CON statute states:

> Mississippi's health planning and health regulatory activities have the following purposes: (1) to prevent unnecessary duplication of health resources; (2) to provide cost containment; (3) to improve the health of Mississippi residents; and (4) to increase the accessibility, acceptability, continuity, and quality of health services.[5]

State CON laws are intended to protect the public from unnecessary hospital services that could increase hospital costs. They also are intended to level the competitive playing field among hospital providers. Health care lawyers who represent individuals or entities that are hospital operators need to be aware of any state CON statutes when advising clients regarding hospital licenses.

Conditions of Participation

Any hospital that participates in the federal Medicare program must adhere to Conditions of Participation regulations[6] of the **Centers for Medicare & Medicaid Services (CMS)**. Regulations on **CoPs** are the minimum health and safety standards that providers and suppliers must meet in order to be Medicare and Medicaid certified. These address such subjects as nursing services, quality assessment, anesthesia, pharmaceutical services, discharge planning, and many other areas. Conditions of Participation also give CMS the authority to make site visits to hospitals for compliance purposes. For more details on CoPs, please refer to Chapter 5.

ACRONYMS

CMS: Centers for Medicare & Medicaid Services

CoP: Conditions of Participation

Accreditation

The Medicare program requires participating hospitals to provide quality care to patients. In order to assure quality, Medicare has a program to inspect hospitals. The process is lengthy, costly, and burdensome. Hence, most hospitals opt to purchase an inspection from an **accrediting** organization that Medicare recognizes. The inspection involves not only a physical site visit, but also an examination of the hospital's policies and procedures and an assessment of the number and qualifications of hospital personnel. The primary accrediting organization for hospitals is the Joint Commission, formerly known as the Joint Commission on Accreditation of Healthcare Organizations. Its accreditation is a nationwide seal of approval that indicates a hospital meets high performance standards.

The process of hospital accreditation is a lengthy one and involves significant preparation time before the Joint Commission actually makes its on-site survey. The Joint Commission recommends that a hospital know and implement its accreditation standards (available in the *Comprehensive Accreditation Manual for Hospitals*) prior to the on-site survey. The standards cover every conceivable subject, including but not limited to patient safety, medical records management, medication management, patient rights, conflict management, leadership, health care staffing levels, and sentinel or unexpected events.

The Joint Commission surveys most of its member hospitals every 3 years, though it may also make unannounced site visits. A hospital may spend considerable time, effort, and money to get ready for this survey by looking closely at its performance improvement efforts and measuring the results to find out if they meet survey requirements. However, some hospitals may return to "business as usual" once the survey is over and may reduce focus on performance improvement, which, unfortunately, may not be in a hospital's best interest.

Accreditation by the Joint Commission gives a hospital "deemed" status for Medicare's Conditions of Participation, meaning that the hospital is deemed to be compliant with Medicare regulations.

REGULATION OF INSURANCE

Hospitals receive the majority of their revenue from insurance. In this section, we will examine the extent of state regulatory authority of private health insurance plans and the limitations the federal government has placed on state authority through other federal laws and regulations.

Basis of State Authority

The primary state authority to regulate the business of insurance is derived from the McCarran-Ferguson Act of 1945.[7] This act specifically exempts the business of insurance from federal antitrust regulations to the extent that states regulate insurance. Though the McCarran-Ferguson Act continues to be the foundation of state regulatory authority in insurance, other subsequent laws have eroded some state power. For example, the **Employment Retirement Income Security Act (ERISA)**,[8] the **Health Insurance Portability and Accountability Act (HIPAA)**,[9] and the **Consolidated Omnibus Budget Reconciliation Act (COBRA)**[10] placed limitations on state authority. These statutes are discussed later in this chapter. The **Gramm-Leach-Bliley Act (GLB)**[11] affected the financial services industry, but also affected the rights of states to regulate insurance. It prohibits states from: (1) preventing or restricting a bank from owning or affiliating with an insurance company, and (2) preventing or interfering with the ability of a bank to engage directly, or in conjunction with others, in insurance sales, soliciting, or cross-marketing. However, states still retain the power to require banks to adhere to consumer protection laws on insurance sales.

ACRONYMS

COBRA: Consolidated Omnibus Budget Reconciliation Act

ERISA: Employment Retirement Income Security Act

GLB: Gramm-Leach-Bliley Act

HIPAA: Health Insurance Portability and Accountability Act

Insurance Contracts

What do we mean by the "business of insurance"? Though the McCarran-Ferguson Act does not define the term, most states provide a statutory definition of insurance as a contract or policy under which one party undertakes on behalf of another to **indemnify** against certain expenses, or pay certain costs, upon the occurrence of certain events. An insurance contract involves five factors: (1) the existence of an **insured** with an **insurable interest**, (2) the insured's interest is subject to a risk of loss upon the occurrence of some specified peril or event, (3) the **insurer** assumes the risk of loss, (4) the assumption of risk is part of a scheme to distribute losses among the group of insureds with similar losses, and (5) the insured pays a **premium** as **consideration** for the insurer's promise to pay.[12]

In other words, an insurance policy covers shifting of risk from an insured to an insurer, for the payment of a fee by the insured to the insurer, when pooling of the payments from the policyholders spreads the risk among them.

In *Union Labor Life Insurance Co. v. Pireno*,[13] the U.S. Supreme Court discussed what elements were necessary to determine whether an activity involved the business of insurance. These were: (1) whether the practice involved the transfer or spreading of risk of policyholders, (2) whether the practice was an integral part of the policy relationship between the insurer and the insured, and (3) whether the practice was limited to entities within the insurance industry. Later cases have affirmed these criteria and they are frequently referred to as the "McCarran-Ferguson factors."

National Association of Insurance Commissioners An organization that addresses the "business of insurance" is the **National Association of Insurance Commissioners (NAIC)**,[14] a nonprofit organization of insurance regulators from all 50 states, the District of Columbia, and the U.S. Territories. Its mission promotes the need for conformity of regulations among its members, the promulgation of model insurance laws, and an accreditation process. Membership is voluntary and the model laws are not binding. However, an NAIC-accredited state enjoys benefits; if a state is accredited, financial examination of a domestic insurer is accepted by other accredited states where the insurer does business. Many insurance companies do business across state lines, making NAIC accreditation a plus. The NAIC accepts the five factors of an insurance contract described previously.

> **ROLE OF THE PARALEGAL**
>
> Health insurance is a huge, complex, and competitive industry that offers many employment opportunities. Paralegals who work for insurers may assist with filing of documents mandated by state regulatory authority or responding to consumer complaints made to state insurance commissioners.

Types of Health Insurance

Several types of health care insurance contracts or policies exist. This section examines the most common types.

Governmental Governmental health insurance plans include Medicare, Medicaid, TRICARE, and CHAMPVA.

Initiated in 1965 through an amendment to the Social Security Act,[15] Medicare and Medicaid are now recognized as the largest health plan insurers in the United States. Medicare originally provided for inpatient hospitalization (Part A) and outpatient medical services (Part B), similar to the BlueCross/BlueShield model. In 1997, the Medicare program was amended to include Part C, Medicare + Choice, a managed care option that beneficiaries could choose in lieu of Parts A and B. In 2003, Medicare + Choice was expanded further and renamed Medicare Advantage. Medicare Part D, for prescription drug coverage, became effective in 2004.

Eligibility for Medicare is limited to those over 65 years of age, the long-term disabled, those with end-stage renal disease, and certain others who may buy into the program. Beneficiaries must pay nominal monthly premiums and must meet a yearly deductible. Medicaid is a joint federal/state program of health insurance for the non-elderly poor and disabled. The federal government sets the minimum standards of coverage but each state runs its own program. Funding of the program is a joint federal and state responsibility. Beneficiary copayments for services and items are minimal or nonexistent.

The Medicare and Medicaid programs and regulations are so complex that the federal government designated the **Center for Medicare and Medicaid Services (CMS)**, an agency in the Department of Health and Human Services, to run the programs. More details on the programs are discussed in the chapter on Medicare.

The TRICARE programs are available to family members of active duty military service members and also to military retirees and their dependents. These dependents include spouses; unmarried children under age 21; unmarried children under age 23 who are full-time students; and legally adopted stepchildren.[16]

CHAMPVA (Civilian Health and Medical Program of the Department of Veterans Affairs) is a health care benefits program for the spouse or widow(er) and children of a veteran who meets one of the following criteria:

- is rated permanently and totally disabled due to a service-connected disability by a Veterans Affairs regional office
- was rated permanently and totally disabled due to a service-connected condition at the time of death
- died of a service-connected disability
- died on active duty

An additional criterion is that the dependents must be not otherwise eligible for Department of Defense TRICARE benefits.

CHAMPVA and the Department of Defense's TRICARE program are quite similar and are often mistaken for each other. CHAMPVA is a Department of Veterans Affairs program; TRICARE is a regionally managed health care program for active duty and retired members of the uniformed services, their families, and their survivors.[17]

Indemnity An indemnity contract is a heath insurance plan where one party (the insurer) agrees to reimburse the other party (the **beneficiary**)

ACRONYM

CMS: Centers for Medicare and Medicaid Services

ACRONYM

CHAMPVA: Civilian Health and Medical Program of the Department of Veterans Affairs for any losses sustained that are covered by the contract. An indemnity health plan charges a monthly premium to the beneficiary in exchange for coverage. A typical indemnity plan is an "80/20," which reimburses 80 percent of claims submitted, with the beneficiary paying for the other 20 percent. Other indemnity contracts plans may be "60/40" or "50/50." With indemnity insurance, beneficiaries may also have to cover expenses subject to a preset deductible before the insurer begins reimbursement. Indemnity plans have lost favor with consumers, though traditional Medicare is an "80/20" indemnity plan.

Managed Care The phrase *managed care* describes a broad category of health insurance plans that are designed to manage the costs, delivery, quality, and access to health care. Common managed care products include **health maintenance organizations (HMOs)**, **preferred provider organizations (PPOs)**, and **point of service (POS)** plans.

In an HMO, a beneficiary pays a monthly premium to the organization, as well as copayments for services and hospitalization. The organization both arranges and provides the services. In HMOs, a beneficiary chooses a primary care physician who acts as a "gatekeeper" for access to specialists and other services and items. Some HMOs are part of integrated delivery systems, owning the insurer, hospital, outpatient clinic, and even the physician practice. Employers quickly embraced HMOs in the 1980s, although consumer demand for freedom of choice has led to development of other managed care products.

Preferred provider organizations negotiate discounted contracts with independent providers and facilities like physician hospital organizations. The level of reimbursement to the beneficiary may vary, depending on whether or not he or she uses physicians and other providers within a specified geographical region or list (the *provider network*). Deductibles may apply.

Point of service plans are those in which beneficiaries do not have to choose services until they are needed. However, most require that a beneficiary designate a primary care physician to coordinate services. These plans often have the characteristics of both indemnity and HMO plans. Maximum benefits are available to beneficiaries when they obtain care within the provider network.

Federal Authority

There are several different federal statutes that regulate and affect health care delivery, including **ERISA**, **COBRA**, **HIPAA**, and the Mental Health

---

ACRONYMS

HMO: health maintenance organization

PPO: preferred provider organization

POS: point of service

ACRONYMS

ERISA: Employment Retirement Income Security Act

COBRA: Consolidated Omnibus Budget Reconciliation Act

HIPAA: Health Insurance Portability and Accountability Act

Parity Act. Some of these may **preempt** state laws. In this section, we will discuss ERISA and COBRA as they affect health insurance.

The Employment Retirement Income Security Act In response to concerns that employer sponsors of welfare and pension plans were not managing their assets properly for plan beneficiaries, Congress passed the Employment Retirement Income Security Act (ERISA)[18] in 1974. Congress wanted both to encourage the voluntary growth of employer-sponsored benefit plans and to protect beneficiaries. ERISA created a federal statutory framework that included a federal preemption provision and that was applicable to most employers. The statute established standards of conduct and mandated reporting and disclosure. It also imposed fiduciary responsibilities on plan administrators, created participation and vesting rights, and imposed criminal and civil sanctions for certain violations.

The preemption provision of ERISA is really three separate clauses which, even when put together, are difficult to synthesize. The preemption provision in ERISA supersedes any and all state laws that "relate to" an employee benefit plan subject to ERISA. ERISA also has a "savings clause" that saves from preemption certain state laws that regulate the business of insurance. Finally, ERISA has a "deemer clause" that creates an exception to the savings clause by providing that no employee-benefit plan may be deemed an insurance company or insurer for purposes of any state law that regulates insurance companies or insurance contracts.

Analysis and application of the preemption clause to state laws on health insurance is a difficult subject, even for judges. Hence, there are a number of cases that wrestle with the meaning of the three clauses described above. In *Metropolitan Life Insurance Co. v. Massachusetts*,[19] the U.S. Supreme Court applied the McCarran–Ferguson factors to determine whether a state law involved the regulation of insurance and whether that "saved" it from ERISA preemption. In another case on the savings clause, *Rush Prudential HMO, Inc. v. Moran*,[20] the U.S. Supreme Court held that ERISA did not preempt an Illinois law that established an independent medical review process for determining medical necessity of services. The *Rush* case has a long history and its outcome has been debated by lawyers for several years.

The Consolidated Omnibus Budget Reconciliation Act In 1986, the Consolidated Omnibus Budget Reconciliation Act (COBRA) was signed into law, amending ERISA, the Internal Revenue Code, and the Public Health

Service Act. This law requires that, under certain conditions, a group health plan must provide former participants and qualified beneficiaries the opportunity to elect and pay for extended health insurance coverage. Employer-sponsored medical expense plans, HMOs, dental plans, vision care plans, prescription drug plans, and some employee assistance plans are governed by COBRA.

Typically, COBRA coverage commences when an employee terminates his employment, voluntarily or involuntarily, with an employer or when the employee is ineligible for benefits due to a reduction in work hours. The employee may then decide to continue to pay for the employer-sponsored health insurance. There are other "qualified" events that trigger COBRA benefits. These include the birth or adoption of a child, marriage or divorce, employee death, entitlement to Social Security (and thus Medicare) benefits, and a dependent child ceasing to be a dependent (i.e., reaching the age when the plan no longer considers the child to be a dependent). When there is a qualifying event, an employer must notify the employee of his or her rights under COBRA to continue coverage of health insurance. Coverage under COBRA expires 18 months after an employee's termination or reduction in hours or 36 months after other qualifying events.

SUMMARY

Legal practitioners must be aware that state and federal laws and regulations often overlap in several areas, such as hospital operations and insurance. All states regulate the operation of hospitals because of their interest in protecting the public. Because operating hospitals is expensive, most acute care hospitals participate in federal government funding programs (e.g., Medicare) and insurance plans to deflect costs.

Opening a hospital requires an application with a state agency. Some states require a Certificate of Need prior to construction of new hospitals or increasing the number of beds available in existing hospitals. Hospitals that accept Medicare payment for services must meet Conditions of Participation. Hospitals that are accredited can bypass visits by Medicare officials.

The business of health care insurance is another area where both state and federal law must be considered. Though states may regulate insurers, regulations must be in conformity with federal laws such as ERISA and COBRA.

Federal laws such as ERISA and COBRA guarantee certain provisions to beneficiaries, while requiring insurance plans to provide some specific coverage and notice elements.

KEY TERMS

accrediting: Giving official status or recognition.

beneficiary: A person to whom an insurance policy is payable.

consideration: Something of value received or promised to induce (convince) a person to make a contract.

indemnify: Compensate or promise to compensate a person who has suffered a loss or may suffer a future loss.

insurable interest: An insured's financial interest in another person or in an object.

insured: One who pays for the protection of risk; the policyholder.

insurer: One who provides protection against risk.

preempt: Have the first right to do something.

premium: Payment by an insured to an insurer.

REVIEW QUESTIONS AND EXERCISES

1. Research your state's law to see if it still has a provision for a Certificate of Need. If so, are there any cases in which a proposed hospital was denied a CON? Report results to your class.

2. Research the hospitals in your community. Are any of them accredited by the Joint Commission? What advantages does accreditation offer?

3. What are the essential components of an insurance contract?

4. If you have health insurance, review your policy. What kind of health insurance plan do you have? Discuss what your plan provides and what and how much you must pay for premiums and services.

5. Explain the different types of governmental health insurance.

ENDNOTES

1. 42 U.S.C. § 11101.
2. La. Rev. Stat. Ann. § 40:2104.
3. Pub. L. No. 109-41 (2005).
4. — So.2d ——, 2007 WL 1121704 (Miss. App., April 17, 2007).
5. Id.
6. 42 CFR § 482.
7. 15 U.S.C. § 1011-1015 (1999).
8. 29 U.S.C. §§ 1001-1461 (1999).
9. Pub. L. No. 104-191, 110 Stat. 1936 (1996).
10. COBRA amended several federal statutes.
11. Pub. L. No. 106-102, 113 Stat. 1338 (1999).
12. Vance, William, Handbook on the Law of Insurance 2 (1951).
13. 458 U.S. 119 (1982).
14. See http://www.naic.org.
15. 42 U.S.C.A. § 1395-1395gg and 1396-1396v.
16. TRICARE Basics, http://www.mytricare.com, accessed June 21, 2007.
17. Health Administration Center, Department of Veterans Affairs, http://www.va.gov/hac/forbeneficiaries/champva/champva.asp, accessed August 8, 2007.
18. 29 U.S.C. §§ 1001-1461 (1999).
19. 471 U.S. 724 (1985).
20. 536 U.S. 355 (2002).

CHAPTER 3

THE PHYSICIAN/PATIENT RELATIONSHIP

CHAPTER OUTLINE

THE DUTY TO TREAT

CONSENT TO MEDICAL TREATMENT

    Exceptions to Obtaining Consent and Other Special Situations

PATIENT DECISION-MAKING

    Right to Refuse Treatment

    Advance Directives

CONFIDENTIAL PATIENT HEALTH INFORMATION

OBJECTIVES

After reading this chapter, students should be able to

- Describe the legal basis for a physician's duty to his/her patient.
- Explain the legal standard for informed consent to treatment and its exceptions.
- Explain patients' rights to make their own health care decisions.
- Identify the different types of advance directives.
- Discuss concepts underlying patient confidentiality.

THE DUTY TO TREAT

Do all physicians have a duty to treat all patients? What initiates the physician/patient relationship? Usually, a patient seeks treatment from a physician and the physician, by rendering that treatment, establishes the physician/patient relationship. It is like a contract. Doctors retain control over the extent of their services, their specialty, their geographic location, their office hours, the types of insurance they accept, and so on. The contract is a voluntary one for both the physician and the patient.

This physician/patient relationship or contract is necessary for a number of other actions to occur or continue: subsequent treatment of the patient by that same physician; the right to physician/patient confidentiality; and the patient's ability to sue the physician in the case of alleged medical **malpractice**. Many states provide limited liability for doctors who, acting as "Good Samaritans," provide emergency care to persons with whom they have no previous or subsequent physician/provider connection. A "Good Samaritan" statute protects doctors from civil damages when they render emergency care when they have no preexisting duty to do so.

Because the contract is a voluntary one, a physician is usually not under an obligation to accept a particular patient for treatment purposes. However, some health insurance plans and hospital staff bylaws may require a doctor to accept a certain number of patients or compel the doctor to accept a percentage of indigent patients. Certain health care facilities that receive federal funding must agree to provide a reasonable volume of services to those who cannot afford to pay for treatment. Emergency on-call physicians may also be required under state or federal law to accept patients in urgent health circumstances. Under the federal **Emergency Medical Treatment and Labor Act**[1] **(EMTALA)**, hospitals that have emergency departments must treat any party in an emergency situation, regardless of the patient's ability to pay for services. For further information about an emergency department's obligations under federal law, please refer to Chapter 10.

Once a physician/patient relationship is established, it may be terminated upon reasonable notice by either the patient or the doctor. However, a doctor may not abandon a patient and must allow sufficient time for a patient to find a suitable substitute for continued treatment.

ACRONYM

EMTALA: Emergency Medical Treatment and Labor Act

CONSENT TO MEDICAL TREATMENT

Every individual has the right of possession and control of his own person. The doctrine of **informed consent** is derived from the concepts of autonomy and self-determination (discussed in detail in Chapter 11). Informed consent has two interdependent elements. First, the right of an individual to control her own person and body includes a right to consent to medical treatment. Second, true and valid consent to medical treatment must incorporate full disclosure of all relevant information, including potential risks. This disclosure, whether verbal or written, should cover information about a patient's condition, the nature of the proposed medical treatment and any benefits or risks of that treatment, and any alternative treatments that the patient could consider. Physicians usually bear the responsibility of obtaining informed consent from patients. Many hospitals and other health care organizations, as well as accrediting bodies, have policies on informed consent. Failure to obtain informed consent prior to treatment may be actionable as a tort.

In some states, specific express consent is required for certain services, tests, or procedures. Examples include abortion services, HIV and AIDS testing, and electroshock therapy. Take a look at the Illinois act on consent for HIV testing, commonly known as the A.I.D.S. Confidentiality Act, at § 305/4[2] which states:

> No person may order an HIV test without first receiving the written informed consent of the subject of the test or the subject's legally authorized representative.

Exceptions to Obtaining Consent and Other Special Situations

It is not always practicable or possible to obtain an informed consent prior to treatment. What do physicians do when they are faced with treating patients who are unconscious or unable to communicate? What does a doctor do when she suspects that a patient may become distraught and refuse treatment if given a life-threatening diagnosis? Three exceptions to implied consent may be used if express informed consent is not easily obtainable.

- In emergencies, informed consent is implied if the doctor presumes that the patient would have given consent to save his/her own life.
- In continued treatment, informed consent is implied if the physician had previously treated the patient for the same condition.
- In special situations, informed consent is implied where giving full information to the patient might be harmful to the patient.

These exceptions do not permit a physician to avoid obtaining an express informed consent, nor may they be used to circumvent a patient's wishes. To qualify for the emergency exception to informed consent, treatment must be necessary to preserve a patient's life or health. Where the risk of full disclosure poses a threat to the patient, the exception applies only if the physician feels that the patient may become so distraught that treatment is severely compromised. However, in the latter situation, the doctor's privilege of withholding full information is limited to occasions on which it is for therapeutic reasons detrimental to the patient; for example, withholding a diagnosis of cancer from a patient who is suicidal.

Minors and Legal Incompetents In general, minors and other **legal incompetents** do not have the ability or **capacity** to make treatment decisions; these are usually left up to parents or guardians. The definitions of minors and legal incompetents vary by state law. Minors are typically those under the age of 18, although in some states, the age of majority is 21. Legal incompetents may be persons who have been judged legally incompetent by a court of law because of their mental or physical handicaps.

If a patient is a minor, informed consent must be obtained from a parent or legal guardian. Of course, this general rule is subject to exceptions. For example, legally emancipated minors (i.e., those minors no longer under the legal control of their parents) may consent to their own medical treatment. Some states also recognize a "mature minor" doctrine, derived from common law, which allows minors to make their own health care treatment decisions if they are sufficiently mature and knowledgeable. The "mature minor" doctrine may be used to protect a doctor from liability for treating a minor without the informed consent of the parent of guardian. In *Cardwell v. Bechtol*,[3] the Superior Court of Tennessee held that a minor had capacity to consent and had given informed consent to treatment by an osteopath. In other instances, if a minor presents himself as an adult of the age of majority to the physician, then the doctor may be protected from a lawsuit by the parents for providing care without their consent. Other exceptions to the general rule that parents or guardians must give informed consent for minors' treatment may be found in specific state statutes that authorize a minor to consent to treatment for substance abuse, alcoholism, venereal disease, or mental illness. A minor's right to make a decision about having an abortion without parental consent was also recognized by the U.S. Supreme Court in *Planned Parenthood of Central Missouri v. Danforth*,[4] which held unconstitutional the Missouri statute that required written consent of a parent to the abortion of an unmarried female under 18 years of age.

Consent in Research Trials A special informed consent is necessary if a patient is to be involved in clinical research trials of drugs or medical devices that are still considered experimental. Patients must be given enough information on the risks involved and any potential medical benefits prior to their involvement in research trials that may involve their medical conditions. Informed consent in clinical research trials is more fully explained in Chapter 11.

PATIENT DECISION-MAKING

Patients not only have the right to consent to treatment; they also have the right to refuse treatment and the right to make advance decisions regarding aspects of their care.

Right to Refuse Treatment

Competent adult patients enjoy a common law right to informed consent and constitutional protection when determining which medical treatment to accept or reject and when to terminate treatment, even if rejection or termination of treatment may be life threatening. Courts have recognized a privacy interest in a person's medical decision-making.

Although incompetent patients do not lose their right to decision-making, it must be exercised through their legal **guardian**. Guardians making decisions to refuse or withdraw treatment must base their decisions on one of three standards: subjective, substituted judgment, or best interest. With the subjective standard, a guardian considers the wishes of the patient. Perhaps the patient has spoken in the past about what she would like done if faced with a life-threatening illness or maybe she has written an **advance directive** (discussed in the following section). The substituted judgment standard is appropriate when a guardian makes a decision on what he believes the patient would want to do if she were competent. The best interest standard allows decisions to be made that are in the best interests of the patient.

Health care decision-making for incompetent patients generates many legal controversies and "right to die" cases. Many states have statutes that address withdrawal or withholding of treatment and nourishment in terminally ill patients.

Advance Directives

Advances in health care technology have extended a physician's ability to prolong and maintain a patient's life. Many people choose to write down their wishes about what kind of medical care they would or would not want should they become incompetent and then develop a terminal illness or experience a life-threatening accident, rather than allowing relatives to make decisions for them or courts to become involved in their treatment. These written statements of patient wishes are known as *advance directives*. Most states have statutes that authorize execution of two different types of advance directives: the **durable power of attorney** and the **living will**.

A *durable power of attorney* for health care is a document that designates an agent who is empowered to make treatment decisions for a patient in the event that the patient is not competent or is unable to make his wishes known. In addition to end-of-life decisions, durable powers of attorney may also be written to cover circumstances that are not life-threatening, such as placement in a nursing home. Some states require that durable powers of attorney expressly authorize the agent to withdraw or refuse life-sustaining treatment if the patient is in a persistent vegetative state or terminal condition.

Durable powers of attorney for health care are often included in the documents that patients may sign upon hospitalization or prior to complex surgical procedures. A general power of attorney may include a clause for health care decision-making that is triggered upon incapacity. See the example in Exhibit 3–1.

> I, JANE C. DOE, appoint JOHN M. SMITH as my agent and attorney-in-fact, and grant him the specific power to make any and all health care decisions for me upon my incapacity or incompetency.

EXHIBIT 3–1: EXCERPT FROM GENERAL POWER OF ATTORNEY

A *living will* is a document that specifies what a person wants to transpire regarding health care and nourishment should the person become incompetent and unable to express her wishes (see Appendix D for a sample living will). Living wills are usually limited to wishes regarding life-sustaining treatment. Most states limit the application of living wills to situations where patients are terminally ill or in persistent vegetative states. For example, look at Louisiana's "living will" statute, which incorporates a sample declaration regarding life-sustaining procedures.

Making of declaration; notification; illustrative form; registry; issuance of do-not-resuscitate identification bracelets

A. (1) Any adult person may, at any time, make a written declaration directing the withholding or withdrawal of life-sustaining procedures in the event such person should have a terminal and irreversible condition.

(2) A written declaration shall be signed by the declarant in the presence of two witnesses.

(3) An oral or nonverbal declaration may be made by an adult in the presence of two witnesses by any nonwritten means of communication at any time subsequent to the diagnosis of a terminal and irreversible condition.

B. (1) It shall be the responsibility of the declarant to notify his attending physician that a declaration has been made.

(2) In the event the declarant is comatose, incompetent, or otherwise mentally or physically incapable of communication, any other person may notify the physician of the existence of the declaration. In addition, the attending physician or health care facility may directly contact the registry to determine the existence of any such declaration.

(3) Any attending physician who is so notified, or who determines directly or is advised by the health care facility that a declaration is registered, shall promptly make the declaration or a copy of the declaration, if written, or a notation of the existence of a registered declaration, a part of the declarant's medical record.

(4) If the declaration is oral or nonverbal, the physician shall promptly make a recitation of the reasons the declarant could not make a written declaration and make the recitation a part of the patient's medical records.

C. (1) The declaration may, but need not, be in the following illustrative form and may include other specific directions including but not limited to a designation of another person to make the treatment decision for the declarant should he be diagnosed as having a terminal and irreversible condition and be comatose, incompetent, or otherwise mentally or physically incapable of communications:

DECLARATION

Declaration made this _____ day of _____ (month, year).

I, _____, being of sound mind, willfully and voluntarily make known my desire that my dying shall not be artificially prolonged under the circumstances set forth below and do hereby declare:

If at any time I should have an incurable injury, disease or illness, or be in a continual profound comatose state with no reasonable chance of recovery, certified to be a terminal and irreversible condition by two physicians who have personally examined me, one of whom shall be my attending physician, and the physicians have determined that my death will occur whether or not life-sustaining procedures are utilized and where the application of life-sustaining procedure would serve only to prolong artificially the dying process, I direct (initial one only):

___That all life-sustaining procedures, including nutrition and hydration, be withheld or withdrawn so that food and water will not be administered invasively.

___That life-sustaining procedures, except nutrition and hydration, be withheld or withdrawn so that food and water can be administered invasively.

I further direct that I be permitted to die naturally with only the administration of medication or the performance of any medical procedure deemed necessary to provide me with comfort care.

In the absence of my ability to give directions regarding the use of such life-sustaining procedures, it is my intention that this declaration shall be honored by my family and physician(s) as the final expression of my legal right to refuse medical or surgical treatment and accept the consequences from such refusal.

I understand the full import of this declaration and I am emotionally and mentally competent to make this declaration.

Signed _____

City, Parish, and State of Residence _____

The declarant has been personally known to me and I believe him or her to be of sound mind.

Witness _____

Witness _____

(2) Should any of the other specific directions be held to be invalid, such invalidity shall not affect other directions of the declaration which can be given effect without the invalid direction, and to this end the directions in the declaration are severable.

(3) (a) Any declaration executed prior to January 1, 1992, which does not contain directions regarding life-sustaining procedures in the event that the declarant is in a continual profound comatose state shall not be invalid for that reason. Such declaration shall be applicable to any terminal and irreversible condition, as defined in this Part, unless it clearly provides to the contrary.

(b) Any declaration executed prior to August 15, 2005, which does not contain an option to specifically initial a choice regarding nutrition and hydration shall not be invalid for that reason nor presumed to mean that the declarant desires the invasive administration of nutrition or hydration.

D. (1) (a) The secretary of state shall establish a declaration registry in which a person, or his attorney, if authorized by the person to do so, may register the original, multiple original, or a certified copy of the declaration.

(b) The secretary of state shall issue a do-not-resuscitate identification bracelet to qualified patients listed in the registry. The do-not-resuscitate identification bracelet must include the patient's name, date of birth, and the phrase "DO NOT RESUSCITATE".

(2) Any attending physician or health care facility may, orally or in writing, request the secretary of state to confirm immediately

the existence of a declaration and to disclose the contents thereof for any patient believed to be a resident of Louisiana. A copy of the declaration or a facsimile thereof transmitted from the office of the secretary of state shall be deemed authentic. However, nothing herein requires a physician or health care facility to confirm the existence of such declaration or obtain a copy thereof prior to the withholding or withdrawal of medical treatment or life-sustaining procedures.

(3) The secretary of state may charge a fee of twenty dollars for registering a declaration and issuing a do-not-resuscitate identification bracelet and a fee of five dollars for filing a notice of revocation. No charge shall be made for the furnishing of information concerning the existence of a declaration, the disclosure of its contents, or the providing of a copy or facsimile thereof.[5]

Note in the preceding statute that two physicians, including the attending doctor, must concur that the patient has a terminal and irreversible condition. Louisiana's law also allows for registration of these declarations with the Secretary of State.

Do Not Resuscitate Orders Many states have legislation that permits doctors to write "Do Not Resuscitate" orders for individuals who may or may not be hospitalized. Typically, a patient in a long-term care facility with a terminal illness or a patient in a hospital who does not want heroic efforts made to save him or her may issue a Do-Not-Resuscitate order. State laws may also address immunity from liability when physicians follow such orders.

Constitutional Protections Does the U.S. Constitution and its Bill of Rights guarantee citizens the right to make their own treatment and end-of life decisions? One of the earliest cases that addressed constitutional issues in end-of-life decisions was that in *Cruzan v. Director, Missouri Dept. of Health.*[6] There, the U.S. Supreme Court addressed the protected liberty interest that grants a person the right to refuse medical treatment, even if that treatment would extend and maintain a person's life. Instead of focusing on the privacy interest, the Court found that this protected liberty interest arises from the Fourteenth

Amendment and that it must be weighed against the state's interests to determine if it is constitutionally permissible.

Under federal law, if a constitutionally protected right to refuse medical treatment is established, the state can only abridge that right and force a patient to accept medical treatment if the state has a **compelling interest**. Compelling state interests that could circumvent an individual's constitutional rights regarding medical treatment include:

- protection of third parties
- prevention of suicide
- preservation of human life
- upholding ethical standards of the medical profession

Courts have also held that incompetents have constitutionally protected rights in health care decision-making. A 1976 case, *In Re Quinlan*,[7] opined that if the personal right to choose or refuse medical treatment is to have any meaning, then it must be maintained during periods of that person's incompetency. However, disputes continue on who has the right to act on behalf of incompetents and which standard of decision making is appropriate.

Many end-of-life decision-making issues with potential constitutional arguments remain unresolved. Some examples include physician-assisted suicide, whether treatment should be given to severely debilitated patients who are not terminally ill, and authorization to remove feeding tubes.

CONFIDENTIAL PATIENT HEALTH INFORMATION

All health care providers must follow a dizzying array of federal and state laws and regulations that govern the disclosure of patient health information. As a general rule, providers must maintain the confidentiality of information about their patients. Of course, this rule is subject to many exceptions.

Physicians may be required under their state's licensing laws to protect the confidentiality of patient information; unwarranted disclosure may expose a doctor to disciplinary actions. Hospitals and other health care organizations also must follow laws on the confidential nature of patient medical records and often must meet the standards of their accrediting agencies, which may require policies on confidential patient information.

Some types of patient health information may be subject to heightened protection, such as laws that restrict release of information on HIV testing or alcohol and substance abuse treatment. The Privacy Regulations of the **Health Insurance Portability and Accountability Act (HIPAA)** set standards and requirements for disclosure of protected patient health information that all health care providers and organizations must follow. These are discussed more fully in Chapter 8.

In general, a patient's medical information cannot be released without the patient's authorization, subject to exceptions. For example, a health care provider may be mandated to disclose certain patient information such as communicable diseases, births, deaths, elder abuse, or other reportable events set out in state law. Likewise, a "duty to warn" may obligate a physician to warn a third party of a patient's contagious condition or violent propensities. The case of *Tarasoff v. Regents of Univ. of California*[8] illustrates the duty to warn third parties. There, a psychiatrist was found to have a duty to warn a third party of a direct threat. The facts of the case were very sad. The psychiatrist was successfully sued by the family of a dead woman who was murdered by one of the psychiatrist's patients after the patient had made a verbal threat to kill the woman during one of his outpatient psychiatric sessions. Many states now have statutes that address a provider's duty to warn and establish the limits of liability.

SUMMARY

In this chapter, we discussed how a physician and patient form a relationship. The physician/patient relationship includes a physician's duty to treat patients and not abandon them, as well as the patient's right to choose a particular physician. Treatment by a physician must include a patient's informed consent, subject to exceptions. Patients have rights to make their own health care decisions to accept or refuse treatment. Incompetent patients also have rights, though their decisions are often made by surrogates. Patients have the right to be involved in end-of-life decision-making and may execute different types of advance directives, such as living wills and durable powers of attorney. Patient confidentiality of health care information must be protected, unless there are mandatory reporting laws or a duty to warn third parties.

ACRONYM

HIPAA: Health Insurance Portability and Accountability Act

KEY TERMS

advance directive: A document such as a durable power of attorney, health care proxy, or living will that specifies your health care decisions and identifies someone who will make decisions for you if you cannot make your own.

capacity: Physical or mental ability to do something; such as make a rational decision.

compelling interest: A strong reason that makes a state law constitutional even though the law classifies persons on the basis of race, color, religion, national origin, veteran status, sex, age, or disability or uses the state's police powers to limit an individual's constitutional rights.

durable power of attorney: When used in the context of advanced directives, refers to a power of attorney that lasts as long as a person remains incapable of making decisions, such as about health care.

guardian: A person who has the legal right and duty to take care of another person or that person's property because that other person (for example, a child) cannot.

informed consent: An agreement to allow something (such as surgery) to happen that is based on a full disclosure or full knowledge of the facts needed to make the decision intelligently.

legal incompetency: The lack of legal ability to do something; the condition of one who lacks the mental ability to manage his or her own affairs and therefore has someone appointed by the state to manage his or her finances and other decisions.

living will: A type of advance directive by which one authorizes one's possible future removal from an artificial life support system.

malpractice: Professional misconduct or unreasonable lack of skill; usually refers to bad, incomplete, or unfaithful work done by a doctor or lawyer.

REVIEW QUESTIONS AND EXERCISES

1. Dr. Dogooder is on his way to work at his office when he passes a three-car crash on the interstate. He stops and tries to help an unconscious woman whose leg is crushed under her car's steering wheel. After an ambulance arrives, Dr. Dogooder leaves the scene

and goes to work. He learns later in the afternoon that the woman he tried to help had to have her leg amputated. Is Dr. Dogooder liable for damages under your state's Good Samaritan law? Was a physician/patient relationship formed when the doctor tried to help the injured woman?

2. Refer to the Illinois statute on consent for AIDS testing (A.I.D.S. Confidentiality Act at § 305/4). Under what circumstances can testing take place without consent?

3. Refer to *Cardwell v. Bechtol* in the Online Companion that accompanies this text. Was the consent verbal or written? Does the case discuss the elements of informed consent?

4. A law associate with whom you work asks for help in drafting advance directives for an elderly couple who are his clients. The wife still lives at home, but the husband is in a nursing home because he has Alzheimer's disease. The wife told the associate that her husband never wanted to prolong his life artificially. What advance directives would your state allow? Are there any problems you foresee with fulfilling the husband's wishes?

5. Research your state's law on health care decision-making. What standards are set out? Who can make decisions for incompetents?

6. Research your state's latest legislative session. Were any laws proposed that addressed end-of-life decision-making?

7. Research your state's laws on mandatory health care reporting. How many statutes did you find?

ENDNOTES

1. 42 U.S.C. § 1395.
2. Il. Stat. Ann. 410 § 305/4.
3. 724 S.W.2d 739, 67 A.L.R.4th 479 (Tenn. Sup. Ct. 1987).
4. 428 U.S. 52 (1976).
5. La. Rev. Stat. § 40:1299.58.3.
6. 497 U.S. 261, 110 S. Ct. 2841, 111 L.Ed. 2d 224 (1990).
7. 70 N.J. 10, 355 A.2d 647 (1976), *cert. den.*
8. 17 Cal. 3d 425, 131 Cal. Rptr. 14, 551 P.2d 334 (1976).

CHAPTER 4

PHYSICIANS, PROVIDERS, AND FINANCIAL RELATIONSHIPS

OBJECTIVES

After completing this chapter, students should be able to

- Describe elements of the process of licensure and credentialing.
- Discuss issues common to physician contracts.
- Distinguish between physicians as employees and physicians as business owners.

LICENSURE AND DISCIPLINE

Graduation from medical school and completing a residency are only part of what is required for physicians to practice medicine. All states now have statutes that require individuals providing medical services to be licensed. States usually have boards of medical examiners that have authority over the licensing process and often over disciplinary procedures as well. Typical application requirements include graduation from an accredited medical school, passing a state examination, completion of a residency, and, perhaps, demonstration of physical and mental soundness. Applicants may also be required to submit fingerprints or agree to a criminal record check, or undergo a physical and mental examination.

State medical boards may also have authority over physician disciplinary procedures. The board's authority may be triggered by an event such as:

- conviction of a crime or entry of a plea of guilty or *nolo contendere*
- fraud, deceit, or perjury in obtaining any diploma, license, or permit
- habitual or recurring substance abuse
- prescription of legally controlled substances without legitimate medical justification
- failure to satisfy the prevailing standards of medical practice
- gross and willful overcharging for professional services
- patient abandonment
- interdiction or commitment

If a doctor's license has been revoked and reinstatement is the issue, factors to be considered usually include:

- the present moral fitness of the petitioning doctor vs. his or her character, maturity, and experience at the time of the misconduct
- recognition of any past misconduct and potential disgrace that might have been brought to the profession, the seriousness of the situation that led to license revocation
- the conduct and rehabilitation of the physician after discipline was imposed.

The burden of proof is on the physician seeking reinstatement. Attorneys representing physicians may find themselves in board-related administrative proceedings regarding retention, revocation, or reinstatement of a physician's license. Therefore, knowledge of board regulations and procedures and state statutes is essential. Since we are in the realm of administrative law, remember that, in general, administrative remedies must be exhausted before judicial review.

An example of a state medical board's revocation of a physician's license can be found in *Dahlquist v. Ohio State Med. Bd.*[1] The Ohio State Medical Board initiated disciplinary proceedings against Glenda Dahlquist, M.D., a pain management specialist, claiming that her care of patients fell below the standard of care. The board alleged that Dahlquist failed to use reasonable care in the administration of drugs and failed to employ reasonable scientific methods in the selection of drugs for treatment. After a hearing, the Board recommended license revocation upon a finding that Dahlquist "prescribed medications in types, amounts, and combinations that were inappropriate," but delayed that decision to allow Dahlquist time to close down her practice. Dahlquist pursued review in the trial court and appellate court, but failed to win reversal of the Board's decision.

Board review of a physician's license is not restricted to activities involving patients. In another case before the State Medical Board of Ohio, proceedings were instituted against Dr. Ahmad Hosseinipour, based on several acts of criminal trespass, domestic violence, and other charges.[2] The hearing examiner determined that the acts demonstrated an inability to practice medicine according to accepted standards, and recommended that plaintiff's license to practice medicine be permanently revoked. About two years later, Hosseinipour petitioned for reinstatement of his license, claiming that he had been diagnosed, post-hearing, with HIV encephalopathy, a form of dementia. He argued that the Board discriminated against him for his HIV status when it revoked his license. The trial court did not agree, finding that Hosseinipour had had not filed his complaint within the two-year statute of limitations under state statute and had not established any reason for tolling the statute of limitations as allowed by the statute. The appellate court affirmed.

For a discussion of state board authority in physician licensing, revocation, and reinstatement, please refer to *In the Matter of Andre Nehorayoff, Respondent, v. Richard P. Mills, as Commissioner of Education of the State of New York, et al.*[3] in the Online Companion that accompanies this text.

MEDICAL STAFF PRIVILEGES AND CREDENTIALING

Doctors in private practices need staff privileges at hospitals and ambulatory surgical centers in order to admit and treat their patients. Often doctors have admitting privileges at several hospitals, and are then considered part of the medical staff responsible for the quality of care for patients.

SPOTLIGHT ON...

All states have laws addressing medical staff privileges at hospitals. For example, Ohio's law provides at ORC Ann. 3727.06:

§ 3727.06. Admission and supervision of patients

(A) As used in this section:
  (1) "Doctor" means an individual authorized to practice medicine and surgery or osteopathic medicine and surgery.
  (2) "Podiatrist" means an individual authorized to practice podiatric medicine and surgery.

(B) Only a doctor who is a member of the medical staff, dentist who is a member of the medical staff, or podiatrist who is a member of the medical staff may admit a patient to a hospital.

(C) All hospital patients shall be under the medical supervision of a doctor, except that services that may be rendered by a licensed dentist pursuant to Chapter 4715 of the Revised Code provided to patients admitted solely for the purpose of receiving such services shall be under the supervision of the admitting dentist and that services that may be rendered by a podiatrist pursuant to section 4731.51 of the Revised Code provided to patients admitted solely for the purpose of receiving such services shall be under the supervision of the admitting podiatrist. If treatment not within the scope of Chapter 4715 or section 4731.51 of the Revised Code is required at the time of admission by a dentist or podiatrist, or becomes necessary during the course of hospital treatment by a dentist or podiatrist, such treatment shall be under the supervision of a doctor who is a member of the medical staff. It shall be the responsibility of the admitting dentist or podiatrist to make arrangements with a doctor who is a member of the medical staff to be responsible for the patient's treatment outside the scope of Chapter 4715 or section 4731.51 of the Revised Code when necessary during the patient's stay in the hospital.

Health care lawyers and their paralegals need to be aware of the laws governing medical staff privileges in their respective states. Often doctors come to health law firms for assistance with cases involving denial of privileges at hospitals where they want to admit and treat patients.

The **medical staff** in a hospital is a self-governing body of practitioners that oversees the quality of care and the services delivered by their peer practitioners. The medical staff must establish bylaws that delineate responsibilities and define the framework within which practitioners are expected to work. The medical staff bylaws may address many different areas: supervision of physicians who are residents, performance improvement, financial conflicts of interest, management of clinical services, telemedicine, and continuing medical education. Bylaws usually address the process of credentialing, which is discussed in the following section, and provide for an appeals process when privileges are denied, revoked, or suspended.

Credentialing

Credentialing the medical staff is an important job that often falls to a health care compliance professional within the hospital or other health care organization (e.g., long-term care facility). A hospital's medical staff must credential and grant staff privileges to all licensed independent health care practitioners who wish to admit or treat patients in the hospital. Credentialing physicians for medical staff privileges involves an assessment of a physician's qualifications to provide patient care in the hospital. Besides licensure by the governing state board, medical staffs may look to relevant training or experience and current competence in an applicant's specialty. Peer recommendations from other practitioners in the same field may be a requirement in some hospitals.

The credentialing process is a detailed one because it includes verification of a physician's license and professional board certifications as well as verification that a physician has not been excluded from federal health care programs or listed in the national databases that track criminal, civil, and other disciplinary matters. Those examining credentials usually check the DHHS **Office of Inspector General's (OIG) List of Excluded Individuals/Entities (LEIE)** database, which provides the health care industry with information regarding individuals and entities currently excluded from participation in Medicare, Medicaid, and other federal health care programs. Statutory authority and the grounds

ACRONYMS

LEIE: List of Excluded Individuals/Entities
OIG: Office of Inspector General

PURPOSE: To ensure that all physicians practicing in (insert health care organization name) are validly licensed by the state(s) in which they practice and have/maintain proper credentials.

SCOPE: This policy applies to physicians providing medical services who are working as employees, independent contractors, or affiliates.

POLICY: All physicians practicing with (insert health care organization name) must maintain current, valid licenses to practice medicine from the state(s) in which they practice. All physicians practicing with (insert health care organization name) must undergo (insert health care organization name)'s initial credentialing review and periodic reviews thereafter during their association with (insert health care organization name). Physicians must notify (insert health care organization name) of any adverse action, including license investigation, suspension, or revocation and/or ineligibility status with federal health care programs.

PROCEDURE: Responsibility for verification of physician licenses and credentials rests with the following departments:

- Human Resources
- Internal Audit
- Compliance

Each department shall develop processes, forms, and other internal guidelines to carry out the intent of this policy. These shall include, at a minimum, methods of verification of physician licensure with the state medical board and verification of no adverse action against a physician through accessing the LEIE databases of the OIG and GSA and the NPDB databank, at the time of the physician's initial association with (insert health care organization name) and periodically thereafter.

EXHIBIT 4–1: SAMPLE PHYSICIAN LICENSURE AND CREDENTIALING POLICY

for exclusion are set out in the Social Security Act[4] and include mandatory and permissive exclusions. Mandatory exclusions range from the very serious (e.g., criminal conviction for patient abuse) to the more mundane (e.g., nonpayment of a federal student loan). Permissive exclusions include misdemeanor convictions, amongst others. Hospitals cannot claim payment for services performed by excluded physicians, so it is easy to understand why checking the OIG LEIE database is essential. More information on exclusions from federal health care programs can be found in Chapters 5 and 6.

SPOTLIGHT ON...

Anyone can search the OIG LEIE database. Go to <http://www.oig.hhs.gov> and follow the links to the exclusions database. These are updated monthly.

The credentials examiner may also check the **National Practitioner Data Bank (NPDB)** for other information that may be relevant to the medical staff's granting of privileges to a physician. The NPDB was created by the **Health Care Quality Improvement Act (HCQIA)** of 1986,[5] originally intended to improve health care by identifying and disciplining physicians who engage in unprofessional conduct. Its data-bank tracks physician licensure, professional society memberships, medical malpractice payment history, and record of clinical privileges. Unlike the LEIE, most of the NPDB is not available to the general public. To access or report physician-specific information, the entity must be an eligible one—a state licensing board, a hospital, a medical malpractice insurer, or a professional society. Self-queries are also allowed for a fee.[6]

SPOTLIGHT ON...

Most health care organizations have policies and procedures in place and designate staff to perform the credentialing process (see Exhibit 4–1). Verification and documentation of a physician's professional credentials at the outset of a business relationship is essential to risk management. No organization wants to find out that a physician is unlicensed or barred from federal health care programs after he or she has been hired.

Physicians may be denied staff privileges or they may later lose them for a variety of reasons: loss of medical license, professional misconduct, negative patient outcomes, financial conflicts of interest, and other reasons that the medical staff committee has identified. Doctors who fail to obtain staff privileges during the credentialing process or later lose them may avail themselves of the hospital's internal fair hearing and appeals process. These allow affected individuals the right to defend themselves. Hospitals that are accredited by the Joint Commission must follow their guidelines for fair hearings and appeals when there are adverse privileging decisions.[7]

One of the hottest legal issues in physician credentialing is known as "economic credentialing." The American Medical Association defines economic credentialing as

> . . . the use of economic criteria unrelated to quality of care or professional competence in determining a physician's qualifications for initial or continuing hospital medical staff membership or privileges.[8]

Some hospitals base credentialing decisions on the number of a physician's referrals or patient admissions, caused, they say, by economic forces in the health care industry. These hospitals may have established conflict of interest policies to ensure that physicians will refer their patients to that particular hospital or risk losing their medical staff privileges. Some hospitals have gone so far as to refuse staff privileges to physicians who have financial interests or leadership positions with competing health care entities.

ACRONYM

AMA: American Medical Association

SPOTLIGHT ON...

The **American Medical Association (AMA)** is an opponent of economic credentialing and has devoted its advocacy resources to fighting its practice. Since 1999, the AMA has worked with the Office of Inspector General to address concerns of fraud and abuse in this area.

A case that many health care lawyers are watching for further developments is *Baptist Health v. Murphy,*[9] which involved application of Baptist Health's economic conflict of interest policy to several cardiologists with ownership interests in competing facilities. The doctors filed suit and were granted a preliminary injunction, enjoining Baptist Health from enforcing the policy, after they had been denied medical staff privileges. Baptist Health's policy mandated the denial of initial or renewed professional staff appointments or clinical privileges to any practitioner who, directly or indirectly, acquires or holds an ownership or investment interest in a competing hospital. Several doctors were deemed ineligible for reappointment under the policy. In their lawsuit, the doctors alleged that Baptist Health violated the federal anti-kickback statute, the Arkansas Medicaid Fraud Act, the Arkansas Medicaid Fraud False Claims Act, the Arkansas Deceptive Trade Practices Act, and that Baptist tortiously interfered with the doctor-patient relationship. The case went up on two interlocutory appeals related to a motion for preliminary injunction, enjoining Baptist from preventing the doctors from practicing medicine at its hospitals. Though the case was remanded for further proceedings, the appellate court noted that the doctors would probably succeed on their claim of tortious interference.

Peer Review

Medical staff bylaws include a provision for peer or professional review of performance of physician duties and related discipline. A health care practitioner's peers in the same discipline conduct reviews of physician performance of duties to ensure that patient care is appropriate. Medical staff bylaws usually identify a minimum set of circumstances before initiating an intensive review of a physician's performance. Negative or adverse decisions may result in the denial or suspension of staff privileges.

The Health Care Quality Improvement Act (HCQIA)[10] requires that health care entities must report adverse actions within 15 days from the date of the adverse action or from the time that clinical privileges were voluntarily surrendered. Reportable events include actions that adversely affect a physician's staff privileges for a period of more than 30 days and acceptance of the physician's surrender or restriction of clinical privileges while an investigation of competence is ongoing or in return for not conducting an investigation. Adverse actions can be reducing, restricting, suspending, revoking, or denying privileges or denial of renewal of privileges.

As might be suspected, challenges to peer review are fairly frequent because an adverse action can impact a physician's future career and livelihood. From the physician's perspective, the peer review process may be onerous and intrusive. From the hospital's perspective, peer review is essential to good physician practice and risk management. Thus, lawsuits are common among physicians against health care entities and their peer review committees. Paralegals can find themselves on either side in peer review lawsuits, depending on whether they work for plaintiff attorneys representing physicians or defense attorneys representing hospitals.

However, HCQIA grants immunity from liability for adverse actions to peer review actions under certain circumstances. In order to receive this immunity, professional review actions regarding a physician's competence or conduct must be taken

- in the reasonable belief that the action was in the furthering of quality health care

- after a reasonable effort to obtain the facts of the matter

- after adequate notice and hearing procedures are afforded to the practitioner involved, or after such other procedures as are fair to the practitioner under the circumstances

- in the reasonable belief that the action was warranted by the facts known, after such reasonable effort to obtaining facts and after meeting the notice and hearing requirements[11]

An example of the peer review process and its appeals can be found in *Lee v. Trinity Lutheran Hospital*,[12] where Trinity Lutheran Hospital was found to be immune from monetary damages when a terminated doctor failed to show that the peer review disciplinary process did not meet standards set forth in the Health Care Quality Improvement Act. Peer review proceedings were brought against Dr. Sharon D. Lee, a member of the medical staff, after she prescribed two drugs to an HIV patient to treat his pneumocystis carinii pneumonia, which triggered an inquiry by the hospital's Pharmacy and Therapeutic Committee and then by the Peer Review on Medicine Committee. Dr. Lee's patient records were reviewed prospectively by a subcommittee and by an independent specialist. Their findings were that she failed to meet the standard of care in four out of five cases reviewed and that she had a consistent problem with "unapproved uses of approved drugs or toxic combinations in HIV patients." Dr. Lee's staff privileges were suspended.

Lee then requested a fair hearing and produced testimony from her own expert, Dr. Joseph Brewer. Following Brewer's testimony, the committee voted to reinstate Lee's privileges conditioned on her attending a physician education program, receiving psychological counseling, and submitting medical records for review. However, an Executive Committee reversed this decision and voted to unconditionally revoke Lee's privileges reasoning, in part, that the suggested conditions would be difficult to enforce and that the hospital could be exposed to liability for granting her privileges. Lee appealed again to an Appellate Review Committee, which unanimously recommended revocation of staff privileges.

Trinity Lutheran then submitted an adverse action report to the National Practitioner Data Bank, listing the reasons why Lee's staff privileges had been revoked. Lee then filed suit in state court alleging defamation and other state law claims. The hospital removed the action to a federal district court, which granted summary judgment in favor of the hospital, finding that the hospital was immune from paying monetary damages under the HCQIA. Lee then appealed. The Eighth Circuit held that Lee had not satisfied her "burden of producing evidence that would allow a reasonable jury to conclude [the hospital's] peer review disciplinary process failed to meet the standards of HCQIA."

The peer review process also raises questions in the area of anti-trust law; these are outside the scope of this book.

EMPLOYMENT

Most doctors have multiple business relationships. Once a doctor is licensed, he or she may join a physician practice, open an individual office, work in a hospital, serve as a medical director of a department within a hospital, engage in clinical research at an academic medical center, consult with health care-related industries, or other possibilities. However, before entering any of these business relationships, a physician must consider whether he or she will be an employee, an independent contractor, or an owner. A paralegal working for a lawyer who represents individual physicians may be called upon to research state laws on professional services contracts. Likewise, health care organizations must consider how they want to structure their business relationships with physicians. Many organizations have policies on professional services agreements (see Exhibit 4–2). For paralegals working with transactional law firms or in large health care organizations, maintenance of contracts is a key role.

PURPOSE: To provide direction as to execution of professional services agreements between affiliates of (insert health care organization name) and physicians and/or physician entities and their immediate family members

SCOPE: This policy applies to all physicians providing patient services with (insert health care organization name) who are employees, independent contractors, or other affiliates.

POLICY: All Professional Services Agreements must be in writing, signed by the parties, and provide for fair market value payments that are set in advance for the services actually rendered. Payments shall not be determined in a manner that takes into account the volume or value of any referrals or other business generated between (insert health care organizations name) and the physician. Professional Services Agreements may only be executed for services actually needed in the community. The term of any Professional Services Agreement should be for at least one year. If the term is for less than 1 year or if the agreement is terminated with or without cause prior to the end of the first year of the agreement, then the parties must not enter into a similar contract until the 1-year term has passed. The Professional Services Agreement shall specify with particularity the services to be rendered.

PROCEDURE: All Professional Services Agreements must be drafted, negotiated, and/or reviewed by the Legal Department. Documentation of fair market valuation by an independent third party appraisal or by reference to a benchmark accepted by the health care industry must be maintained. All Professional Services contracts must be executed by the CEO of (insert health care organization).

The Legal Department shall identify additional processes for renewal of existing contracts, in accordance with the intent of this policy.

EXHIBIT 4–2: SAMPLE PROFESSIONAL SERVICES POLICY

Both parties to the contract have different legal considerations, which are set out in this chapter. The courts have considered three main categories of facts in determining whether a worker is an independent contractor or an employee:

- behavioral control—when, where, and how to work
- financial control—how the business pays the worker
- type of relationship—permanency of business relationship

Employee

As a general rule, an employee is subject to the control of his or her employer. Employers are responsible for

- withholding federal income tax
- withholding and paying the employer social security and Medicare tax
- paying federal unemployment tax (FUTA)
- issuing Form W-2, Wage and Tax Statement, annually
- reporting wages on Form 941, Employer's Quarterly Federal Tax Return

Before entering into a contract for employment, attorneys representing physicians and contracts managers working for health care organizations must have a clear understanding of the duties and responsibilities of each party. The contract should be as specific as possible and include applicable terms regarding

- work and on-call schedule
- staff privileges at hospital(s)
- location(s) of employment
- any supervisory or administrative responsibilities
- compensation
- benefits
- term (as in length) of agreement and any termination clause
- restrictive covenants
- ownership opportunities

This list is not exclusive, but does give most of the considerations necessary prior to drafting an employment agreement.

Compensation Setting physician compensation can be a complicated process. Compensation varies depending on physician specialty, years of experience, professional certifications, geographic location, and the type of entity that is the employer. Employment agreements should include the amount and timing of compensation, as well as the actual dollar amount. Many agreements may set a base salary or a formula that includes productivity measures (e.g., number of patients seen or procedures done). Some agreements include bonuses for physicians who achieve preset goals.

Fringe benefits make up a fair amount of the total compensation package and may include malpractice and other insurance, continuing medical education, beeper or cell phone, reimbursement of moving expenses, retirement plan, and other perks. Many benefits can be structured separately from strict compensation; doing so may allow the employed physician to save money in taxes.

When malpractice insurance is included in the compensation package, it is important to distinguish whether it is "occurrence" or "claims made" coverage. Occurrence malpractice insurance covers incidents on the date they occurred, regardless of the date the claim is made. Claims made malpractice insurance covers incidents on the date the claim is made. It is recommended that physicians with claims made insurance purchase "tail" insurance for protection against malpractice actions that occurred while employed, but after the claims made policy lapsed.

SPOTLIGHT ON...

Let's consider an example of the effects different types of malpractice insurance have when a claim is filed. Suppose that Dr. Goodwrench at Doc in the Box Hospital left a sponge in a patient during a surgery on 8/25/07. Dr. Goodwrench had occurrence coverage during his employment, but left Doc in the Box on 9/25/07 for a competing hospital. On 12/15/07, the patient files a malpractice claim. With occurrence coverage, the claim would be honored (setting aside any notions that there would be protracted litigation!). On the other hand, the claim would not be covered if there were only claims made coverage as the policy lapsed when Dr. Goodwrench left the employment of Doc in the Box. Tail insurance would have provided the additional needed coverage

Ownership Opportunities Physicians joining private practices may be looking for long-term business relationships, rather than merely employment. It is advisable to work out in advance any terms and conditions that affect ownership opportunities in the practice. Because many employers may be reluctant to be bound to such an arrangement with a new employee, an expression of intent to periodically review the physician's performance with an eye towards a future partnership track may be the only reference to a share of ownership of the practice in the employment agreement.

Term and Termination Employment agreements should include a commencement and expiration date. Many agreements include "evergreen" clauses that allow agreements to automatically renew year after year. If an evergreen clause is included, be sure that it provides for periodic review of compensation.

Most employment agreements are "at will"—that is, either party can terminate the employee/employer relationship at any time, for no reason. However, some agreements may specify circumstances when an employee may be terminated for cause (e.g., criminal conviction, license suspension, etc.). It is important, from the employed physician's perspective, that the agreement include a notice provision, as well as a time period to cure any breaches.

Restrictive Covenants Employment agreements usually include a **restrictive covenant** that incorporates both non-competition and non-solicitation clauses. Restrictive covenants may prohibit practice in a certain geographic area or for a certain length of time and may also prevent a physician from soliciting patients or referrals. To be enforceable, however, the restrictive covenant must be reasonable in duration and scope, not injure the public, and not prohibit the physician from pursuing activities that the employer does not engage in. A restrictive covenant may not be so broadly drawn that it prevents a physician from practicing his profession. Attorneys and paralegals should check state law for specific statutes on the enforceability of restrictive covenants.

Independent Contractor

Sometimes, both the employer and the physician prefer that a business relationship be that of an **independent contractor**, rather than that of an employee. The Internal Revenue Service states:

> A general rule is that you, the payer, have the right to control or direct only the result of the work done by an independent contractor, and not the means and methods of accomplishing the result."[13]

For a worker who is considered an independent contractor, an employer is responsible for issuing Form 1099-MISC, Miscellaneous Income, to report compensation paid.

For physicians who are involved in a variety of settings and who wish to control their hours, an agreement to work as an independent contractor may be the preferred arrangement. For example, a teaching physician employed full-time as faculty at an academic medical center may also serve part-time as a medical director at a private hospital or provide coverage for a vacationing doctor. In those situations, an agreement for the physician to be an independent contractor would work well. Duties and responsibilities must be delineated in the agreement, with many of the same provisions as in an employment contract.

THE ROLE OF THE PARALEGAL

Since attorneys are intimately involved in many physician financial relationships, paralegals can find themselves called upon to research state licensing regulations and case law for license revocation/reinstatement; assist with a physician's contract drafting and management; and provide credentialing information.

OWNERSHIP

Many doctors in the United States work for themselves in private or group practices, often indicating financial independence. Ownership in a practice includes decision-making power, shared profits and losses, and equity in the practice's value.

Purchase Agreements

Physician practices can be as simple as sole proprietorships, which require no formal documentation, or as complex as partnerships, limited liability companies (LLC), or corporations, depending on state law.

A number of documents may evidence a physician's "buy-in" into an existing practice. Foremost among these is the purchase agreement, which details the physician's ownership percentage, purchase price, and payment terms, as well as representations and warranties about assets, liabilities, taxes, etc. The ownership percentage may be evidenced by stock, partnership interest, or LLC member interest. Other documents may include an operating agreement for an LLC, a partnership agreement, or bylaws if the practice is organized as a corporation.

Ownership Agreements

Ownership agreements usually address both management and control issues and ownership interests. Management and control issues depend on the size of the practice and the roles and duties of those assuming management; thus, these should be clearly defined. For example, if a physician-owner is the treasurer of the corporation, what specifically can the treasurer do? Write checks for business expenses? Sign payroll for non-physician employees? Award a bonus to himself? In larger practices, there may be a management committee that handles everyday operations such as hiring/firing employees and executing contracts with insurance companies.

Ownership interests imply voting rights in management of the practice. Owners may have equal say or voting may be weighted according to seniority, productivity, or other factors. Ownership is not generally transferable, though ownership agreements should address transferability to other owners due to a physician's disability, retirement, relocation, or death. Likewise, ownership agreements often include methodology for valuation of a physician's share of the practice if any of the preceding events occur.

Compensation

Physician-owners share the risk of profit and loss; thus, their base compensation may be lower than a physician-employee. However, remaining funds can be distributed as bonuses. Ownership agreements should spell out how compensation and fringe benefits are determined, as well as calculation formulas for bonuses. Physician-owners may also be compensated for a longer period of disability than a physician-employee. Another consideration is how a physician-owner may be terminated from the practice. Unlike physician-employees, physician-owners are generally terminated only for cause. "For cause" provisions can include loss of license, criminal activities, regulatory violations, low productivity, damage to the practice's reputation, loss of hospital privileges, bankruptcy, moral turpitude, incompetent practice of medicine, failure to maintain malpractice insurance, or other reasons spelled out in the ownership agreement.

Dissolution

Although ownership agreements usually prohibit or restrict transfer of ownership interests, most physician-ownership agreements recognize a physician's professional life cycle: disability, relocation, retirement, and death. Any triggering event should be clearly defined, along with a provision that addresses buy-out of shares by the remaining physician-owners. Voluntary **dissolution** of a practice is also an area that should be explored and defined in the ownership agreement.

SUMMARY

In this chapter, we have examined the major areas that impact a physician's practice. Graduation from medical school is just the beginning of a career. Physicians must be licensed by the state in which they practice and they must be credentialed by the hospitals where they admit patients. Physicians in private practice must first consider whether they want to be employees or owners. Health care organizations must consider how they want to contract with doctors. Both employment and ownership agreements must be detailed contracts, with consideration for compensation, benefits, malpractice insurance, and termination.

Licensure is regulated by state boards or agencies. Credentialing is a process controlled by a hospital's medical staff. Employment and ownership agreements are contracts and must meet any state law requirements.

KEY TERMS

credentialing: Verifying and evaluating the qualifications (education, license, etc.) of a health care practitioner who provides patient care services in a hospital or other health care organization.

dissolution: Ending or breaking up. For example, dissolution of a contract is a mutual agreement to end it; dissolution of a corporation is ending its existence.

independent contractor: A person who contracts with an "employer" to do a particular piece of work by his or her own methods and under his or her own control.

medical staff: Individual health care practitioners who are subject to the bylaws, rules, and regulations of an organized medical staff, usually in a hospital.

restrictive covenant: A clause in an employment contract that prohibits the employee from working for the employer's competitors for a certain time period after the contract ends.

REVIEW QUESTIONS AND EXERCISES

1. Following Hurricane Katrina in August 2005, many physicians wanted to volunteer to help in the Gulf Coast states that were affected by the disaster. This raised problems of licensure and credentialing for the volunteers. Check your state's licensing board or entity and the Department of Health and Human Services to see what emergency orders or measures were put into place at that time.

2. An essential function of a health care paralegal is contract management. Suppose that you work for a hospital system with the following:
   - One thousand physician contracts of different duration and different begin/end dates
   - agreements are a mix of employee and independent contractors
   - physicians who practice in 30 different specialties

Design a template or spreadsheet that would allow you to review contract renewals at least 60 days in advance.

3. Many large health systems publish their medical staff bylaws online. See if you can find the staff bylaws regarding credentialing for a hospital in your area.

4. Research your state's law to find the licensing regulations for physicians. Are there any provisions that surprised you? Discuss.

5. You are the paralegal to an associate at a health law firm. The associate's newest client is Dr. Smithjohn, who has just undergone a negative peer review process and has been recommended for denial of staff privileges at East County General Hospital. Dr. Smithjohn feels that he has been unfairly treated because he used an experimental, unapproved (and very expensive) drug in his medical management of diabetes in about a dozen patients. All of the patients have shown improved conditions. What is Dr. Smithjohn's next course of action? What must he prove? How likely is a successful lawsuit? Identify what types of evidence may be helpful to produce to aid Dr. Smithjohn's case.

6. Assume that Dr. Smithjohn is unsuccessful in his lawsuit. What repercussions may he suffer?

7. West County General Hospital wants to develop a solid credentialing and medical staff privileges policy. What resources, websites, and databases should be included as references to the policy? What federal laws and regulations must be considered?

8. Refer to *In the Matter of Andre Nehorayoff, Respondent, v. Richard P. Mills, as Commissioner of Education of the State of New York, et al* in the Online Companion that accompanies this text. What was the physician's professional misconduct? What did the doctor submit as proof of his rehabilitation? What is the petitioner's burden of proof?

ENDNOTES

1. No. 04AP-811 (Ohio Ct. App. May 10, 2005).
2. *Hosseinipour v. State Med. Bd. of Ohio,* No. 03AP-512, 2004 WL 503941 (Ohio Ct. App. Mar. 16, 2004).
3. 95 N.Y.2d 671, 746 N.E.2d 169, 723 N.Y.S.2d 114 (2001).
4. 42 U.S.C. §§ 1128 and 1156.
5. Publ.L. 99-660, 45 C.F.R. § 60 *et seq.*
6. "Eligible Entities," NPDB Handbook, Department of Health and Human Services Publication No. HRSA-95-255.
7. Standard MS 4.50, Joint Commission on Accreditation of Hospitals, Comprehensive Accreditation Manual for Hospitals: The Official Handbook (2005).
8. American Medical Association Policy H-230.975.
9. No. 04-430 (Ark. Sup. Ct. February 2, 2006).
10. 42 U.S.C. § 11112(a).
11. "Fact Sheet on Professional Review Immunity," National Practitioner Data Bank, Healthcare Integrity and Protection Data Bank, available at http://www.npdb-hipdb.com/factsheet.html, accessed June 26, 2007.
12. No. 04-1553 (8th Cir. May 24, 2005).
13. "Independent Contractors vs. Employees," available at http://www.irs.gov/businesses/small, accessed June 26, 2007.

CHAPTER 5

MEDICARE

OBJECTIVES

After reading this chapter, you should be able to

- Identify and distinguish the different parts of Medicare.
- Understand the roles of beneficiaries, providers and suppliers, physicians, and Medicare Advantage organizations.
- Differentiate payment methods for physicians and other providers.
- Master the steps of the appeals process for the different parts of Medicare.

MEDICARE COVERAGE AND ELIGIBILITY

Medicare, the country's largest third-party payer, continues to evolve its programs and policies to meet the needs of its beneficiaries, while struggling with politics, economics, and technology. To say that the Medicare program is enormous is a gross understatement. The Medicare program processes over one billion fee-for-service claims per year, is the country's largest purchaser of managed care services, and, as of 2006, accounts for 19 percent of the federal government's budget. There are now more than 43 million beneficiaries enrolled in Medicare.[1]

Originally enacted during President Lyndon B. Johnson's administration, Medicare has since expanded its coverage from those over age 65 to include the disabled and anyone with end-stage renal disease. During President George W. Bush's administration, Medicare received an "overhaul" of its programs with the enactment of the Medicare Prescription Drug, Improvement, and Modernization Act of 2003 (commonly referred to as the MMA).[2] This act added a new Part D to Medicare (see Exhibit 5–1), a prescription drug benefit, and made other significant changes that we will discuss in this chapter.

Part	Coverage
A	Hospital services, etc.
B	Professional services, etc.
C	Medicare Advantage plans
D	Prescription drugs

EXHIBIT 5–1: MEDICARE QUICK REFERENCE

The Centers for Medicare and Medicaid Services (CMS) is the federal health oversight agency charged with administration of the Medicare and Medicaid programs. Though CMS is quite large, it is part of a cabinet-level agency, **the Department of Health and Human Services (DHHS)**. Later in this chapter, we will discuss the parameters of the agency's authority.

ACRONYMS

CMS: the Centers for Medicare and Medicaid Services

DHHS: the Department of Health and Human Services

With the aging of the United States population and the retirement of the "baby boomer" generation, continued Medicare expansion is inevitable. However, the financial burden on the federal government will also continue to grow.

Although outside the scope of this chapter, Medicare must be distinguished from the Medicaid program. While Medicare is a program primarily for those retired from employment, Medicaid serves the population with no or little work history. Medicaid is a health insurance program for low income, disabled persons. The Centers for Medicare and Medicaid Services set minimum standards for eligibility and benefits. However, states administer the programs and benefits can vary from state to state, based on the relative wealth or poverty of the state budget. In recent years, many states have inaugurated programs for the medically needy, including pregnant women, children, and the working poor.

Part A: Hospital Services

Medicare Part A is often called Hospital Insurance. Part A covers inpatient hospitalization, **skilled nursing facility (SNF)** care, some **home health agency (HHA)** services, and hospice care.

ACRONYMS

HHA: home health agency

SNF: skilled nursing facility

Coverage Hospital covered services include a semi-private room, meals, regular nursing services, laboratory tests, X-rays, operating and recovery room, in-patient prescriptions, intensive care, in-patient rehabilitation, psychiatric care, and other medically necessary services and supplies.

Following hospitalization, a patient may need a lengthy rehabilitative stay in a non-acute setting, such as a skilled nursing facility. If a patient has been in a hospital for at least three consecutive days, he/she may be discharged directly or within 30 days to a SNF for extended services of up to 100 days. A doctor, clinical nurse, or nurse practitioner must certify services as medically necessary.

Home health care services are available to **beneficiaries** who need intermittent and non-acute medical, nursing, or therapeutic care. These services are provided in the beneficiary's home or in another outpatient setting. Beneficiaries may receive 100 days of HHA services following a three-day hospitalization. In order to qualify for HHA services, a beneficiary must be

- confined to the home.
- under the care of a physician
- receiving services under a plan of care established and periodically reviewed by a physician.
- in need of skilled nursing care on an intermittent basis, physical therapy, speech-language pathology, or occupational therapy

However, housekeeping, transportation, drugs, and biologicals are not covered HHA services.[3]

Hospice care is provided to terminally ill patients who have decided to forego aggressive treatment and, instead, have opted for palliative care, such as pain relief, social services, physical therapy, and nursing services. A physician must certify that a patient is terminally ill, i.e., that he/she has six months or less to live if the illness is allowed to run its normal course. Beneficiaries receive hospice care in two periods of 90 benefit days each, followed by unlimited 60-day benefit periods. By electing to receive hospice care, beneficiaries waive their rights to all other Medicare services.[4]

Eligibility Every individual over the age of 65 who is eligible for Social Security retirement or survivor benefits is presumably eligible for Part A. Federal, state, and local government employees over the age of 65 may also be eligible, if their employment was "Medicare qualified." Until the mid-1980s, government workers did not pay payroll taxes into the Part A trust fund as they do now. Permanent residents who are over the age of 65 and have resided in the United States for five years, but who would not otherwise be eligible for Medicare, may voluntarily enroll in Part A by paying a monthly premium. Other eligible Part A beneficiaries are those under the age of 65 who have end-stage renal disease or those who have received disability benefits for at least 20 months under Social Security or Railroad Retirement programs.

Funding Part A is funded by payroll taxes paid into the federal Hospital Insurance Trust Fund. The trust fund's financial health is dependent on income exceeding outlay; thus, the vagaries of health care trends and current demographics influence its financial stability.

Part B: Physician Services

The title of this section may be misleading. Part B includes services that doctors may order, as well as actual physician visits.

Coverage Medicare Part B, also known as Supplementary Medical Insurance, covers

- physician services
- outpatient hospital department care
- services at ambulatory surgical centers
- ambulance services
- rural health care services
- surgical dressings
- laboratory tests and diagnostic X-rays
- outpatient physical, occupational, and speech therapy
- rental or purchase of **durable medical equipment (DME)**
- prosthetic and orthotic devices
- some home health care not covered under Part A
- certain other supplies

ACRONYM

DME: durable medical equipment

For Medicare purposes, physicians are either medical doctors or doctors of osteopathic medicine and certain limited license practitioners (e.g., chiropractors, dentists, optometrists, oral and maxillofacial surgeons, and podiatrists). Physician services include diagnosis, therapy, surgery, consultation, and treatment of the patient.

Part B services generally fall into one of three categories:

- those provided by outpatient providers and freestanding suppliers
- those rendered by non-physician practitioners who work under physician supervision or with physician collaboration
- professional services, including supplies, that are "incident to" physician services

"Incident to" services are often the subject of interpretation and misinterpretation, necessitating the Centers for Medicare and Medicaid Services to issue a rule in 2002 to clarify "incident to" billing provisions.[6] "Incident to" services are not performed by a physician, but are considered an essential element of his or her professional service. They may be rendered by a non-physician practitioner, such as a physician assistant or nurse practitioner, under the supervision of a physician in the physician's office suite or in the patient's home. Examples include cardiac rehabilitation and administration of certain drugs and biologicals that cannot be self-administered.

SPOTLIGHT ON...

Despite the health care community's emphasis on preventative care, Medicare did not cover a basic physical exam for new Part B beneficiaries until January 1, 2005. Beneficiaries must get the "Welcome to Medicare" physical exam within the first six months of Part B coverage. Other newly covered services include cardiovascular and diabetes screening, PET scans for Alzheimer's disease, and a one-time ultrasound screening for Abdominal Aortic Aneurysm for beneficiaries who are at risk.[7]

Eligibility Part B is a voluntary program available to Part A beneficiaries who must pay a monthly premium, deducted from their Social Security checks. Additionally, Part B services are subject to a yearly deductible; beneficiaries may also incur co-payments for certain services. The cost of the Part B premium changes annually.

Funding Unlike Part A, which is funded through the Hospital Insurance Trust Fund, Part B is funded through the Supplementary Medical Insurance Trust Fund. Besides the monthly premiums, Part B receives general tax revenues. Thus, bankruptcy of Part B is unlikely.

Part C: Medicare Advantage

Medicare Advantage (MA) is a popular managed care plan offered under Medicare.

Coverage In 1997, the Balanced Budget Act added Medicare Part C to the Social Security Act.[9] Medicare Part C established a new private health plan option for Medicare beneficiaries similar to a managed care plan. Originally known as Medicare + Choice, Part C's name changed to Medicare Advantage with the passage of the Medicare Prescription Drug, Improvement, and Modernization Act of 2003.[10]

Part C beneficiaries receive all of the benefits of Parts A, B, and D, subject to some limitations. Benefits are basic and supplemental. Basic benefits consist of those in Parts A and B. Supplemental benefits are either mandatory or optional, depending on the plan approved by the Centers for Medicare and Medicaid Services. Typical supplemental benefits may include wellness programs and discounts on eyeglasses.

Services are delivered to Part C beneficiaries by the plan, which may be a preferred provider organization, private fee-for-service plan, provider-sponsored organization, or an insurance plan operated in conjunction with a medical savings account. Beneficiaries may pay co-payments for services or may pay monthly insurance premiums to the plan. Like private managed care for non-Medicare beneficiaries, Medicare Advantage plans require beneficiaries to choose services from a pre-approved list of doctors and hospitals, or network. Going outside of the network generally requires pre-approval and/or higher co-payments by the beneficiary.

Eligibility Beneficiaries who are eligible for Part A and enrolled in Part B may elect Medicare Advantage coverage during designated enrollment periods in their geographic areas. Medicare Advantage plans are now

ACRONYM

MA: Medicare Advantage

able to serve regions of an entire state or multi-state areas. All 50 states now have MA plans, although enrollment is less dense in rural areas.[11]

Enrollment in a Medicare Advantage program is accomplished by an affirmative request by the beneficiary during the plan's enrollment period. Those individuals with **end-stage renal disease (ESRD)** are not eligible to join a MA plan; however, if an individual develops ESRD while enrolled, he or she may continue to receive MA benefits.

Medicare Advantage beneficiaries may decide to **disenroll** during specified periods and then elect to enroll in another MA plan or return to traditional Medicare. However, beginning in 2006, MA beneficiaries will be subject to "lock-in" periods when enrollment and disenrollment may be restricted.

Medicare Advantage organizations may terminate a beneficiary from the plan for several reasons: late premium payments, disruptive behavior, or termination of the service area by the plan. In cases of termination, a beneficiary's coverage reverts to traditional fee-for-service Medicare.

Funding The Centers for Medicare and Medicaid Services pay MA organizations from the Hospital Insurance and Supplementary Medical Insurance Trust Funds. Medicare Advantage organizations may also charge premiums and co-payments to beneficiaries; these must be approved by CMS as part of the MA plan.

Special Requirements Medicare Advantage plans are the only organizations required to have compliance plans under Medicare regulations.[12] The compliance plan must include all elements recommended by the Sentencing Guidelines; please refer to Chapter 7 for more information on compliance programs. Medicare Advantage Prescription Drug Plans must have comprehensive programs to combat and prevent fraud, waste, and abuse.[13]

The Centers for Medicare and Medicaid Services also regulate the marketing and enrollment practices of MA organizations.[14] All marketing materials must be reviewed and approved by CMS in advance of distribution. Marketing materials include any and all materials distributed to beneficiaries that promote the MA plan, inform beneficiaries of enrollment procedures and eligibility, or explain coverage of services. Organizations are prohibited from having marketing practices that discriminate against beneficiaries on the basis of their health status. In particular, the Office of Inspector General for DHHS is concerned with

ACRONYM

ESRD: end-stage renal disease

"cherry-picking" beneficiaries during enrollment—selective marketing that targets healthier individuals.[15]

Part D: Prescription Drugs

Prescription drug coverage has been a long-awaited benefit for Medicare beneficiaries.

Coverage The Medicare Prescription Drug, Improvement, and Modernization Act of 2003 established a voluntary outpatient prescription drug benefit for prescription drugs, biologicals, and vaccines. After passage of the MMA, CMS authorized a temporary drug discount program for Part B beneficiaries from June 2004 through the end of 2005. Since Part C beneficiaries usually receive discounted drugs through their MA plans, they were not eligible to participate in a separate discount program. The drug discount card was offered by pharmacy benefit managers, insurers, and other qualified sponsors. Beneficiaries paid a $30 enrollment fee. Low-income beneficiaries were eligible for a $600 subsidy. After the effective date of Part D regular coverage, the discount drug card program was phased out.

Coverage under Part D for enrolled beneficiaries was effective January 1, 2006. Costs vary depending on the plan chosen, but the average is about $37 monthly, with a $250 yearly deductible. Beneficiaries also have to pay co-insurance amounts. Part D limits drug coverage at $2,250 yearly, but then picks up coverage again if a beneficiary's total out-of-pocket expenses reach $3,600 yearly. Beneficiaries with limited income and resources may be eligible for government subsidies.[16]

Eligibility Beneficiaries eligible for Part A and enrolled in Part B are eligible for this new benefit that became operational in 2006. Beneficiaries enrolled in MA plans must access the drug benefits that their plans offer.

Funding The Part D benefit is financed through a separate account in the Supplementary Medical Insurance Trust Fund and through beneficiary premiums.

Electronic Prescribing At some point in the not-too-distant future, paper records and prescriptions will give way to electronic media. The MMA provides that electronic prescriptions, or e-prescribing, must be based on national standards and will be mandatory for drug plans participating in the new Medicare Part D prescription drug benefit by 2009. The Centers for Medicare and Medicaid Services required an initial set of well-established standards when the Medicare benefit began in 2006.[17]

Miscellaneous Provisions

Some little-known but important features of the Medicare program are described briefly in this section.

Low-Income Assistance The Qualified Medicare Beneficiary program, the Specified Low Income Medicare Beneficiary program, and the Qualifying Individual program all offer financial assistance for low-income **Medicare beneficiaries** who cannot afford to pay premiums, coinsurance, and/or deductibles. Beneficiaries must have total annual incomes that match or fall below 135% of the federal poverty level in order to qualify for assistance. Medicare refers to these beneficiaries, eligible for Part A and/or B as well as Medicaid, as "dual eligibles."[19]

Secondary Payor Rule Medicare only pays for services when it is the primary **payer**. Items or services that may be covered under other health insurance plans or programs (e.g., employer-sponsored health insurance, worker's compensation coverage, etc.) are not eligible for payment. In such circumstances, Medicare's liability is secondary to that of the primary payer or insurer.

Medigap Beneficiaries who are covered under Parts A and B may purchase supplemental policies known as Medigap policies. These private commercial insurance polices are intended to fill in the "gaps" in Medicare coverage. Typically, the Medigap policies cover coinsurance, deductibles, and prescription drugs. No Medigap policies solely for Part D coverage could be issued or renewed after January 1, 2006, the effective date of the prescription drug coverage in Part D. However, other Medigap or supplement policies for co-insurance and other benefits may still be available.

National Coverage Decisions The Medicare Coverage Manuals list broad areas of covered items and services and may lag behind in identifying new areas of coverage because of rapid advances in medicine and treatment modalities. The Secretary of DHHS has the authority to make coverage determinations for specific items and services. A **National Coverage Decision (NCD)** is basically a policy statement that grants, limits, or excludes Medicare coverage for a specific item or service or extends or denies coverage for a specific patient population. The NCD directs Medicare contractors or fiscal intermediaries how to process claims. The Center for Medicare and Medicaid Services issues NCDs in manual instruction, memoranda, rulings, or notices in the *Federal Register*. After publication, these NCDs are binding.

> **ACRONYM**
> NCD: national coverage decision

Health care organizations, providers, and suppliers, as well as individual beneficiaries, may request a National Coverage Determination. However, the request is a formal, detailed process outlined in the *Federal Register*. The Centers for Medicare and Medicaid Services prefer to receive informal questions first regarding the current coverage of a particular item or service, the kinds of data needed for submission with the request, the appropriate format of the request, or the typical timelines to complete a request. The Centers for Medicare and Medicaid Services also offer suggestions to the requestor to clarify the kind of information necessary for an evaluation of whether an item or service is "reasonable and necessary."[20]

Medicare contractors may make **local coverage decisions (LCD)**,[21] often on a claim-by-claim basis, in the absence of NCDs. The LCDs provide guidance on coverage and coding of services and items for providers and suppliers in their specific geographic region. An LCD may not conflict with an NCD, but it may supplement it.

> **ACRONYM**
> LCD: local coverage decision

Advance Beneficiary Notice Beneficiaries are entitled to receive an **Advance Beneficiary Notice (ABN)** from a doctor or supplier when payment for a service or item is likely to be denied by Medicare. The ABN must be provided in writing and in advance to be considered effective notice. Beneficiaries may appeal ABN decisions.

> **ACRONYM**
> ABN: advance beneficiary notice

CERTIFICATION

The Medicare programs obligate those providers, physicians, and suppliers who wish to participate in and receive reimbursement for items and services to be certified as eligible to do so. In fact, all claims contain a section for certification that a service or item was reasonable and medically necessary.

Providers

Medicare requires that providers and suppliers meet certain eligibility conditions to participate in the Medicare program. These are referred to as "conditions of participation," or CoPs, and are standards that facilities must adhere to in order to receive payment from Medicare. A state agency usually inspects facilities and certifies them as approved providers. Private accreditation groups such as the Joint Commission on Accreditation of Healthcare Organizations may give "deemed" status to providers whose facilities they have inspected and certified, thus negating the need for a state agency inspection.

Providers that have met required standards must then execute a written agreement, or "provider agreement," with DHHS in which they agree to abide with all Medicare program requirements. These provider agreements are automatically renewed each year unless the provider is excluded from Medicare participation for reasons of criminal or civil misconduct or substantial noncompliance with program requirements.[22]

Each provider is issued a provider identification number which must appear on every claim for reimbursement of services, as well as any correspondence.

Physicians and Suppliers

Physicians and **suppliers** must complete detailed applications before they are approved for participation in the Medicare program. These applications include information on professional licensure, ownership, prior practice, and practice location(s). A Medicare contractor for the geographic region in which the physician practices processes applications. Physicians and suppliers must sign authorizations for electronic funds transfer for payment and may also sign agreements for electronic data exchange. Implementation of regulations issued pursuant to the Health Insurance Portability and Accountability Act of 1996[23] has nearly eliminated the paper claim and paper check. Like the facility providers mentioned in the previous section, suppliers are issued provider identification numbers. Physicians receive a unique physician identification number that must appear on their claims.

Medicare Advantage Organizations

In order to qualify as an MA organization, and then enroll beneficiaries and be paid for services on their behalf, an MA plan must enter into a contract with Medicare. A condition of participation is assumption of financial risk on a prospective basis for health care services for the plan's members. A Medicare Advantage organization must provide proof of appropriate state licensure (e.g., **HMO**, **PPO**, etc.) and authority to accept prepaid capitation for comprehensive health care services. Contracting organizations must also meet certain minimum enrollment numbers and have a satisfactory administrative and management plan.

ACRONYMS

HMO: health maintenance organization

PPO: preferred provider organization

Contracts are issued for one year and are renewable. Like facility providers, an MA may be given "deemed" status if it meets the standards of an accrediting organization such as the National Committee for Quality Assurance or Utilization Review Accreditation Commission.

Prescription Drug Providers Providers who wish to participate in Part D sponsorship must file an application with DHHS for a particular geographic region. A **Prescription Drug Provider (PDP)** must be state-licensed as a health insurer or other risk-bearing organization. Plans may assume full-risk, limited risk, or be fallback plans (i.e., does not bear insurance risk). As with Medicare Advantage plans, PDP sponsors must adhere to certain administrative and management standards, as well as rules on enrollment, marketing, contracting periods, and beneficiary protections. The Centers for Medicare and Medicaid Services have published special guidances for PDP sponsors, along with a drug formulary.[24]

ACRONYM

PDP: Prescription Drug Provider

MEDICARE PAYMENT

Medicare uses several methods of payment for services.

Introduction to Reimbursement Methodology

Paralegals without accounting expertise may find Medicare's methods of reimbursement to be as baffling and frustrating as calculus written in Cyrillic script. Prior to 1983, Medicare paid for services on a retrospective cost basis, meaning that hospitals and doctors and other providers were paid the amount that they charged for services that had been completed. Faced with spiraling health care costs that were borne by the federal government, Congress passed the Social Security Amendments of 1983 and the creation of a prospective payment system for Medicare in-patient services.[25]

Medicare reimbursement attorneys and their staff must be well informed about reimbursement methodology in order to ensure that payments to their health care providers are correct.

Prospective Payment System

The **Prospective Payment System (PPS)** pays for in-patient hospital services on a prospective rate, usually the nationwide average of treating a patient with a particular medical condition. Each case or condition is categorized into a **diagnostic-related group (DRG)**.

The Prospective Payment System is used for acute hospital care, rehabilitation hospitals, long-term care hospitals, psychiatric hospitals, and rural-area hospitals. Some hospitals such as children's hospitals, cancer hospitals, and Veterans Administration hospitals are excluded from the PPS system because a workable PPS methodology could not be developed. These are paid on a reasonable cost basis, subject to limits imposed by the Tax Equity and Fiscal Responsibility Act (TEFRA) of 1982.[26]

Diagnostic-Related Groups

A diagnostic-related group (DRG) is

> a classification system that groups patients according to diagnosis, type of treatment, age, and other relevant criteria. Under the prospective payment system, hospitals are paid a set fee for treating patients in a single DRG category, regardless of the actual cost of care for the individual.[27]

Each DRG has a payment weight assigned to it, based on the average resources used to treat Medicare patients in that DRG. The base payment rate is divided into a labor-related and non-labor share. The labor-related share is adjusted by the wage index applicable to the area where the hospital is located.

Certain diagnostic services performed on an outpatient basis during the three days immediately preceding a patient's hospital admission are not billable to Medicare as separate services. They are considered part of the "72-hour DRG payment window" and must be billed as part of the DRG.

ACRONYMS

DRG: Diagnostic-Related Group

PPS: Prospective Payment System

Special Adjustments

Medicare makes several payment adjustments in certain areas to help compensate for special programs.

Low-Income Patients Hospitals that have a high number of low-income patients are eligible to receive an add-on payment to the DRG base rate. This addition is known as "disproportionate share;" such a hospital is often referred to as a **disproportionate share hospital (DSH)**. Congress established the DSH add-on payment as recognition of the relatively higher costs of providing care to low-income patients, often resulting from the generally poorer health of these patients. Hospital financial analysts must submit detailed cost reporting each fiscal year so that their hospitals receive the appropriate amount due to them under the disproportionate share addition.

ACRONYM

DSH: disproportionate share hospital

The decision in *Monmouth Medical Center v. Thompson*[28] was significant for hospitals that provide health care services to low-income patients. First, it invalidated the government's previous ruling that prohibited the reopening of cost reports to recalculate the disproportionate share payment. It also allowed any Medicare hospital in any part of the country to bring suit in the jurisdiction of the District of Columbia district court.

Medical Education Programs Medicare subsidizes the costs of educating new doctors and allied health professionals in teaching hospitals through direct graduate medical education and indirect medical education adjustments. Certain residency programs qualify for graduate medical education payments. Approved teaching hospitals receive an indirect medical education adjustment for each patient's case. The MMA made changes to the calculation of the appropriate rates and the programs covered.[29]

Outliers Special payments above the usual Medicare rates can be made for extraordinarily high cost cases. These are known as **outlier** payments; DHHS adjusts the threshold criteria for determining outliers annually.

Introduction to Reimbursement for Physicians

Medicare payments to physicians were originally based on the lesser of the reasonable or customary charges. However, as with Part A services, stricter payment methods became necessary to control costs to the government. Physician payments can now be one of three types:

- resource-based relative value
- blended capitation
- market-based system

ACRONYM

RBRVS: Resource Based Relative Value Scale

Resource Based Relative Value Scale In 1989, Congress established a new payment methodology for physician services called the Resource Based Relative Value Scale. The **Resource-Based Relative Value Scale (RBRVS)** bases fees on the relative value of a physician's work (i.e., skill level, intensity of effort, and medical judgment), which are then adjusted for variations by geographic area, practice area, and potential malpractice expenses. Each medical procedure is assigned a relative value, which is then multiplied by the conversion factor to determine the Medicare payment. The Medicare Economic Index updates the conversion factor annually.

Medicare-participating physicians are paid the full RBRVS amount, while non-participating physicians are paid 95 percent of the allowable RBRVS amount. Non-participating physicians are subject to a maximum limit on what they can charge Medicare beneficiaries over the fee schedule amount; they are also subject to sanctions if they repeatedly bill Medicare beneficiaries in excess of the limiting charge.

ACRONYM

HCPCS: HCFA Common Procedural Coding System (pronounced "hick-pix")

The RBRVS has been compiled into a coding arrangement known as the **HCFA Common Procedural Coding System (HCPCS)**. Proper coding and documentation of office visits, hospital stays, medical consultations, and case management services is taken very seriously by CMS. Failure to provide adequate documentation in a patient's chart can trigger unwanted events such as reduced reimbursement or allegations of false claims to Medicare.

Capitation Capitation is an advance monthly payment made by CMS. Physicians receive a per-member-per-month payment for those patients who are enrolled in Medicare Advantage programs. The payment is equal to 1/12 of the annual MA capitation rate for the particular geographic region that the MA organization serves.

Capitation payments vary across the country. Congress attempted to even out variations by allowing MA organizations the greater of

- a blend of national and local rates
- a guaranteed minimum payment floor
- a minimum increase over the prior year's payment floor of at least 2 percent
- One hundred percent of the average fee-for-service amount in the original Medicare

Capitation is a risky payment method as physicians must serve as "gatekeepers" for beneficiaries seeking frequent office visits, expensive tests, and lengthy in-hospital stays. To make capitation a profitable venture, healthier beneficiaries are more attractive.

Market-Based System Beginning in 2006, the MMA established a competitive, market-based system for certain services. Part B has a competitive acquisition program for drugs and biologicals to be supplied directly to physicians. Likewise, payment for DME and other supplies are also subject to a competitive bidding process. Medicare Advantage plans under Part C are also required to use a competitive bidding process for benefits under Parts A and B. Part D will incorporate bidding and benchmark rates into payments for prescription drugs.

Assignment and Reassignment

Students familiar with insurance law may recognize the concepts of assignment and reassignment of insurance claim proceeds. Medicare has its own rules.

Assignment Medicare considers assignment as an agreement between the physician or supplier and the Medicare beneficiary. The beneficiary transfers his or her rights to benefits for covered services to the physician or supplier. In return, the physician or supplier agrees to accept the approved Medicare rate as payment in full for services rendered.

No direct payments to beneficiaries are allowed under Part A. Under Part B, however, beneficiaries have the choice of assignment or of receiving direct payment from Medicare and then paying the physician or supplier himself. Physicians and suppliers who accept assignment may not charge beneficiaries anything other than required co-insurance and Medicare deductibles. Under Part C, only the MA organization is entitled to receive payments.

Reassignment In general, Medicare prohibits reassignment of benefits to anyone other than the original provider of services. However, the MMA liberalized the reassignment rules regarding site of service.[30] Now, physicians and suppliers may reassign payment, wherever the service was performed, as long as the physician or supplier is an employee or independent contractor of the entity that will be billing for services.

The rule that prohibits Medicare reassignment may be eroding. Exceptions to this general rule are fairly numerous. These include payments

- to an inpatient facility,
- to an organized health care delivery system,
- to an employer,
- to an agent,
- under a reciprocal billing arrangement,
- under a ***locum tenens*** arrangement,
- for purchased diagnostic tests,
- for diagnostic test interpretation,
- to a bank, and
- to certain others (e.g., a medical school or government agency).

MEDICARE APPEALS

For a quick primer on administrative law and procedure, please refer to Appendix C.

The Medicare appeal process has several twists and turns, depending on which party appeals a decision and the type of dispute being appealed. Paralegal students may find it interesting to learn that appeals under Parts A and B generally involve disputes between providers or suppliers and the Medicare program. Health law sections of law firms often have staff devoted to these complex reimbursement issues. Individual beneficiaries also have the right to appeal disputes of coverage and payment, though attorneys are seldom involved in these.

Both the Benefits Improvement and Protection Act of 2000 (BIPA)[31] and the Medicare Prescription Drug, Improvement, and Modernization Act of 2003 (MMA)[32] made procedural and substantive changes to the appeals process. The BIPA changes included timing of review and appeal requests, as well as establishment of an appeals process for coverage determination.

Medicare now contracts with private insurance companies, called Fiscal Intermediaries for Part A and carriers for Part B, to carry out many of the administrative functions of the appeals process. The MMA also shortened time limits for appeals.

Appeals by Providers, Physicians, and Other Suppliers for Parts A and B

Medicare offers five levels in the Part A and Part B appeals process (see Exhibit 5–2). The levels, listed in the order in which they occur, are

- redetermination by the **Fiscal Intermediary** or the carrier
- reconsideration by a **Qualified Independent Contractor**
- hearing before an **Administrative Law Judge**
- review by the Medicare Appeals Council within the Departmental Appeals Board
- judicial review in U.S. District Court.

First Level of Appeal: Redetermination A redetermination is an examination of a claim by the FI or carrier personnel who are different from the personnel who made the initial determination. The appellant has 120 days from the date of receipt of the initial claim determination to file an appeal. There is no minimum amount in controversy to request a redetermination.

ACRONYMS
ALJ: Administrative Law Judge
FI: Fiscal Intermediary
QIC: Qualified Independent Contractor

- Reconsideration by Qualified Independent Contractor (QIC)
- Hearing before Administrative Law Judge (ALJ)
- Appeals Council/Departmental Appeals Board (DAB) review
- Judicial review in U.S. District Court
- Redetermination by Medicare Administrative Contractor (MAC)

EXHIBIT 5–2: FIVE LEVELS OF THE APPEALS PROCESS

A request for a redetermination may be filed on Form CMS-20027 or in a written request that includes

- beneficiary name
- Medicare Health Insurance Claim number
- specific service and/or item(s) for which a redetermination is being requested
- date(s) of service
- name and signature of the party or the authorized or appointed representative of the party

The appellant should attach any supporting documentation to the redetermination request. The FI or carrier will usually issue a decision (either a letter or a revised remittance advice) within 60 days of receipt of the redetermination request.

Second Level of Appeal: Reconsideration A party to the redetermination may request a reconsideration if dissatisfied with the decision made during the redetermination process. A Qualified Independent Contractor (QIC) will conduct the reconsideration through an independent review of medical necessity issues by a panel of physicians or other health care professionals. Like the redetermination, a minimum monetary threshold is not required to request reconsideration.

A written reconsideration request must be filed within 180 days of receipt of the redetermination. The Medicare Redetermination Notice gives instructions for reconsiderations. A request for reconsideration may be made on Form CMS-20033 or by written request with the same details as are required by the reconsideration. The request must explain why the party disagrees with the redetermination decision. A copy of the Medicare Redetermination Notice and other useful documentation must be included.

Reconsiderations are conducted on-the-record and, in most cases, the QIC will send its decision to all parties within 60 days of receipt of the request for reconsideration. The decision will contain detailed information on further appeals rights if the decision is not fully favorable. If the QIC cannot complete its decision in the applicable timeframe, it will inform the appellant of the right to escalate the case to an Administrative Law Judge hearing.

Third Level of Appeal: Administrative Law Judge Hearing If the claim is at least $110 and the QIC's decision is unsatisfactory, a party to the reconsideration may request a hearing presided over by an Administrative

Law Judge (ALJ). The request must be made within 60 days of receipt of the reconsideration. Appellants must also send notice of the ALJ hearing request to all parties to the QIC reconsideration.

ALJ hearings are generally held by video-teleconference or by telephone. In-person hearings are available if the appellant can demonstrate good cause. Appellants may also ask the ALJ to make a decision without any hearing ("on the record"). The ALJ will generally issue a decision within 90 days of receipt of the hearing request, though the timeframe may be extended for a variety of reasons including, but not limited to, the case being escalated from the reconsideration level, the submission of additional evidence not included with the hearing request, the request for an in-person hearing, the appellant's failure to send notice of the hearing request to other parties, and the initiation of discovery if CMS is a party. The amount in controversy required to request an ALJ hearing is increased annually by the percentage increase in the medical care component of the Consumer Price Index for all urban consumers.

Fourth Level of Appeal: Appeals Council Review If a party to the ALJ hearing is dissatisfied with the ALJ's decision, the party may request a review by the Appeals Council. There are no requirements regarding the amount of money in controversy. The request for Appeals Council review must be submitted in writing within 60 days of receipt of the ALJ's decision, and must specify the issues and findings that are being contested. In general, the Appeals Council will issue a decision within 90 days of receipt of a request for review.

Fifth Level of Appeal: Federal District Court If a party is dissatisfied with the Appeals Council's decision, the next level of appeal is to file suit in federal district court within 60 days of receipt of the decision. The amount in controversy must be at least $1,090, an amount that is increased annually in accordance with the Consumer Price Index.[33]

ROLE OF THE PARALEGAL

Law firms with health care sections may represent large health care providers in reimbursement issues to ensure correct payments to their clients. Paralegals may research current Medicare regulations and PRRB cases to assist in this important legal function.

ACRONYM

PRRB: Provider Reimbursement Review Board

SPOTLIGHT ON THE PROVIDER REIMBURSEMENT REVIEW BOARD

In addition to appeals of final determinations of fiscal intermediaries, the **Provider Reimbursement Review Board (PRRB)** reviews disputed claims of at least $10,000. The PRRB is an independent panel to which a certified Medicare provider may appeal if it is dissatisfied with a final determination by its fiscal intermediary. A decision by the PRRB may be affirmed, modified, reversed or vacated and remanded by the CMS Administrator within 60 days of notification to the provider.[34] Written decisions of the PRRB are available online for research and review.

An interesting provider appeal case is *In Re: Medicare Reimbursement Litigation.*[35] In this case, 26 hospitals serving Medicare and Medicaid patients filed suit to reopen Notice of Program Reimbursements that they received for previous fiscal years, setting the DSH add-on payments.

SPOTLIGHT ON...

One of the most newsworthy supplier appeals involves the Scooter Store, a large supplier of power mobility devices. In April, 2005, the Department of Justice filed suit against the company for fraudulent billing, alleging that the Scooter Store steered Medicare beneficiaries away from scooters to more expensive power wheelchairs. In June, 2005, the Scooter Store filed a motion to dismiss that lawsuit, arguing that the suit admits the company included all legally required paperwork and physician certifications in its claims. The company also filed a countersuit claiming that CMS contractors continue to disallow valid claims for power chairs and scooters.[36] The Center for Medicare and Medicaid Services amended its rule on who can prescribe these power mobility devices and now requires a face-to-face examination of the beneficiary by a physician.[37]

Appeals by Beneficiaries for Parts C and D

Beneficiaries have rights to Medicare appeals. Though beneficiaries have rights to appeals in Parts A and B, this section examines the special rules for Parts C and D.

Appeals in Medicare Advantage Programs Beneficiaries enrolled in Medicare Advantage organizations also have appeal rights regarding coverage denials, claims payments, and general grievances. Grievances are those issues that do not involve a "determination" and are usually handled internally by the MA. Grievances are often related to quality of care issues or complaints about long waiting times on the telephone or in waiting rooms.

Determinations for coverage of specific services or items must be made expeditiously, but not later than 14 days after a request is received. Some MA plans require prior authorization of expensive services or items that a beneficiary may be seeking. The MA may have a **gatekeeper** who makes decisions on these prior authorizations. The beneficiary may request an expedited determination, or within 72 hours, if his or her medical condition is at serious risk.

Beneficiaries may request reconsideration of an adverse determination within 60 days of the initial determination notice. The MA must complete its reconsideration within 30 to 60 days, depending on the circumstances. If the beneficiary is not satisfied with the reconsideration, he/she may appeal to the MA's contracted independent entity, a Qualified Independent Contractor (QIC). If the amount in controversy is over $100, the beneficiary may appeal to the administrative law judge. Further review by the DAB and federal court are available if the ALJ's decision is not favorable.

Sometimes an MA beneficiary may be hospitalized and the MA determines that the hospital stay is no longer necessary. In that situation, a beneficiary is entitled to receive a notice of end of coverage. A beneficiary who is hospitalized may request an immediate review by the QIC and not incur additional financial liability during the QIC process.

Appeals in Prescription Drug Plans Appeals of Part D issues started in January, 2006, the date of implementation. In general, the MMA requires that beneficiaries be afforded the same expedited determinations, reconsiderations, and other review available under Parts A and B. Beneficiaries enrolled in MA organizations will follow appeal procedures for Part C. Beneficiaries are allowed to appeal decisions that exclude coverage of specific drugs or coverage of non-preferred drugs in favor of preferred drugs. Complaints that do not involve coverage or payment issues are called grievances and must be filed within 60 days of the event that led to the complaint. If the prescription drug plan does not cover a particular drug, a beneficiary can request a coverage determination to see if an exception applies. The PDP sponsor has 72 hours for standard requests and 24 hours for expedited requests to render a decision.

Further appeals follow a process similar to other Medicare appeals. A beneficiary may request a redetermination within 60 days of the plan's coverage determination. If the decision is unfavorable to the beneficiary, the next level is a request for an reconsideration by an **Independent Review Entity (IRE)**, made within 60 days. Further appeal steps are then to the Administrative Law Judge, the Medicare Appeals council, and finally, to federal court.[38]

ACRONYM

IRE: Independent Review Entity

Case Study *Hospital Serv. Dist. No. 1 of the Parish of LaFourche v. Thompson*[39] is a good example of the appeals process, medical necessity of health care services, and certification of that necessity by a physician. The plaintiff, Hospital Service District No. 1 of LaFourche Parish (i.e., county), Louisiana, d/b/a/ Lady of the Sea General Hospital, filed claims for Medicare reimbursement for psychiatric partial hospitalization services that it provided to eight Medicare beneficiaries. The Medicare fiscal intermediary denied the claims and review was brought before an administrative law judge who agreed with the denial. Plaintiff then appealed to the Departmental Appeals Board, which also denied the claims.

Having exhausted administrative remedies, the plaintiff filed suit in federal court against the defendant, Tommy Thompson, then Secretary of DHHS. Plaintiff raised a number of errors with the ALJ's opinion, including that the findings of fact were not supported by substantial evidence. What was at issue was interpretation of Medicare's regulations on medical necessity and physician certification.

In its analysis, the court noted that the Medicare statute requires a physician to certify that the beneficiary would require inpatient psychiatric care if partial hospitalization were not provided as a prerequisite for approval of reimbursement for PHP services. The ALJ had determined that seven of the eight beneficiaries lacked any physician certification, which supported a technical denial of the claims. Thus, the court concluded that the ALJ evaluated the medical evidence and properly denied the claims because of lack of medical necessity.

SUMMARY

Medicare continues to be a viable force in the direction of health care policy in the United States as well as a large economic force in the delivery of health care services. Despite all of its complicated rules, it continues to provide the elderly and disabled population with needed health care services and items. Payment methodology continues to evolve to assure fairness in reimbursement to providers, while maintaining solvency of the program.

Health care lawyers and administrators continue to face challenges when working with the Medicare program, especially with the certification process for providers and with obtaining the correct payment for services and supplies.

It is unlikely that this generation or the next will see the demise of Medicare. It is woven into the health care industry and into the populace's mindset that dismantling it would be unheard of.

KEY TERMS

Note: Definitions for key terms in this chapter were adapted from the Centers for Medicare & Medicaid Services website (www.cms.hhs.gov).

disenroll: End health care coverage with a health plan, including Medicare.

disproportionate share hospital: A hospital with a disproportionately large share of low-income patients. Under Medicaid, states augment payment to these hospitals. Medicare inpatient hospital payments are also adjusted for this added burden.

gatekeeper: In a managed care plan, this is another name for the primary care doctor. This doctor gives you basic medical services and coordinates proper medical care and referrals.

***locum tenens* arrangement:** A substitute physician.

medicare beneficiary: A person who has health care insurance through the Medicare or Medicaid program.

outlier: Additions to a full episode payment in cases where costs of services delivered are estimated to exceed a fixed loss threshold. HH PPS outliers are computed as part of Medicare claims payment by Pricer Software.

payer or **payor:** In health care, an entity that assumes the risk of paying for medical treatments. This can be an uninsured patient, a self-insured employer, a health plan, or an HMO. The terms *payer* and *payor* may be used interchangeably.

provider: Any Medicare provider (e.g., hospital, skilled nursing facility, home health agency, outpatient physical therapy, comprehensive outpatient rehabilitation facility, end-stage renal disease facility, hospice, physician, non-physician provider, laboratory, supplier, etc.) providing medical services covered under Medicare Part B; any organization, institution, or individual that provides health care services to Medicare beneficiaries. Physicians, ambulatory surgical centers, and outpatient clinics are some of the providers of services covered under Medicare Part B.

supplier: Generally, any company, person, or agency that provides a medical item or service, such as a wheelchair or walker.

REVIEW QUESTIONS AND EXERCISES

1. In *Hospital Serv. Dist. No. 1 of the Parish of LaFourche v. Thompson*, why was it important for the plaintiff to aggregate the claims before filing suit? Plot the time delays of each step of the administrative appeal process in this case.

2. Your office has a chiropractic practice as a client. The Fiscal Intermediary or carrier contractor has denied numerous claims of the practice, saying that they are not medically necessary. The claims were generally for maintenance after a spinal manipulation. How would you appeal the denials? Where would you look for the regulations that cover spinal manipulation? Are there any other resources that you found that may help you determine whether these claims are eligible for Medicare reimbursement? Prepare a memo for your supervising attorney outlining all of the steps that need to be taken, the timeframe of each step, and the documents required. Include references and analysis of any applicable research in your memo.

3. Give examples of the types of issues that are reviewable in a Medicare appeal.

4. In general, who is eligible for Medicare?

5. When is an Advanced Beneficiary Notice used?

6. Describe the differences in Medicare Parts A, B, C, and D. Give relevant examples of program description, eligibility, and coverage.

7. The administrator of the hospital that you work for wants to reopen its Notice of Program Reimbursements for the fiscal year that ended in 2006 to see if the appropriate DSH amount was given to the hospital. She asks you to research the Medicare regulations to see if the PRRB has changed its procedures following the *In Re: Medicare Litigation* case (see the Online Companion that accompanies this text). Prepare a memo with your findings.

8. The small health insurer for whom you work wants to apply to become a Medicare Advantage organization. Identify the steps necessary to qualify as an MA organization. What additional requirements are of particular concern in MA plans?

9. You are a paralegal at Health Care Lawyers, LLC, which represents Healthy Living Partners, Inc., a DME company that supplies motorized wheelchairs. Healthy Living Partners has been denied a claim, numbered DCN# 00456789-D, for payment for a motorized wheelchair. The claim was already reviewed once and the denial notice, dated June 13, 2007, stated that the wheelchair was not "medically necessary" for the patient. Healthy Living Partners has received a number of denials of payment for similar claims and the company fears that it will go out of business if it cannot recover payment. Prepare a memo, outlining the steps of the appeal process. Be sure that you include relevant time limits and references to any outside sources. Identify any documents that you feel are necessary for the appeal.

ENDNOTES

1. "CMS Financial Report, Fiscal Year 2006," Center for Medicare and Medicaid Services, available at http://www.cms.hhs.gov/CFOReport/Downloads/2006_CMS_Financial_Report.pdf, accessed August 4, 2007.
2. Publ. L. No. 108-173, 117 Stat. 2066 (2003).

3. 42 U.S.C. § 1395x(m), 1395f(a)(2)(C); 42 C.F.R. § 409.47,.42,.49.

4. 42 U.S.C. § 1395x(dd)(1), 42 C.F.R. § 418.3, .20-30.

5. "2006 Medicare Trustees Report," CMS Press Release, May 1, 2006, available at http://www.cms.hhs.gov/apps/media/press/release.asp, accessed August 4, 2007.

6. 42 C.F. R. §§ 410.26, 414.34, Medicare Carriers Manual § 2050.1.

7. "Guide to Medicare's Preventive Services," available at http://www.medicare.gov/Publications/Pubs/pdf/10110.pdf, accessed July 31, 2007.

8. "The CMS Quarterly Provider Update," available at http://www.cms.hhs.gov/QuarterlyProviderUpdates/, accessed July 31, 2007.

9. Publ. L. No.105-33, 111 Stat. 251 (1997), 42 U.S.C. §§ 1851-1859.

10. Publ. L. No. 108-173, 117 Stat. 2066 (2003).

11. "Medicare Advantage in 2007,"available at http://www.cms.hhs.gov/hillnotifications/downloads/MedicareAdvantagein2007.pdf, accessed August 5, 2007.

12. 42 C.F.R. § 422.503(b)(4)(vi).

13. 42 C.F.R. § 423.504(b)(4)(vi)(H).

14. 42 C.F.R. § 422.80 *et seq.*

15. M+CO Guidance, 64 Fed. Reg. at 61898 (§II.A.2.b).

16. "Prescription Drug Coverage—General Information," available at http://www.cms.hhs.gov/PrescriptionDrugCovGenIn/, accessed August 6, 2007.

17. "E-Prescribing Overview," available at http://www.cms.hhs.gov/EPrescribing/, accessed August 5, 2007.

18. "HHS Issues Report to Congress on E-Prescribing: Electronic Prescribing to Cut Errors and Costs," available at http://www.hhs.gov/news/press/2007pres/04/pr20070417b.html., accessed August 5, 2007.

19. "Glossary," http://www.cms.hhs.gov/glossary, accessed July 31, 2007.

20. "CMS Issues Draft Guidance Documents Related to National Coverage Process," March 1, 2005 CMS Press Release, available at http://www.cms.hhs.gov/apps/media/press/release.asp?Counter=1377, accessed August 6, 2007.

21. "Local coverage decisions" were previously known as "local medical review policies." See Benefits Improvement and Protection Act (BIPA) of 2000 at § 522 (a)(2) (B), Publ. 106-554, 114 Stat. 2763 (2000).

22. Exclusions from federal health care programs can be either mandatory or permissive. The subject of exclusions is covered more extensively in Chapter 6.

23. Publ. L. No. 104-191, 100 Stat. 1936 (1996).

24. "Prescription Drug Coverage Contracting," available at http://www.cms.hhs.gov/PrescriptionDrugCovContra/ 01 Overview.asp#TopOfPage, accessed August 6, 2007.

25. Publ. L.No. 98-21, 97 Stat. 65 (1983); 42 U.S.C.A. § 1395www(d).

26. Publ. L. No. 97-248, 96 Stat. 324 (1982); 42 U.S.C.A. § 1395x(v); 42 C.F.R. §§ 412.22, 413.40.

27. "Glossary," available at http://www.cms.hhs.gov/glossary/, accessed July 31, 2007.

28. 257 F.3d 807 (D.C. Cir. 2001).

29. Publ. L. No. 108-173, 117 Stat. 2066 (2003), at § 712.

30. MMA at § 952.

31. Pub. L. 106-554, 114 Stat. 2763 (2000).

32. Pub. L. 108-173, 117 Stat. 2066 (2003).

33. "The Medicare Appeals Process," Medicare Learning Series, July 2006.

34. "Overview: The Provider Reimbursement Review Board," available at http://www.cms.hhs.gov/PRRBReview/, accessed August 6, 2007.

35. No. 04-5203, D.C. Cir. decided July 1, 2005.

36. Crotreau, Roger, "Scooter Store trying to get suit by government tossed," San Antonio Express-News, June 2, 2005.

37. CMS- 3017-IFC.

38. "Medicare Prescription Drug Coverage: How to File a Complaint, Coverage Determination, or Appeal," available at http://www.cms.hhs.gov/partnerships/downloads/11112.pdf, accessed July 31, 2007.

39. No. 03-0415 (E.D. La. Aug. 25, 2004).

CHAPTER 6

FRAUD AND ABUSE

OBJECTIVES

After completing this chapter, students should be able to

- Discuss the concepts of false claims and prohibited referrals.
- Recognize health care programs and providers to which statutes and regulations apply.
- Identify potential liability issues.
- Research federal regulations and federal agency materials regarding fraud and abuse and their penalties.

INTRODUCTION

Four physicians agreed to pay a $32.5 million settlement in connection with claims that they performed unnecessary cardiac surgeries at Redding Medical Center in California in exchange for non-prosecution of criminal charges against them. Two of the doctors have agreed never to perform any cardiology procedures or surgeries on Medicare, Medi-Cal, or TRICARE patients. However, the settlement preserved the rights of the Medical Board of California and the U.S. Department of Health and Human Services to revoke the physicians' licenses and exclude them from participating in Medicare. The whistleblowers will share over $9.88 million.[1]

In November, 2005, the U.S. Attorney for the District of Delaware and the Delaware Attorney General reached a $150,000 settlement and a Corporate Integrity Agreement with Harbor Healthcare concerning inadequate care provided to disabled children in the late 1990s. Harbor Healthcare allegedly submitted false claims in violation of both the state and federal **False Claims Acts (FCA)**.[2]

In Florida, Richard E. Cox was convicted for his role in a conspiracy to transport and sell various prescription medical devices, knowing the devices to have been stolen, converted, or taken by fraud; and of impeding and obstructing the lawful and legitimate functions of the **FDA** in enforcing federal laws and regulations applicable to prescription medical devices. Cox was a former sales representative for Ethicon Endosurgery, Inc., a company specializing in the development and distribution of prescription medical devices for use in surgical procedures. As part of his plea agreement, Cox agreed to pay approximately $716,616 in restitution to Ethicon, the amount of the profit he realized from the criminal conduct.[3]

ACRONYMS

FCA: False Claims Act

FDA: Food and Drug Administration

All of these situations involve health care **fraud and abuse** and show the seriousness of the consequences for health care providers and organizations if their conduct deviates from federal requirements. Billing for unnecessary services or engaging in prohibited financial transactions exposes health care providers to a variety of civil, criminal, and administrative penalties. In the following sections, we will look at some of the different laws and regulations that apply to health care program–related violations and examine the basic principles of liability. Paralegals working in health law firms need to be aware of the different types of civil lawsuits, criminal prosecutions, and administrative proceedings that the firm's health care clients could face.

FALSE CLAIMS ACT

What is a false claim? The basic rule in billing for health care services is: "No payment shall be made for services or items, which are not reasonable and necessary for the diagnosis and treatment of the patient."[4] A false claim, then, is a request for payment for a service or item that is not reasonable or necessary for the diagnosis or treatment of the patient. Some blatant examples of false claims would be billing for

- lab equipment that you don't have
- services of unlicensed doctors
- surgery if the doctor performing surgery is out of the country
- procedures on organs that the patient doesn't have,
- medical errors (e.g., wrong side surgeries)

Statutory Authority

Misconduct that is related to the submission of claims to federal health care programs (i.e., Medicare, etc.) can be grounds for civil suit, criminal prosecution, or administrative remedies under the False Claims Act.[5] The FCA applies to any person or entity who knowingly presents a fraudulent or false claim to the government for approval or payment. Now would be a good time to review Chapter 1 to see the government health care programs and the different providers who might be submitting claims for payments to them.

Civil suits under the FCA may be brought by the federal government or by private individuals, known as *qui tam* relators. In actuality, *qui tam* relators are usually employees or former employees of health care organizations, who, through their job responsibilities, learn of fraudulent activity. These kinds of *qui tam* relators are also known as **whistleblowers**. As an attractive incentive for reporting fraud, *qui tam* relators share in the money recovered by the government through successful litigation or settlement, plus obtain reimbursement for costs, expenses, and attorney fees.

When a private citizen brings a civil FCA suit, the U.S. Department of Justice is notified and may join as a party to the lawsuit. The FCA complaints must show that the defendant presented or caused to be presented a claim for approval or payment, that the claim was false or fraudulent, and that the acts were knowingly undertaken. A defendant who is found liable under the FCA must pay treble damages, or three times the amount of loss to the federal government, as well as civil fines of up to $11,000 for each false claim. The amount of liability can yield dramatic total dollar amounts, because, for example, each CMS Form 1500[6] submitted for a single request for payment of a single service to an individual patient constitutes a claim under the FCA. Imagine a $40 false charge for an office visit that did not take place. Multiply the charge by three, and then add $11,000; now repeat that for multiple patients and see how high the dollar amount becomes.

SPOTLIGHT ON...

In June, 2004, Rite Aid Corporation paid $7 million to settle allegations that it submitted false prescription claims to government health insurance programs between January 1987 and December 2001.

Case Law

While large settlements garner press releases and headlines, cases brought under the FCA are also noteworthy. One of the most interesting for students to read is *United States v. Krizek,*[7] a case that addresses interpretation of the FCA's "knowingly and willingly" requirement. This FCA civil suit was brought by the government for two types of misconduct: **upcoding** and billing for medically unnecessary services. The government alleged that Krizek's billing hours approached 24 hours in a given day. The District Court found the defendant psychiatrist and his wife liable for knowingly submitting false claims, but did not find evidence that the services were medically unnecessary. However, the Court noted that Dr. and Mrs. Krizek relied on shoddy bookkeeping and "failed utterly" to review bills. The government sought an astronomical $81 million of damages, though actual losses were $245,392. The case was remanded for recalculation of damages.

Several FCA cases involve an implied certification theory of liability, that is, when a claim is submitted and certified by signature, services rendered are considered as having been medically necessary and delivered. An example exists in *U.S. ex rel. Mikes v. Straus*,[8] a suit filed by a *qui tam* relator. Dr. Mikes, a former employee of Pulmonary and Critical Care Associates, sued her employers, alleging that the submission of Medicare reimbursement claims for spirometry procedures not performed in accordance with the relevant standard of care violated the FCA. She alleged that the procedures were not of the desired quality, but not that they were medically unnecessary. She contended that submitting the Medicare Form 1500 and completing its certification implied that the service was of a high standard of care. Unfortunately, the court did not agree with Dr. Mikes's theory and dismissed the case.

Not only can people be sued under the FCA; municipalities can be sued as well. In *Cook County v. United States ex rel. Chandler*,[9] Dr. Chandler brought a *qui tam* suit against Cook County Hospital, alleging misconduct in the handling of a $5 million research grant from the National Institute of Drug Abuse to fund a program called "New Start" for drug-dependent pregnant women. The county moved to dismiss the case, claiming that it was not a person within the meaning of the FCA and, thus, could not be sued under the statute. The Seventh Circuit disagreed; Justice Souter, writing for the U.S. Supreme Court, affirmed. The Court noted that

> . . . municipal corporations and private ones were simply two species of 'body politic and corporate,' treated alike in terms of their legal status as persons capable of suing and being sued.

EXCLUSIONS, CIVIL MONETARY PENALTIES, AND OTHER ADMINISTRATIVE REMEDIES

Health care fraud and abuse is a multibillion dollar "industry" in the United States. Loopholes in regulations have allowed providers and organizations to "game" the system. Congress responded by allowing enforcement agencies to impose a wide range of penalties. In this section, we will explore administrative remedies other than civil suits and criminal **sanctions**. However, administrative sanctions are not exclusive; penalties in civil suits and criminal sanctions may also apply.

Exclusions

Exclusion from participation in federal health care programs can have a devastating financial effect on a provider or organization who receives this penalty. Most health care providers and organizations derive a significant portion of their business from beneficiaries who are enrolled in Medicare, Medicaid, CHAMPVA, or TRICARE. Payment for services or items furnished by any excluded individual or entity cannot be made.

SPOTLIGHT ON...

The Office of Inspector General for DHHS maintains an exclusions database at http://www.oig.hhs.gov/fraud/exclusions.html. The website also maintains a list of administrative actions.

Exclusion authority rests in different sections of the Social Security Act. Please refer to the Table of Authorities in Appendix E. There are two types: mandatory and permissive. Mandatory exclusions include those for certain types of criminal convictions such as patient abuse or felonies related to controlled substances. A mandatory exclusion is for no less than 5 years. Permissive exclusions include a variety of lesser offenses, such as claims for excessive charges or default on medical student loans.

When CMS proposes to exclude a provider, the provider may submit a response disputing the reasons for the exclusion within 60 days of receipt of the notice. Providers may appeal exclusion decisions by filing a request with the ALJ within 60 days of the notice of the exclusion. They may also ask for reinstatement no sooner than 120 days prior to the terminal date of the exclusion.[10]

Civil Monetary Penalties

In the early 1980s, Congress gave authority to the Department of Health and Human Services to impose penalties for health care fraud and abuse through administrative proceedings. These proceedings are handled by the **Office of Inspector General (OIG)** of the Centers for Medicare and Medicaid Services. Statutory authority resides in the Social Security Act.[11] The maximum **civil monetary penalty (CMP)** is $10,000 per claim, though greater penalties may apply for certain offenses. A CMP is considered to be a fraud upon a government program. Typically, the fraud relates to noncompliance with specific billing requirements or other program (i.e., Medicare, etc.) requirements. The standard for imposition of a CMP is that the person taking action knew or should have known that the action is a departure from usual conduct. For example, a CMP for upcoding may be imposed if there is a pattern of submitting claims for an item or service based on a code that the person knew or should have known would result in a greater payment than submitting a claim using the correct code. Potential sanctions extend to a person acting with deliberate ignorance or reckless disregard of the truth or falsity of the information, but not to someone who acts with reasonable diligence, but still makes a mistake.

A CMP administrative hearing is initiated when the OIG issues a demand letter to the provider or organization, describing the factual basis or misconduct for the sanction sought. The respondent has the right to request a hearing before an **administrative law judge (ALJ)** within DHHS, at which time the OIG and the respondent have the right to present evidence and make arguments to the ALJ, who issues a written decision. The ALJ's decision may be appealed administratively and to federal court.[12] Prior to initiating formal administrative CMP proceedings, the OIG may try to resolve matters amicably through negotiation. In fact, most CMP cases are resolved through settlement with no decision having been made on the merits.

> In each CMP case resolved through a settlement agreement, the settling party has contested the OIG's allegations and denied any liability. No CMP judgment or finding of liability has been made against the settling party.[13]

Other Administrative Remedies

The government has additional remedies for fraudulent conduct.

Assessment in Lieu of Damages In addition to CMPs, the government can recover compensation for actual losses sustained. This kind of recovery is called an "assessment in lieu of damages sustained" and is usually not more than three times the amount claimed for each item or

ACRONYMS

CMP: civil monetary penalty
OIG: Office of Inspector General

ACRONYM

ALJ: administrative law judge

service in question. Like CMPs, the assessment in lieu of damages penalty is authorized in the Social Security Act.

Termination or Nonrenewal of Agreement Remember from Chapter 5 that providers usually have a provider or participation agreement. Another penalty in the government's arsenal against health care fraud and abuse is termination or nonrenewal of that agreement with the government. Financially, this can be a serious consequence for a provider or organization if it no longer has this agreement and thus, can no longer bill for items or services. Loss of a provider or participation agreement can also flow from a criminal conviction for health care fraud and abuse, as will be discussed in the following section.

Intermediate Sanctions The government has even more measures to penalize individuals or entities who have committed health care fraud and abuse. These are called "intermediate sanctions" and include nonpayment or suspension of payment, suspension of member enrollment, appointment of temporary management, and corrective action plans.

CRIMINAL PENALTIES IN GENERAL

Prosecutors have a variety of laws to invoke in health care fraud cases.

Statutory Authority

A good starting point is the standard fraud provisions in Title 18 of the U.S. Code. Most commonly used in cases of health care fraud are prohibitions against the following offenses:

- false claims, or applications to the government for payment[14]
- false statements, or representations or disclosures made to the government[15]
- mail fraud and wire fraud[16]

All of these offenses carry the following serious penalties:

- five years' imprisonment
- a fine of $250,000 for an individual or $500,000 for an organization, or twice the gross gain or loss from the offense, whichever is greater[17]

Another source of law for a criminal health care fraud prosecution can be found in the **Health Insurance Portability and Accountability**

Act (HIPAA). HIPAA's criminal provision prohibits false statements related to health care matters.[18] HIPAA also enhanced penalties to allow for a potentially longer prison sentence—up to 10 years.

Section 1128B of the Social Security Act also provides harsh punishment for serious offenses by individuals or entities. The Act provides that it is a felony to:

ACRONYM

HIPAA: Health Insurance Portability and Accountability Act

- knowingly and willingly make or cause to be made any false statement of a material fact in any application for any benefit or payment, or for use in determining rights to such payment, under a federal health care program,

- conceal information from or fail to disclose information to the government—specifically, information of an event affecting the initial or continued right to a benefit or payment under a federal health care program,

- apply to receive federal benefit or payment for the use and benefit of another and knowingly and willingly and willfully converting such payment to another use, or present (or cause to be presented) a claim for physician services knowing that the person who furnished the services is not a licensed physician, or counsel or assist an individual to dispose of assets (including by any transfer in trust) in order for an individual to become eligible for medical assistance, or

- knowingly and willfully make, cause to make, induce, or seek to induce, any false statement or representation of a material fact as to the conditions or operation of any institution, facility, or entity:

  (i) in order to qualify for certification or recertification as any entity for which certification is required, including a hospital, critical access hospital, skilled nursing facility, intermediate care facility for the mentally retarded, home health agency, health maintenance organization or competitive medical plan; or

  (ii) in response to required disclosure of information under § 1124A of the Social Security Act.[19]

Penalties for any of these violations include fines that range upwards to $25,000 as well as up to 5 years in prison.

Criminal charges are investigated by the DHHS OIG or CMS and then referred to the Department of Justice for prosecution. Criminal charges often accompany False Claims Acts violations and their civil actions.

ROLE OF THE PARALEGAL

Just as in other types of criminal cases, paralegals working on health care fraud cases can expect to be involved in obtaining documents and witness statements for evidentiary purposes.

Case Law

Although most criminal convictions flow from violations of the anti-kickback and Stark laws discussed in the following sections, an interesting case of health care conspiracy, fraud, and theft can be found in *United States v. Herring*.[20] John and Martha Herring owned a chain of home health agencies in Louisiana that served mostly Medicare patients. Each year, cost reports were filed for Medicare reimbursement. Some costs, such as pension plan contributions, could be accrued and listed as debts but had to be paid within one year of reporting. The Herrings had purchased pension plans for the agencies' employees. Through a series of transactions, the Herrings borrowed money from these plans to finance the agencies' business operations. Later at trial, the government presented evidence that the Herrings used funds of the agencies for personal expenses, disallowed under Medicare rules. Prior to the criminal case, the Herrings filed for bankruptcy for their home health agencies, but did not disclose that they owed the agencies money for personal expenses. The Herrings were convicted and fined and the U.S. Court of Appeals for the Fifth Circuit affirmed on appeal.

ANTI-KICKBACK LAW

Capitalism usually supports sharing profits of collective economic activity. For example, sales agents usually receive commission or merchants give discounts for volume purchases. But in health care, these practices have been frowned upon.

The federal **Anti-Kickback Statute (AKS)** is another prosecutorial tool in the government's battle against health care fraud and abuse. It targets financial incentives that induce or reward referrals. AKS applies

ACRONYM

AKS: Anti-Kickback Statute

to any referrals for all services or items that will be paid by a federal health care program.

Statutory Authority

Federal anti-kickback law makes it a felony to knowingly and willfully solicit or receive remuneration in return for referring an individual to a person for the furnishing or arranging for the furnishing of an item or service, or in return for purchasing, leasing, ordering, or arranging for or recommending purchasing, leasing, or ordering any good, facility, service, or for which payment may be made in whole or in part under a Federal healthcare program.[21] Each offense is punishable by a fine of up to $25,000 and/or imprisonment up to 5 years. Violators are also subject to exclusion from federal health care programs as well as civil monetary penalties up to $50,000 for each violation and a fine three times the amount of the claim. All health care providers are subject to the Anti-Kickback Statute.

Regulations and Safe Harbors

Congress established statutory exceptions, known as "safe harbors," for certain payment practices that it considers not to be prohibited referrals. Most of these are common sense exceptions that must be properly disclosed. If a financial arrangement between health care providers meets one of these safe harbors, it is fully protected from civil and criminal liabilities under AKS.

The Office of Inspector General passed safe harbor regulations in 1991 that identified permissible payment practices in the following areas:

- investment interests
- space rental
- equipment rental
- personal services and management contracts
- sale of a practice
- referral services
- warranties
- discounts
- employees

- group purchasing organizations
- waiver of coinsurance and deductibles for Part A inpatient hospital services and certain federally qualified and funded health care facilities[22]

SPOTLIGHT ON...

The OIG has passed and proposed additional areas for safe harbors. These are available on their website in the Fraud Prevention & Detection section.

Advisory Opinions and Fraud Alerts

A health care provider or other party can request an OIG advisory opinion about the application of fraud and abuse authorities to the party's existing or proposed business arrangement. Congress established the OIG advisory opinion process as part of the Health Insurance Portability and Accountability Act of 1996. Once issued, an OIG advisory opinion is legally binding on the Department of Health and Human Services and the requesting party, but not on any other governmental department or agency or other party. A provider that receives a favorable advisory opinion is protected from OIG administrative sanctions, so long as the proposed arrangement is conducted in accordance with the facts submitted to the OIG. However, no person or entity can rely on an advisory opinion issued to someone else.[23] Seeking an advisory opinion is voluntary.

Most advisory opinion requests seek guidance regarding the anti-kickback statute or its safe harbor regulations. However, the OIG may also issue advisory opinions regarding exclusions, civil monetary penalties, and criminal penalties.

The OIG occasionally issues fraud alerts or bulletins to warn providers of impermissible practices in the health care industry. These are posted on the OIG's website and are distributed directly to providers.

Case Law

Two questions arise in AKS cases involving remuneration for referrals: (1) if the purpose of the payment is to induce referrals and (2) if the defendant's conduct is knowing and willful.

The leading AKS case is *United States v. Greber*.[24] Dr. Greber, an osteopath who was board certified in cardiology, was president of Cardio-Med, Inc., a company that provided diagnostic services regarding Holter monitors. When Cardio-Med performed a service for a referring physician, the company forwarded a portion of the Medicare reimbursement (about 40%) to the referring physician. The fee was characterized by Cardio-Med as an "interpretation fee" by the referring physician, but, in fact Dr. Greber did all of the interpretations. Dr. Greber was convicted of tendering kickbacks in violation of the AKS. The Third Circuit Court of Appeals affirmed his conviction, noting that "if one purpose of the payment was to induce future referrals, the Medicare statute has been violated."

In *Hansleter Network v. Shalala*,[25] the court interpreted the statute's "knowingly and willfully" language. Three clinical laboratories established joint ventures with physicians to form a network. The government proposed to exclude several individuals and entities involved with the network. In examining the issues, the court held that the statute's "knowingly and willfully" language required the government to prove not only that the defendant intentionally engaged in conduct prohibited by the statute, but also that the defendant did so with the knowledge that his conduct violated the law. Under the Court's standard, the government must prove that: (1) the defendant intentionally entered into referral agreements later determined to violate the statute, and (2) when the defendant entered into the referral arrangement or when he benefited from it, he or she knew that the arrangement violated the Anti-Kickback Statute.

The Eleventh Circuit did not follow the *Hansleter* court's interpretation. In *United States v. Starks*,[26] the Court held that specific knowledge of the statute was not required to uphold the convictions of Angela Starks and Andrew Siegel, defendants involved in patient referrals by community health aides to a chemical dependency unit.

STARK LAW

Yet another consideration in a physician's practice is the "Stark Law," a prohibition against certain physician referrals. The statute and its regulations are referred to as the "Stark Law"[27] in deference to Congressman Pete Stark (D-CA) who introduced and supported the legislation. The Stark Law prohibits referrals by physicians to entities with which they have a financial relationship. This law is an attempt to deal directly with overutilization of services by targeting referrals by financially interested physicians.

The Stark Law is important for health care attorneys and their paralegals who draft, review, or negotiate contracts between physicians and other entities. Review of the law's exceptions is critical in professional services agreements, leases and rentals, joint ventures, and other common business arrangements.

Statutory Authority

The Ethics in Patient Referrals Act, the basis for the Stark Law, made it illegal for physician referrals for Medicare-financed services to clinical laboratories in which the physician or immediate family member has a financial relationship. This prohibition was later expanded by the 1993 Omnibus Budget Reconciliation Act to apply to other **designated health services (DHS)** paid for by Medicare and Medicaid.

The law includes both compensation agreements and ownership or investment interest in its definition of "financial relationship." The designated health services are

- physical therapy services
- occupational therapy services
- radiology, including magnetic resonance imaging, computerized axial tomography scans, and ultrasound services
- durable medical equipment and supplies
- parenteral and enteral nutrients, equipment, and supplies
- prosthetics, orthotics, and prosthetic devices
- home health services and supplies
- outpatient prescription drugs
- inpatient and outpatient hospital services

Unlike AKS, Stark adopts a "**bright-line**" test when determining violations. There is no requirement that the conduct involve the knowing and willful receipt of a kickback.

Penalties for Stark violations may include

- denial of payments
- refund of monies received by physicians and facilities for amounts collected

- payment of civil penalties of up to $15,000 for each service that a person "knows or should know" was provided in violation of Stark Law, and three times the amount of improper payment the entity received from the Medicare program

- exclusion from the Medicare program and/or state health care programs including Medicaid

- payment of civil penalties up to $100,000 for each attempt to circumvent the Stark Law

Regulations and Exceptions

In 1995, the **Centers for Medicare and Medicaid Services (CMS)** published final regulations, known as Stark I, that implemented the law's prohibition against ordering clinical laboratory services from an entity with which a physician has a financial relationship.[28] In 1998, CMS published proposed regulations, known as Stark II, regarding the other designated health services. Stark II regulations were finalized and became effective in July, 2004.[29] Stark Phase III regulations were still pending in 2007, though they are likely to address tightening loopholes and prohibiting certain "per click" leases and percentage compensation arrangements; eliminating many "under arrangements" joint ventures; and curtailing the use of the in-office ancillary services exceptions.[30]

Stark Law broadly prohibits physician self-referrals, but then it legitimizes numerous specific arrangements that it calls "exceptions." These exceptions operate in a manner similar to that of the safe harbors of the Anti-Kickback Statute. The exceptions are quite complicated and require specific details to be applicable. In general, the exceptions fall into three categories: (1) ownership and investment, (2) compensation, and (3) generic exceptions that apply to all financial arrangements.

Case Law

Physicians and their lawyers try to avoid litigation involving Stark regulations, often preferring to seek an OIG advisory opinion before a physician becomes involved in a financial relationship that could be prohibited. Nevertheless, there are cases that involve interpretation of the Stark regulations. A case that is frequently cited is *American Lithotripsy Society v. Tommy G. Thompson.*[31] In that case, a group of physicians sued the then-Secretary of CMS, alleging many violations of CMS's rule-making authority and interpretation of exceptions to Stark regulations.

ACRONYM

CMS: Centers for Medicare and Medicaid Services

Physicians were prohibited under the regulations from referring patients for lithotripsy services to entities with which they had a "financial arrangement" unless they could prove that they met one of the statutory exceptions. You can find this case in the Online Companion.

SUMMARY

Fraud and abuse in the health care industry focuses on three general areas: fraudulent claims for reimbursement, illegal kickbacks, and the prohibition against physician self-referrals. The federal government has several enforcement tools to combat health care fraud and abuse: civil *qui tam* lawsuits, criminal statutes, and administrative remedies such as health care program exclusion and civil monetary penalties.

The three laws that are most frequently invoked in health care fraud and abuse are the False Claims Act, Anti-Kickback Statute, and Stark Law, though there are other federal fraud statutes that may be applicable.

KEY TERMS

bright line: A rule or principle that is simple and straightforward; a rule that avoids or ignores ambiguity.[32]

fraud and abuse: *Fraud:* To purposely bill for services that were never given or to bill for a service that has a higher reimbursement than the service produced. *Abuse:* Payment for items or services that are billed by mistake by providers, but should not be paid for by Medicare. This is not the same as fraud.[33]

***qui tam*:** *Who* (for himself) *as well as* (for the government). Describes a lawsuit brought by an individual on behalf of the government, or brought by the government based on an informer's tip. If the government collects a fine or penalty from the lawsuit, the informer may get a share.[34]

sanctions: Administrative remedies and actions (e.g., exclusion, civil monetary penalties, etc.) available to the OIG to deal with questionable, improper, or abusive behaviors of providers under Medicare, Medicaid, or any state health programs.[35]

upcoding: Using improper billing codes to charge Medicare or Medicaid for an item or service to receive higher payments than would ordinarily be due for the treatment of a patient.[36]

whistleblower: An employee who brings organizational wrongdoing to the attention of government authorities. Government laws protect some whistleblowers.[37]

REVIEW QUESTIONS AND EXERCISES

1. Explain the differences between civil and criminal actions in health care fraud and abuse. Who investigates health care fraud and abuse? Who may initiate each type of action? What are the penalties for each?

2. Who is subject to the Anti-Kickback Statute? Who is subject to the Stark law?

3. Dr. DoGood is a physician on the Gulf Coast, trying to establish his practice. His idea is to give $3 to FEMA housing inspectors for each person's name and address that they are able to provide to him. Then he will prepare a letter to each person, offering his physician services. If that person comes into his office for a service, he will give an additional 5 percent of the Medicare-billable amount to the FEMA inspector making the referral. What problems do you see with Dr. DoGood's proposal?

4. The history of the Stark Law and its regulations pose a challenge to the regulatory researcher. Using the information on administrative law provided in Appendix C, as well as the endnotes in this chapter, see if you can provide citations and dates to the actual federal law, the proposed and final regulations in the Federal Register, and the codification of those regulations in the Code of Federal Regulations. Does your research lead you to any additional material on the Stark Law?

5. Does it surprise you that the Stark Law's definition of financial relationship extends to a physician's immediate family? Why do you think it is important that financial arrangements of a physician's immediate family be scrutinized?

6. Best Practice, LLC is a large, multi-specialty practice with 60 doctors. Best Practice's Compliance Officer investigated a complaint that showed that four doctors in the Urology Department had been upcoding billing for urology services for the past 3 years. The doctors insist that they did not know that the billing codes were

incorrect. Can the Compliance Officer voluntarily report this information to the federal government? What laws or regulations may have been violated? What legal standard applies to each?

ENDNOTES

1. News Release dated November 15, 2005, U.S. Department of Justice, Eastern District of California, available at http://www.usdoj.gov/usao/cac/news/pr2005/, accessed August 19, 2007.

2. Press Release dated November 10, 2005, U.S. Department of Justice, District of Delaware, available at http://www.usdoj.gov/usao/cac/news/pr2005/, accessed August 19, 2007.

3. Press Release dated November 10, 2005, U.S. Department of Justice, Southern District of Florida, available at http://www.usdoj.gov/usao/cac/news/pr2005/, accessed August 19, 2007.

4. Social Security Act § 1862(a)(1)(A).

5. 32 U.S.C. §§ 3729-3731.

6. CMS Form 1500 is the Health Insurance Claim Form for Medicare reimbursement.

7. 111 F.3d 934 (D.C. Cir. 1997), 192 F.3d 1024 (D.C. Cir. 1999).

8. 274 F.3d 687 (2d Cir. 2001).

9. 589 U.S. 119 (2003).

10. 72 FR 39754, July 20, 2007.

11. Social Security Act § 1128A, 42 U.S.C. § 1320a-7a.

12. 42 C.F.R. § 1005.

13. "Background on Civil Monetary Penalties," available at http://www.oig.hhs.gov/fraud/enforcement/administrative/cmp/cmp.html, accessed July 31, 2007.

14. 18 U.S.C. § 287.

15. 18 U.S.C. § 1001.

16. 18 U.S.C. § § 1341, 1343.

17. 18 U.S.C. § 3571.

18. 18 U.S.C. § 1035.

19. 42 U.S.C. § 1320a-7b.

20. No. 02-30533 (5th Cir. July 17, 2003).

21. 42 U.S.C. § 1320a-7b (b).

22. 42 C.F.R. § 1001.952(a)-(k).

23. FAQs About Advisory Opinions, available at http://www.oig.hhs.gov/ fraud/advisoryopinions.html, accessed August 18, 2007.

24. 760 F.2d 68 (3d Cir. 1985), *cert. den.*, 474 U.S. 988 (1985).

25. 51 F. 3d 1390 (9th Cir. 1995).

26. 157 F. 3d 833 (11th Cir. 1998).

27. 42 U.S.C. § 1395 nn.

28. 60 Fed. Reg. 41,914 (1995), codified at 42 C.F.R. § 411.

29. 66 Fed. Reg. 905 (2001), codified at 42 C.F.R. § 411.

30. Quarterly Provider Update-Regulations, July 1–September 30, 2007, available at http://www.cms.hhs.gov/QuarterlyProviderUpdates/ downloads/Regs-3Q07QPU.pdf, accessed August 18, 2007.

31. 215 F.Supp.2d 23 (D.C. Cir. 2002).

32. Oran, Daniel, Dictionary of the Law, 3d ed., Delmar/West Legal Studies, 2000.

33. Glossary, available at http://cms.hhs.gov/apps/glossary, accessed July 31, 2007.

34. Oran, Daniel, Dictionary of the Law, 3d ed., Delmar/West Legal Studies, 2000.

35. Glossary, available at http://cms.hhs.gov/apps/glossary, accessed July 31, 2007.

36. Caldwell, Donald H., Jr., "Terminology," Fundamentals of Health Law, 3d ed., American Health Lawyers Association (2004).

37. Oran, Daniel, Dictionary of the Law, 3d ed., Delmar/West Legal Studies, 2000.

CHAPTER 7

HEALTH CARE COMPLIANCE PROGRAMS

OBJECTIVES

After reading this chapter, students should be able to

- Identify the essential elements of compliance.
- Describe the role that compliance plays in health care organizations.
- Identify situations when noncompliance may lead to charges of fraud or abuse.
- Discuss the role of federal oversight agencies in health care compliance.

HEALTH CARE COMPLIANCE PROGRAMS

Why should a health care organization have a **compliance** program? Shouldn't we leave concerns about compliance with law and regulations to lawyers? Health care organizations must have programs to address risks associated with patient care and safety, infectious diseases, biohazards, and workplace injuries. One of the newest "risks" in the health care industry is noncompliance with federal and state laws and regulations that govern the industry's business practices. As you proceed through the chapters of this book, you will become familiar with the complexity of such laws as the False Claims Act,[1] the Health Insurance Portability and Accountability Act,[2] and the multitude of regulations that are issued by governmental agencies. In response to these legal and regulatory challenges, health care organizations have begun to implement corporate compliance programs to combat internal criminal conduct.

Too often organizations establish compliance programs as a formality, but then fail to instill the values of compliance and ethics into the corporate culture. Corporate governance and accountability frequently make headlines in today's news. For example, in the last few years, scandals surrounding business practices at Health South and Tenet Healthcare Corporation have been investigated and reported widely in the media. Both of these companies had (and continue to have) compliance programs, yet these programs' existence did not guarantee conformity with law. Nevertheless, compliance programs can serve an important function in health care organizations by reducing fraud and by requiring them to conform to law. These programs also help to fulfill organizations' ethical obligations to the communities and patients they serve and to the payers and shareholders with whom they have a financial interest.

Paralegals working in health care law firms and in-house in health care organizations must understand the important purpose that compliance programs fulfill in maintaining legal accountability. Compliance programs are often the first line of defense in preventative legal medicine.

ACRONYMS

DHHS: Department of Health and Human Services

OIG: Office of Inspector General

Role of the Office of Inspector General

The **Office of the Inspector General (OIG)** of the **Department of Health and Human Services (DHHS)** is the agency charged with preventing and detecting fraud and abuse in federal health care programs. Most health care organizations and providers participate in the Medicare program or other federally funded health plans such as Medicaid, TRICARE, and CHAMPVA. The only type of entity that is required by law to have a compliance program is a managed care plan for Medicare recipients that falls under Medicare Part C. However, the OIG firmly recommends that anyone who participates in these federal health care programs establish compliance and ethics programs voluntarily.

The OIG has issued several **Compliance Program Guidances (CPGs)** for different segments of the health care industry to help establish and guide their compliance programs. These documents have been issued for hospitals, clinical laboratories, home health agencies, hospices, nursing homes, ambulance suppliers, durable medical equipment suppliers, third-party billing companies, pharmaceutical manufacturers, and Medicare Part C managed care plans. All of the guidances offer suggestions for dealing with problematic or risky areas in each industry segment.

The OIG has adopted the elements of effective compliance programs, detailed in the U.S. Sentencing Guidelines and discussed in the following section, to apply to health care organizations and providers. This assures conformity between the OIG's own enforcement goals and those of other federal law enforcement authorities, including the Department of Justice.

Elements of Compliance Programs

Defined simply, a compliance program is a mechanism or operation whose aim is to ensure that the health care organization and its employees and contractors follow applicable laws and regulations. Often, standards or best business practices are incorporated into a compliance program. In the health care industry, the majority of compliance programs must develop a framework that ensures the submission of consistently accurate claims for reimbursement of patient services to federal and state payers and private insurers. Doing so lessens the risks of litigation under the False Claims Act, for example. Though compliance programs in the health care industry usually address health care laws, they often may include environmental, research, antitrust, or other laws as well.

Health care organizations must consider both substantive and structural components when devising a compliance program that meets the organization's needs.[3] The substantive component must address the specific body of laws and regulations that apply to the particular health care organization. For example, hospitals must comply with Medicare and Medicaid regulations if they bill those programs. Academic medical centers that engage in clinical research must observe federal regulations arising from the "Common Rule"[4] regarding human subject protection. Other types of laws and regulations that it may be appropriate to review for applicability include those related to state

ACRONYM

CPG: Compliance Program Guidance

licensing of medical professionals, employee benefits, environmental safety within hospitals and laboratories, antitrust issues (a concern in large health care systems), and many others. Organizations have the flexibility to designate which laws their compliance programs will oversee, often leaving to other departments the responsibility for compliance with laws that are not health care specific.

The structural component builds the framework necessary for continuous operation of an effective compliance program. An organization may create a compliance program as part of administration or as a separate department; it chooses the staff, funds its efforts, and promotes its objectives. In the health care industry, this structural component must incorporate the elements identified as necessary by the Office of Inspector General. These elements are drawn from the U.S. Sentencing Guidelines of 1991 and fall into the following seven areas, which we will discuss in detail later in the chapter:

- compliance standards
- high-level responsibility
- education
- communication
- monitoring and auditing
- enforcement and discipline
- response and prevention

To be effective, a compliance program must be more than just a manual of policies and procedures that is dusted off when government regulatory enforcers or accreditation agencies are reviewing an organization's practices. A compliance program must demonstrate an organization's meaningful commitment to its legal obligations and its continuing efforts to make its employees active participants in the corporate compliance endeavor.

Source of Authority: U.S. Sentencing Commission Guidelines

Corporate compliance programs originated after publication of the 1991 U.S. Sentencing Commission Guidelines. Though the primary purpose of the guidelines was to standardize sentences for federal criminal defendants, Chapter 8 of the Guidelines addresses the sentencing of organizations and discusses principles for how effective compliance and ethics programs can be a means of lessening the consequences of corporate criminal behavior. Thus, most health care organizations, especially large entities, voluntarily establish compliance and ethics programs.

The guidelines were strengthened in 2004 in response to the 2002 Sarbanes-Oxley Act's directive to the U.S. Sentencing Commission to ensure that the guidelines were "sufficient to deter and punish organizational criminal misconduct."[5] Sarbanes-Oxley was passed by Congress to provide additional corporate transparency for publicly traded companies. Though many companies in the health care industry are organized as not-for-profit entities, the safeguards of Sarbanes-Oxley may serve as models of accountability.

SPOTLIGHT ON...

In 2004, the Department of Justice indicted Richard M. Scrushy, former chief executive of HealthSouth Corporation, on numerous counts of fraud, conspiracy, obstruction of justice, perjury, money laundering, and false reporting in the first test of the Sarbanes-Oxley Act. The case went to trial in 2005. Mr. Scrushy was convicted of bribery and sentenced to federal prison; he has appealed his sentence.

The guidelines allow for a reduction in culpability if an organization can prove that an offense occurred despite the existence of a program designed to prevent and detect violations of law. The seven elements, listed in the previous section, comprise the minimum requirements that the federal government recognizes as essential to a good compliance program. The 2004 amendments also require that organizations promote a culture of compliance with the law. In 2005, the American Bar Association urged the U.S. Sentencing Commission to study the attorney-client waiver in Chapter 8 of the Sentencing Guidelines.

SPOTLIGHT ON...

In *United States v. Booker*,[6] the U.S. Supreme Court ruled that the mandatory sentencing requirements for criminal defendants contained in the U.S. Sentencing Commission Guidelines were not valid. Though this decision may affect future health care criminal defendants, it did not change or invalidate any part of the suggested compliance program concepts in the sentencing guidelines.

Compliance Standards

> The organization shall establish standards and procedures to prevent and detect criminal conduct.[7]

Health care organizations typically have standards and procedures for those areas that pose liability risks and that can generate criminal and civil consequences if violations occur. A representative sampling of policies and procedures in a hospital will include billing and claims processing, medical necessity of services, and patient privacy and confidentiality, among others. Another important source may be a code of conduct that puts employees and contractors on notice of behavioral expectations and intolerance of legal and ethical violations. The code of conduct may also detail **whistleblower** protection against retaliation. The role whistleblowers play in compliance is detailed in Chapter 6.

In order to effectively meet this element of a compliance program, standards and procedures must be written in language that is comprehensible to the whole range of an organization's employees, from the housekeeper to the CEO. Posting and distribution of materials is necessary, as is certification by employees that they have read, understood, and agree to abide by the standards and procedures. Many large health care organizations post their standards and procedures on their websites or provide personnel with handbooks. Lastly, because legal requirements may change and procedures may vary, organizations must ensure that published material is updated regularly.

High-Level Responsibility

> Specific individual(s) within high-level personnel of the organization shall be delegated operational responsibility for the compliance and ethics program. Individual(s) with operational responsibility shall report periodically to high-level personnel and, as appropriate, to the governing authority, or an appropriate subgroup of the governing authority, on the effectiveness of the compliance and ethics program.[8]

Every health care organization should designate a compliance officer to manage activities related to its compliance efforts. Depending on the size of the organization, the compliance officer's responsibility may be his or her sole duty, or the position may be supplemental to the individual's existing duties. However, those other duties should not pose a conflict of interest with the mission of the compliance program. For example, the marketing director of a health insurance plan may not be a good choice for a compliance officer because he or she may be in a position to manipulate an organization's message to the best public relations advantage, but not necessarily the best legal and ethical one. The Health Care Compliance Association estimates that 31 percent of compliance officers have master's degrees, 31 percent have bachelor's degrees, 18 percent have Juris Doctor degrees, and 17 percent have a master's in business administration.[9] The Office of Inspector General has suggested that the compliance officer's function should be separate from that of the general counsel or chief financial officer to assure independence, though not all health care organizations have followed that suggestion. Regardless of who assumes the role of compliance officer, that person must be trustworthy and approachable, possess good judgment, and serve as an example of integrity.

SPOTLIGHT ON...

Should an organization's general counsel serve as its chief compliance officer as well? In 2003, during intense governmental scrutiny, Tenet Healthcare's general counsel and chief compliance officer was forced to step down. A U.S. senator had criticized her for her conflicting roles in the company: serving as general counsel while overseeing compliance with governmental rules. In 2007, the U.S. Department of Justice filed a complaint against Christi Sulzbach, Tenet's former general counsel, alleging that she violated the False Claims Act by submitting false certifications to the Medicare program.

The compliance officer must have access to the organization's board of directors or chief executive officer if the compliance program is to have authority and meaning within the organization. Many organizations follow the recommendation of the OIG and establish a compliance committee to assist the compliance officer with program implementation and oversight. Members of the compliance committee are typically senior staff members with different perspectives within the organization. For example, personnel from finance, human resources, and clinical operations may be good committee members because their views of the organization reflect their knowledge of the operations of their departments. The committee members reinforce the organization's commitment to compliance and can bolster compliance efforts from within their respective departments.

The 2004 amendments to the U.S. Sentencing Guidelines highlight management's obligation to not only be involved in the development of compliance programs, but also to be active in oversight of implementation and effectiveness. This proactive approach envisions due diligence on the part of the compliance officer, committee members, the board of directors, and other high-level personnel to detect problems and address solutions on an ongoing basis.

Education

The organization shall take reasonable steps to communicate periodically and in a practical manner its standards and procedures, and other aspects of the compliance and ethics program to members of the governing authority, high-level personnel, substantial authority personnel, the organization's employees, and as appropriate, the organization's agents by conducting effective training programs and otherwise disseminating information appropriate to such individuals' respective roles and responsibilities.[10]

A health care organization must communicate and educate its staff on the standards, policies and procedures, and code of conduct that are the essence of the compliance program. The sentencing guidelines make clear that all levels of full-time and part-time employees, from senior management to service personnel, must receive training and periodic retraining. The guidelines also suggest that organizations have a requirement that employees certify that they have received the training and agree to comply with its objectives.

Many organizations have formal training programs or departments whose sole function is to train and develop staff. Training programs and written material should be designed to reach a broad-based audience of employees with different skills and educational levels. An employee's introduction to the compliance program may come during an initial orientation session. The content presented during new employee orientation may include a session that summarizes the standards, policies and procedures, and the code of conduct, as well as a general introduction to laws on fraud and abuse. Delivery methods can include live training by professionals, videos, and computer-based sessions.

Training that is specifically targeted to employees whose job responsibilities correspond with significant financial risks, such as coding and billing for health care services, should be part of any organization's training plan. Other potential problematic areas include grants management, accounting and finance, contracting, and clinic operations. Employees in these departments are entrusted with responsibilities that expose the organization to liability. Likewise, it may be prudent to include independent contractors and outside vendors in compliance training programs, especially if an organization relies on temporary staff or consultants, a practice that is not uncommon in the health care industry.

Written material on compliance must be presented in a clear, unambiguous manner and must be readily available for staff's use. Many organizations now keep policies and procedures in electronic format on their websites while smaller entities may keep hard copies of compliance documents in looseleaf binders. Like training curricula, compliance material must be updated and revised to reflect legal and regulatory changes. A regular compliance newsletter or a section in an existing publication is an effective way to communicate and promote the compliance message and to disseminate new information.

Some organizations build compliance into employee performance evaluations. Managers and supervisors should be sure that employees understand how compliance affects their roles, advise that compliance is a condition of employment, and disclose any disciplinary action that noncompliant employees may be subject to, including termination.

Communication

> The organization shall take reasonable steps to have and publicize a system, which may include mechanisms that allow for anonymity or confidentiality, whereby the organization's employees and agents may report or seek guidance regarding potential or actual criminal conduct without fear of retaliation.[11]

The creation and maintenance of effective, open channels of communication between an organization's staff and those charged with compliance oversight is another element of a dynamic compliance program. Employees must feel comfortable reporting incidents of noncompliance and must be assured that they will not suffer retaliation for doing so. Please refer to Chapter 6 to see how employees who report misconduct—often referred to as whistleblowers—can initiate lawsuits when they suspect fraud or abuse in federal health care programs. The sentencing guidelines emphasize that whistleblowers shall be afforded special protection against retaliation. Though first-line supervisors should still respond to employee concerns, employees must have the freedom to directly access the compliance officer to report infractions and obtain guidance on regulatory matters and organizational policies. Reporting noncompliance to someone who is outside of an employee's direct line of command can lessen the employee's fear of negative repercussions. Other stakeholders, such as contractors, vendors, and patients, also have the right to report allegations of wrongdoing and should also be encouraged to do so.

Internal reporting mechanisms such as a hotline, suggestion box, or e-mail mailbox are all valuable in aiding communication. Whatever mechanisms are chosen, correct phone numbers or addresses must be made available to staff, contractors, vendors, patients, and the general public through posters, announcements, websites, and other media.

The compliance officer must maintain a log of all reports received and must promptly initiate investigations. To encourage communication, reports may be made on an anonymous basis. All reports are confidential and sharing of them must be limited. Reports of investigations that validate suspected wrongdoing should be shared with any internal governing authority, such as the CEO, the compliance committee, and the board of directors.

Auditing and Monitoring

> The organization shall take reasonable steps to ensure that the organization's compliance and ethics program is followed, including monitoring and auditing to detect criminal conduct.[12]

Once a compliance program has been put into place, periodic audits or risk assessments must be used to evaluate the program's effectiveness at detecting violations. These audits can help identify problem areas that may need additional training or guidance and can also help reduce errors. The OIG recommends that compliance programs make an initial assessment of departments' operations that can be used as a baseline against which future progress can be compared.

Audits have two primary areas of focus: (1) compliance with federal, state, and other governing laws, regulations, and program requirements, and (2) assessment of the compliance program's processes.[13] Several consulting companies offer manuals and software on issues and areas suitable for compliance audits. Audit tools include surveys, on-site visits, personnel record checks, interviews, sampling protocols, and other techniques. Compliance audits may be scheduled at intervals appropriate to the level of risk that a particular area poses. For example, random audits of claims by a particular physician may be done monthly because correct claims processing is essential to avoid potential legal penalties and to maintain cash flow. However, an audit of compliance training may be only a yearly event. The OIG has prepared guidance on audit methodology, available through its Office of Audit Services.

Personnel performing audits must be adequately trained and experienced in identifying compliance issues and addressing corrective measures. Auditors may be either external or internal; however, they must be independent of the operational program that they are auditing. Auditors often have accounting or other financial backgrounds.

Enforcement and Discipline

The organization's compliance and ethics program shall be promoted and enforced consistently throughout the organization through (A) appropriate incentives to perform in accordance with the compliance and ethics program; and (B) appropriate disciplinary measures for engaging in criminal conduct and for failing to take reasonable steps top prevent or detect criminal conduct.[14]

Disciplinary policies that describe the consequences of violations of the standards of conduct, other internal policies and procedures, and applicable laws and regulations are essential to the effectiveness of the compliance program. Levels of discipline can vary among health care organizations but most include verbal warnings and supervisory conferences for minor infractions to financial penalties, suspension or termination from employment, or loss of hospital privileges for medical staff for more serious violations. Internal disciplinary sanctions may be in addition to penalties imposed by federal and state regulatory agencies charged with oversight of health care programs. Both failure to detect a violation and intentional, egregious noncompliance can trigger disciplinary sanctions.

Employees must be aware of disciplinary policies and their ramifications; thus, dissemination of this information to all employees is required. In order for the disciplinary policy to be a deterrent of noncompliant conduct, it must be consistently enforced. All levels of employees must be treated in the same manner when noncompliance is an issue. The organization's disciplinary policy should detail appropriate responses for handling specific types of problems as well as elaborate on who bears the responsibility for enforcing any actions taken. Supervisors and upper-level management must be aware of their role in the instruction and discipline of their subordinates. They must also be personally accountable to the organization.

While disciplinary policies cannot extend to outside contractors, an organization has the obligation to ensure that it does not hire or enter into contracts with ineligible persons or organizations. Under the Social Security Act's requirements, excluded providers or entities who furnish services or items to federal health care beneficiaries (*e.g.*, persons eligible for Medicare, Medicaid, TRICARE, or CHAMPVA) are subject to governmental sanctions, including denial of claims payment and civil monetary penalties. These penalties are discussed in detail in Chapter 6. Health care organizations that do not take the time to review the Office of Inspector General's and General Services Administration's exclusion and debarment lists may find federal government enforcers knocking on the door of their corporate headquarters.

Organizations should have policies and procedures in place to assure that staff and contractors possess the appropriate professional licenses and to review adverse reports on health care practitioners, other providers, and suppliers from agencies, courts, and health plans. In particular, hiring or contracting of persons in certain high-risk or vulnerable areas, such as nursing homes or hospices, may be the subject of intensive employment screening.

Response and Prevention

> After criminal conduct has been detected, the organization shall take reasonable steps to respond appropriately to the criminal conduct and to prevent further similar conduct, including making any necessary modifications to the organization's compliance and ethics program.[15]

While the other elements of a compliance program can be viewed as "preventative medicine," this component of corrective action acknowledges that organizations must fix what is broken. If a violation has been detected, the organization must take care that an investigation and response are prompt and appropriate. Corrective action is especially important if the noncompliance has resulted in inappropriate or inadequate patient care.

The OIG often uses **corporate integrity agreements (CIAs)** when negotiating settlements with health care providers and organizations accused of wrongdoing in federal health care programs.

ACRONYM

CIA: corporate integrity agreement

A provider or entity consents to these obligations as part of the civil settlement and in exchange for the OIG's agreement not to seek an exclusion of that health care provider or entity from participation in Medicare, Medicaid and other Federal health care programs. False claims submitted in violation of the False Claims Act or Civil Monetary Penalties Law give rise to the OIG's permissive exclusion authority under 42 U.S.C. §1320a-7(b)(7). Providers who settle these cases often deny that they were liable or that they committed the alleged conduct.[16]

The typical duration of a CIA is five years. The OIG maintains a list of CIAs on its website. Providers and organizations subject to CIAs run the gamut from individual physicians to health plan insurers to pharmaceutical manufacturers. No one type of provider or entity can escape the scrutiny of the OIG.

Corporate integrity agreements typically include adherence to the essential compliance elements, for a start. But many CIAs include specific provisions related to the identified risks. For example, in 2000, the University of Chicago, its hospitals, and its faculty physician practice paid $10.9 million to the federal government to settle allegations of false Medicare claims. In their CIA, any third-party billing company that the University of Chicago used was subject to the OIG's plan for periodic audits.[17]

Importance of Compliance and Ethics Programs

Despite the troubles of the headline-making organizations mentioned earlier in the chapter, most health care entities manage to stay out of legal trouble. Why would an organization expend financial and human resources to establish a compliance program that is *generally not required by law*? The potential benefits of a compliance and ethics program are many and varied. These include:

- Preventing misconduct by employees and contractors.
- Guarding against negative impacts on patients when misconduct is related to patient care.
- Enhancing and safeguarding an organization's or provider's reputation.
- Avoiding the costs associated with legal defense of criminal, civil, or administrative suits.
- Influencing enforcement agencies' decisions regarding prosecution.

- Mitigating liability, whether in civil monetary penalties or cases of breach of fiduciary responsibility.
- Abating penalties under the U.S. Sentencing Guidelines.[18]

All of these benefits, individually or collectively, compensate for any expenditure of time, personnel, or money that implementing and maintaining a compliance program entails.

CORPORATE COMPLIANCE

The government does not have the only enforcement tools in health care compliance. Private legal actions, such as shareholder **derivative actions**, are available where corporate misconduct occurs in for-profit health care entities that are incorporated.

In Re Caremark[19] was one of the earliest cases where the court discussed corporate compliance programs. Caremark was a Delaware corporation headquartered in Illinois that provided both managed care and patient care services. The managed care business included prescription drug programs and the operation of physician practices. The patient health care services included infusion therapy, growth hormone therapy, HIV/AIDS-related treatment, and hemophilia therapy. Both the U.S. Department of Justice and the OIG were involved in an investigation of Caremark's business practices, including physician contracts, as a substantial portion of Caremark's revenues were derived from the Medicare and Medicaid programs. In 1994, Caremark was charged with multiple felonies. It entered into agreements with the governmental agencies, including a Corporate Integrity Agreement, and was required to pay civil and criminal fines.

A shareholder derivative action was filed in 1994, purporting to seek recovery of the losses incurred by the company from the individual defendants who constituted Caremark's board of directors. The court eventually approved a settlement in the case. Part of the settlement included provisions for a Compliance and Ethics Committee to meet four times annually and for corporate officers in business segments to serve as compliance officers and report semiannually to the Committee. The court examined the plaintiffs' allegation of "liability for failure to monitor" by the board of directors. In other words, the court considered whether the board was liable for the fraudulent business practices because it failed to maintain a sufficient level of oversight of the organization's daily operations. At page 968, the court noted:

> . . . As the facts of this case graphically demonstrate, ordinary business decisions that are made by officers and employees deeper in the interior of the organization can, however, vitally affect the welfare of the corporation and its ability to achieve its various strategic and financial goals.

The court discussed the incentives that the Federal Sentencing Guidelines provide for corporations to have in place ". . . compliance programs to detect violations of law, promptly to report violations to appropriate public officials when discovered, and to take prompt, voluntary remedial efforts." Though ultimately the court concluded that the board's directors were not guilty of a sustained failure to exercise their oversight function, this case has been used by the U.S. Department of Justice as an example of the evaluation process of a corporate compliance program when deciding whether to prosecute corporations.[20] The entire opinion can be found in the Online Companion that accompanies this text.

SUMMARY

If a compliance and ethics program is to be successful, a provider or organization's leadership must exhibit an enduring dedication to nurturing a climate of integrity and responsiveness. The seven essential elements of a good compliance program in the U.S. Sentencing Commission Guidelines form the framework on which entities can build a program that is specific to their needs, while maintaining a goal of reducing noncompliant and/or illegal conduct. The transparency required by the Sarbanes-Oxley Act places additional demands on compliance and ethics programs in publicly traded companies.

The Office of Inspector General serves important roles in the oversight of health care delivery and financing. The OIG provides Compliance Program Guidances for risks in industry-specific areas. The OIG often uses Corporate Integrity Agreements as part of settlement agreements with organizations accused of wrongdoing in federal health care programs. The OIG also maintains a website for its compliance guidance, as well as a list of providers and organizations subject to Corporate Integrity Agreements.

KEY TERMS

compliance: Acting in a way that does not violate a law or terms of an agreement.

derivative action: A lawsuit by a stockholder of a corporation against another person (usually an officer of the company) to enforce claims the stockholder thinks the corporation has against that person.

whistleblower: An employee who brings organizational wrongdoing to the attention of government authorities. Government laws protect some whistleblowers.

REVIEW QUESTIONS AND EXERCISES

1. What are the seven elements of an effective compliance program?

2. Visit the website of a large health care organization such as Humana or Tenet Healthcare. See if you can you find their policies on compliance and ethics. Has the organization addressed the seven essential compliance elements?

3. Visit the website of the Office of Inspector General for the Department of Health and Human Services. See if you can find the Compliance Program Guidances mentioned earlier in this chapter.

4. Visit the website of the Office of Inspector General for the Department of Health and Human Services again. See if you can locate the list of Corporate Integrity Agreements. These are arranged in reverse chronological order. Do you see any health care organizations on the list that are in your geographical area?

5. The U.S. Sentencing Commission Guidelines apply to corporations. Do you think that the seven elements of compliance programs should be applied to the other types of business organizations that are discussed in the chapter on health care organizations? Why or why not?

6. Shepardize the *Caremark* decision found in the Online Companion. Are there other cases of corporate misconduct that involve for-profit health care organizations?

ENDNOTES

1. 31 U.S.C. § 3801 *et seq.*

2. 45 C.F.R. §§ 160 and 164.

3. See generally, "Evaluating and Improving a Compliance Program," Health Care Compliance Association, 2003.

4. 45 C.F.R. § 46.

5. P.L. 107-204, § 805 (a)(2)(5).

6. *United States v. Booker*, 543 U.S. 220 (2005) No. 04—104, 375 F.3d 508, affirmed and remanded; and No. 04—105, vacated and remanded. Note that the case was vacated on grounds.

7. United States Sentencing Commission, Guidelines Manual, § 8B2.1(b)(1).

8. United States Sentencing Commission, Guidelines Manual, § 8B2.1(b)(2)(C).

9. 2004 Profile of Health Care Compliance Officers, Health Care Compliance Association, PricewaterhouseCoopers LLP, 2004.

10. United States Sentencing Commission, Guidelines Manual, § 8B2.1(b)(4)(A).

11. United States Sentencing Commission, Guidelines Manual, § 8B2.1(b)(5)(C).

12. United States Sentencing Commission, Guidelines Manual, § 8B2.1(5).

13. See generally, "Compliance Program Basics," Health Care Program Compliance Guide, Bureau of National Affairs, Inc., 2004.

14. United States Sentencing Commission, Guidelines Manual, § 8B2.1(b)(6).

15. United States Sentencing Commission, Guidelines Manual, § 8B2.1(b)(7).

16. "Corporate Integrity Agreements," www.oig.hhs.gov/fraud/ cias.html, accessed July 31, 2007.

17. "Institutional Compliance Agreement Between the Office of the Inspector General of the Department of Health and Human Services and the University of Chicago and the University of Chicago Hospitals," 1/13/2000.

18. See generally, "Compliance Program Basics," <u>Health Care Program Compliance Guide</u>, Bureau of National Affairs, Inc., 2004.

19. 698 A.2d 959 (Del. Ct. Chan. 1996).

20. "Principles of Federal Prosecution of Business Organizations," U.S. Department of Justice Memorandum to Heads of Department Components and United States Attorneys, dated December 12, 2006, available at <u>http://www.usdoj.gov</u>.

CHAPTER 8

HEALTH INSURANCE PORTABILITY AND ACCOUNTABILITY ACT

CHAPTER OUTLINE

OBJECTIVES

After completing this chapter, students should be able to

- Describe the health insurance portability requirements for employers.
- Identify which health care providers and entities are subject to HIPAA privacy and security regulations.
- Define basic HIPAA privacy terminology.
- Apply privacy regulations to factual situations.
- Discuss the security measures necessary for guarding protected health information.

HISTORY OF LEGISLATION

Students need to be wary of the many myths and misconceptions about the **Health Insurance Portability and Accountability Act (HIPAA)** that they may have heard. Despite intense publicity, few realize how much HIPAA has changed the landscape of health care. A brief review of HIPAA's original intent might shed some light on what the fuss has been about.

The Health Insurance Portability and Accountability Act[1] of 1996 originated as a bipartisan bill (the Kennedy–Kassenbaum bill) in Congress and was signed into law by President Clinton in 1996. As originally introduced, its purpose was

> "to amend the Internal Revenue Code of 1986 to improve portability and continuity of health insurance coverage in the group and individual markets, to combat waste, fraud, and abuse in health insurance and health care delivery, to promote the use of medical savings accounts, to improve access to long-term care services and coverage, to simplify the administration of health insurance, and for other purposes."[2]

What started out as primarily a law to address health insurance portability and guaranteed insurance coverage expanded to other areas such as patient privacy, patient information security, medical savings accounts, and electronic transmission of patient health data.

As originally enacted, HIPAA affected many sections in the U.S. Code including the Internal Revenue Code, the **Employment Retirement Income Security Act (ERISA)**, **Consolidated Omnibus Budget Reconciliation Act (COBRA)**, and the Public Health Service Act. In 2001, President Bush signed a major amendment to HIPAA, the **Administrative Simplification Compliance Act (ASCA)**[3] to ensure that covered entities comply with the standards for electronic health care transactions and code sets previously adopted under the Administrative Simplification Subtitle of HIPAA.

Many segments of the health care industry tried to eliminate, change, or delay adoption of HIPAA. Insurers were forced to offer health insurance coverage to high-risk groups. Employers had to adapt to additional requirements of health insurance eligibility for employees, dependents, and former employees. Medical liability reform became a hot-button issue in the 2004 presidential election. Many providers were (and still are) resistant to using standardized electronic transactions for health care, rather than using old-fashioned paper to conduct business. Privacy regulations in particular generated intense controversy, with insurers, lawyers for health care organizations, and the general public engaged in vociferous debate about the merits and flaws of patient privacy.

HIPAA Subtitles

HIPAA is organized into five subtitles:

- Title I: health insurance reform
- Title II: prevention of health care fraud and abuse and administrative simplification
- Title III: tax-related health provisions
- Title IV: group health plan requirements
- Title V: revenue offsets

In this chapter, we will focus on Titles I and II since they present the most compelling compliance challenges for the legal professional practicing in the health care area. Title III's tax provisions as they relate to health care law and compliance issues are briefly discussed.

TITLE I: PORTABILITY, ACCESS, AND RENEWABILITY

Most of us do not stay with one employer for 30 years as our parents did; we move from job to job and sometimes experience periods of unemployment. Our expectation is that our health insurance coverage will continue uninterrupted when we change employers or are between jobs. For those of us who are small business owners or self-employed, the ability to purchase a health insurance policy is a necessity. Once we have insurance coverage, we want to be assured that it cannot be taken away because of a disease or disability that we may develop. HIPAA guarantees portability, access, and renewability and has changed the provision of health insurance in significant ways. This section describes employer obligations and employee rights in health insurance coverage.

Guarantees

HIPAA guarantees can be summarized as

- limitation on preexisting condition exclusions
- access to coverage for small employers
- enhanced COBRA benefits

- mental health parity if that coverage is offered
- protection against discrimination in offering or renewing coverage

Limitation on Preexisting Condition Exclusions An important aspect of HIPAA insurance reform is the limitation on exclusions for preexisting conditions for which an individual received treatment within the previous 6 months. A preexisting medical condition is ". . . any physical or mental condition resulting from an illness, injury, pregnancy, or congenital malformation."[4] A group health plan or insurer cannot impose an exclusion from coverage for a preexisting condition for a period of more than 12 months from the date of the individual's enrollment. A preexisting exclusion may not be imposed on account of pregnancy, on newborns or newly adopted children if subsequently enrolled within 30 days of birth or adoption, and with respect to genetic information.

The time period of preexisting condition exclusion can be shortened if an individual can prove that he or she had prior creditable coverage, through a Certificate of Creditable Coverage (described more fully in the next section). **Creditable coverage** can be used to reduce or eliminate preexisting condition exclusions that might be applied under a future insurance plan or policy. In general, if a person had other health coverage of any kind, the new plan's preexisting condition exclusion period must be reduced by the period of the previous coverage, provided that there was no break in insurance coverage of over 63 days.[5] Group health plans and health insurance issuers are required to furnish a certificate of creditable coverage when an individual leaves a plan. The certificate describes the amount of creditable coverage and the date the coverage ended.

Access to Coverage for Small Employers Small employers benefited by the enactment of HIPAA. Employers with at least 2 but less than 50 employees are guaranteed access to health insurance coverage. However, HIPAA does not require any employer to offer health insurance coverage as a benefit. As of July 1997, insurers were required to renew coverage to all employer groups, regardless of the health status of any group members. Unfortunately, HIPAA does not guarantee affordability. The free market forces small employer groups to pay higher premiums for coverage.

Enhanced COBRA Benefits COBRA guarantees benefits for continued health insurance coverage to terminated employees or employees who voluntarily leave their employers. Employees who leave their employment and who participated in their employer's group health plan must be provided with a Certificate of Creditable Coverage, without charge and within a reasonable period of time. A Certificate of Creditable Coverage is a written document specifying the period of an employee's creditable coverage. Certificates must be furnished automatically to an employee whose group coverage has ended, such as when leaving or quitting a job; an individual who loses health coverage and who is not entitled to elect **COBRA continuation coverage**, such as in small-employer plans that are not subject to COBRA; and an individual who is qualified for COBRA and has elected COBRA continuation coverage or after the expiration of any grace period for the payment of COBRA premiums. Certificates may be furnished on request to employees and their dependents if they ask for them.

Effective January 1, 1997, HIPAA made changes to COBRA continuation coverage, regardless of when the event occurs that entitles the individual to continuation coverage. First, a disabled individual, as determined under the Social Security Act, is entitled to 29 months of COBRA continuation coverage, instead of the usual 18 months given to terminated or separated employees. Under prior law, the individual had to be disabled at the time of termination of employment or reduction in hours in order to receive this extended coverage. Under HIPAA, an individual is entitled to 29 months of COBRA coverage if he or she became disabled at any time during the first 60 days of COBRA coverage. The extension of continuation coverage to 29 months also is available to any other family members of the disabled individual who are entitled to COBRA continuation coverage.

In general, COBRA coverage is discontinued when an individual becomes covered under another group health plan. However, COBRA cannot be terminated because of other coverage where the plan limits or excludes coverage for any preexisting condition of the individual. HIPAA limits the circumstances under which a plan may impose a preexisting condition exclusion period on individuals. If a plan is precluded under HIPAA from imposing an exclusion period on an individual, COBRA continuation coverage may then be terminated.

HIPAA also modified COBRA rules to provide that children who are born, adopted, or placed for adoption with the covered employee during the continuation coverage period are treated as "qualified beneficiaries" and thus eligible for coverage.

Mental Health Parity Another benefit related to HIPAA's access, portability, and renewability provisions is mental health parity in insurance coverage. The **Mental Health Parity Act** of 1996 (**MHPA**)[6] prevents group health plans from placing annual or lifetime dollar limits on mental health benefits that are lower, or less favorable, than what the plan offers for annual or lifetime dollar limits for medical and surgical benefits. For example, if a health plan has a $1 million lifetime limit on medical and surgical benefits, it cannot put a lesser amount, say $100,000, as a lifetime limit on mental health benefits.

Group health plans may impose some restrictions on mental health benefits and still comply with the law. For example, some plans increase copayments or co-insurance or limit the number of visits for mental health benefits. As we have seen with guaranteed access, the law does not guarantee affordability.

Although the law requires parity, or equivalent dollar limits, MHPA does not require group health plans and health insurance issuers to include mental health coverage in their benefits package. Thus, the MHPA applies only to group health plans that offer mental health coverage in their benefits packages. Dollar amounts for treatment of substance abuse or chemical dependency are not counted when adding up the limits for mental health benefits and medical and surgical benefits to determine if parity exists. The law applies to most group health plans with more than 50 workers, but is not applicable to individual health insurance coverage in the market. However, insurance laws in some states may also require mental health parity in plans offered to smaller groups and/or individuals.

The protections of the MHPA expired at the end of 2004. In the 2005 Congress, several bills were introduced to take its place: the Mental Health Equitable Treatment Act of 2005,[7] the Medicare Mental Health Modernization Act of 2005,[8] and the Health Security for All Americans Act.[9] None of these bills passed both houses.

Protection against Discrimination HIPAA prevents group health plans from using an individual's health factors as a reason for disparate treatment from other similarly situated individuals in the health plan. However, insurance issuers may consider all relevant health factors of all individuals in the group when determining the rates for a group health plan during the underwriting process.

These nondiscrimination rules are valuable in a variety of situations. Suppose that you were diagnosed with a chronic illness that will require frequent doctor visits. A group health plan may not deny payment for needed services or increase premiums. Likewise, group health plans may not discriminate against individuals who learn that they have inherited a disease or condition. Their health insurance coverage must remain intact.

TITLE II: ADMINISTRATIVE SIMPLIFICATION AND FRAUD AND ABUSE PREVENTION

Administrative Simplification is the great oxymoron of HIPAA—it's jokingly referred to as Administrative Complication. The main parts of Administrative Simplification—transactions, code sets, privacy regulations, security regulations, and national provider identifiers—comprise a bulk of regulatory material that has kept the health care industry busy with implementation for the last few years. Each area offers the compliance or health care professional the opportunity to develop expertise and provides a significant amount of work for lawyers in health care practices.

The goal of Administrative Simplification is improved efficiency and effectiveness of the nation's health care system through the use of electronic data exchanges. Administrative Simplification provisions direct that the **Department of Health and Human Services (DHHS)** establish initiatives to fulfill legislative intent as follows:

> **ACRONYM**
>
> DHHS: Department of Health and Human Services

- national standards for electronic health care transactions
- unique, national identifiers for providers, health plans, and employers
- privacy and security of health data[10]

It has taken several years for DHHS to implement these initiatives. Each area has required legal, financial, and operational analysis; proposed regulations; comments by health care providers and the general public; finalization of regulations; and enforcement provisions.

Covered Entity Before we get into a detailed discussion of the subparts of Administrative Simplification, it's time to step back and think about who is subject to this section of HIPAA. The Administrative Simplification standards apply to any entity or individual that is a

- health care provider that conducts certain transactions in electronic form
- health care clearinghouse
- health plan

A business entity or individual that fits into one or more of these categories is referred to as a **covered entity (CE)** in the Administrative Simplification regulations.

ACRONYM

CE: covered entity

> **SPOTLIGHT ON...**
>
> CMS provides decision tools on its website to determine whether an individual or a business entity is a covered entity under HIPAA Administrative Simplification. By answering a series of questions, the decision tool will render its determination of covered entity status.

Remember from our discussion in Chapter 5 that health care delivery involves a number of different general and specialized medical services. In the Code of Federal Regulations, health care is defined as

> . . . care, services, or supplies related to the health of an individual. It includes, but is not limited to, the following: (1) Preventive, diagnostic, rehabilitative, maintenance, or palliative care, and counseling, service, assessment, or procedure with respect to the physical or mental condition, or functional status, of an individual or that affects the structure or function of the body; and (2) Sale or dispensing of a drug, device, equipment, or other item in accordance with a prescription.[11]

It is easy to see, then, that Administrative Simplification has a wide reach. The key additional requirement, however, is that health care providers must conduct certain health care transactions in electronic form.

A health care clearinghouse is

> . . . a public or private entity . . . that does either of the following functions: (1) processes or facilitates the processing of health

information . . . in a nonstandard format or containing non-standard data content into standard data elements or a standard transaction, [or] (2) receives a standard transaction . . . and processes or facilitates the processing of health information [in the standard transaction] into nonstandard format or nonstandard data content for the receiving entity.[12]

In other words, a health care clearinghouse helps health care providers change paper information about patient enrollment, claims, etc. into electronic information.

A health plan provides or pays for the costs of health services. Private, employer-sponsored, and government health plans such as Medicare and TRICARE are all health plans. But not all health plans are covered entities for HIPAA purposes. Group health plans with less than 50 participants and certain self-administered plans are excluded from HIPAA's Administrative Simplification requirements.

Transactions and Code Sets

For those already involved in the business side of the health care industry, knowledge of **transactions and code sets (TCS)** is an essential component of getting paid the correct amount for health care services.

Rather than rely on bad handwriting on a variety of paper forms to conduct common activities regarding patient financial information, Administrative Simplification mandates standardization of those actions through the use of **electronic data interchange**. And so that we are all on the same page as far as disease classification, diagnosis, and treatment procedures, Administrative Simplification requires use of two recognized coding systems.

Standardization of electronic transactions applies to the following common business activities:

- enrollment/disenrollment in a health plan
- claims/encounters with health care providers or services
- eligibility for health care services
- payment/remittance for health care services
- premium payment to plans
- claim status for health care services already rendered
- referral certification/authorization for certain health care services

ACRONYM

TCS: Transactions and Code Sets

- coordination of benefits when more than one health plan may be liable for payment
- first report of injury when a patient is involved in an accident
- claims attachment for additional information that may be needed to process a claim for payment

Administrative Simplification requires that health care providers and suppliers code information on their patients using the **Healthcare Common Procedural Coding System (HCPCS)** and **International Classification of Diseases (ICD-9 and 10)**. Both of these manuals were in widespread use prior to adoption of Administrative Simplification. The HCPCS procedure and modifier codes apply to items and supplies and non-physician services not covered by the **Current Procedural Terminology (CPT)** codes that physicians use in daily practice. The ICD-9 lists diagnosis codes, while the ICD-10 lists codes for procedures.

Privacy Rule

Computerized records of 562,000 US troops, dependents and retirees, including names, addresses, telephone numbers, birth dates and Social Security numbers, are stolen from TriWest Healthcare Alliance, Pentagon contractor in Phoenix, exposing them to risk of identity theft; company advises potential victims, thousands of whom face deployment in Persian Gulf, to seek free credit reports and flag their credit records.[13]

Prosecutors seeking leads in gruesome killing of newborn baby in Storm Lake, Iowa, subpoena names of hundreds of women who had pregnancy tests at local Planned Parenthood clinic and who might have been due to give birth shortly before baby's death late May, but organization is fighting subpoenas in court; organization argues that young women must have confidential source of help to turn in difficult situations; other clinics and local hospital provided information; Planned Parenthood has support of American Civil Liberties Union and American College of Obstetricians and Gynecologists.[14]

Prozac, drug used as antidepressant, is mailed unsolicited to Michael Grinsted, West Palm Beach, Fla., resident; manufacturer Eli Lilly, which apologized for earlier mailings, says it is unaware of new incident; parents weigh joining class-action lawsuit against company, Walgreen drug chain and several doctors for misusing patients' records and invading their privacy.[15]

Privacy is a hot-button issue. With the wealth of consumer information available and the ease of access to information via the Internet, the intent of HIPAA's Privacy Rule—to protect individually identifiable health information—is a noble and necessary one. Privacy Rule regulations of HIPAA[16]

- give patients certain rights and protections regarding their health care information
- require health care providers to guard privacy of their patients/clients
- limit access to health care information by some outside entities

History of the Privacy Regulations The regulatory rulemaking process in administrative law may shed some light on the length of time that proposal of privacy regulations and actual implementation of them has taken. The first notice was published in November, 1999,[17] inviting comments. The government received over 52,000 public comments. The final rule, establishing standards for privacy of individually identifiable health information, was published in the Federal Register[18] on December 28, 2000. DHHS continued to receive comments regarding the impact and operation of the proposed rule on different segments of the health care industry, as well as on individual patients. The Secretary of DHHS then invited additional comments until March, 2001.[19]

The original effective date for the privacy rule was April 14, 2001.[20] However, confusion and misunderstanding about the privacy rule continued, so DHHS began development of guidelines on implementation and clarification on requirements so that potential problems could be addressed.

In July 2001, DHHS published the first in a series of guidances designed to answer common questions and provide assurances for resolving any unintended consequences that the privacy rule might have. Public hearings were held in August 2001 and January 2002, sponsored by the National Committee for Vital and Health Statistics, an advisory body to DHHS. As a result of these hearings, DHHS proposed modifications to the privacy rule in the following areas:

- consent
- uses and disclosures for treatment, payment, and operations

- notice of privacy practices
- minimum necessary uses and disclosures
- oral communications
- business associates
- uses and disclosures for marketing
- parents as personal representatives of minors
- uses and disclosures for research purposes
- uses and disclosures for which a patient authorization is required
- deidentification of patient data

That's a pretty exhaustive list. Notice of modifications in these areas was published on March 27, 2002.[21] Only 30 days were allowed for additional comments, as the implementation date of the privacy rule's protections was on the horizon. Although the privacy rule was effective in 2001, its implementation date was April 14, 2003 for most affected entities and providers.

SPOTLIGHT ON...

A new subspecialty in the health care industry was spawned to handle the change in operations that HIPAA privacy regulations necessitated—the HIPAA privacy professional. Lawyers, health information managers, privacy and security consultants, trainers, auditors, and other professionals offered niche services in HIPAA privacy compliance.

ACRONYM

PHI: protected health information

Patient Rights The HIPAA privacy rules grant a number of rights to individuals regarding **protected health information (PHI)**.

Access to Protected Health Information[22] Patients have the right to ask for copies of their medical information contained in a **designated record set**, with some limited exceptions for psychotherapy notes, information prepared for use in or in anticipation of litigation, and information kept by the covered entity that is subject to and/or exempt from the Clinical Laboratory Improvements Amendments of 1988.[23] Covered entities generally have policies that detail the procedures, forms, and fees to be used when a patient wants information from his or her record.

Request an Amendment to PHI[24] Patients have the right to amend protected health information in their designated record sets. Covered entities must have a process in place to review these requests and decide whether the requested amendment will be made.

Request Restrictions on Certain Uses and Disclosures and Receive Confidential Communications[25] Patients may request that certain uses and disclosures of their protected health information, as outlined in the Notice of Privacy Practices, be restricted. As with the amendment process described above, the covered entity must have a process in place to handle these patient requests. Patients may also request that the health care provider communicate with them confidentially or at an alternate address.

Request an Accounting of Disclosures of their PHI[26] Patients may request that a covered entity provide them with an accounting or list of disclosures of their PHI that was legitimately released, but without their express patient authorization. This accounting must cover the 6 years prior to the date of the request, although not for any years prior to the Privacy Rule implementation date of April 14, 2003. An accounting could include disclosures such as

- communicable diseases to public health agencies
- reports of child or domestic abuse
- other reports required by law
- disclosures made pursuant to court order or subpoena
- limited disclosures to law enforcement
- reports to coroners and funeral directors about a decedent
- donations to cadaveric organ, tissue, or eye procurement organizations
- some research activities; disclosures made in the interest of public health or safety; information provided in workers' compensation cases
- certain disclosures for specialized government functions, such as public benefits determinations, and military activities, amongst others

Each covered entity may have different information on patients; thus, each accounting of disclosures will look different. However, the regulations specify that dates, descriptions, names, etc. be included in the accounting. Patients have the right to receive an accounting of any disclosures yearly, without charge.

Certain patient rights require that individuals have the opportunity to agree or object to the use or disclosure of their PHI. Some of these are highlighted below.

Opting Out of a Facility Directory[27] Patients may choose to opt out of listing name and room number in a facility's directory when they are inpatients. Covered entities must have processes in place to accommodate these requests.

Notification of Persons Involved in Patient Care[28] In certain circumstances, health care providers may disclose information to a patient's family members, close personal friend, or someone else involved in the patient's care. If the patient is present, the health care provider can ask if he or she is in agreement with the disclosure. In other circumstances, such as notification of general condition or death, the health care provider may infer consent based on professional judgment.

Duties of the Covered Entity Covered entities have a number of affirmative duties regarding protecting health information. Here are the most important ones.

Notice of Privacy Practices (NPP)[29] What individual has not received a notice of a business's privacy practices? In health care, too, patients must receive a notification of a covered entity's privacy practices. These detail what the CE does with a patient's protected health information. The NPP must also be posted at the provider's site.

Privacy Official and Complaint Contact[30] Covered entities must designate a Privacy Official to oversee and implement privacy policies and procedures and work to ensure compliance with the requirements of the HIPAA Privacy Rule. The Privacy Official may also be responsible for receiving complaints about matters of patient privacy.

Accounting of Disclosures of Protected Health Information[31] Patients are entitled to receive accountings of disclosures for purposes other than treatment, payment, and operations. Practically speaking, covered entities must develop systems, procedures, and forms to track these disclosures to be able to meet patient requests.

Whistleblower/Nonretaliation[32] Covered entities must ensure that employees who report perceived misconduct (i.e., whistleblowers), including actual or potential violations of state and federal laws and regulations, are protected against any retaliation.

Mitigation after Improper Protected Health Information Use or Disclosure[33] The covered entity has a duty to ensure the proper use and/or disclosure of PHI. The CE must mitigate any harmful effect that becomes known if PHI is used or disclosed improperly.

Training and Education Requirements for Workforce Members[34] All of a CE's workforce, including students and volunteers, must be trained on the CE's HIPAA privacy policies.

Documentation Requirements[35] The CE must adhere to all documentation requirements, generally 6 years.

Safeguards[36] The CE must have the appropriate administrative, technical, and physical safeguards to protect the privacy of protected health information and to minimize the risk of unauthorized access, use, or disclosure.

Business Associates[37] A covered entity often has business associates, or outside vendors, who have been hired to do work that may involve the disclosure or exchange of PHI. Typical business associates may be third-party administrators, actuaries, lawyers, some software vendors, etc. The HIPAA Privacy Rule requires that covered entities have written contractual agreements with their business associates that specifically provide for uses, disclosures, and safeguards of PHI. See Appendix G for a sample business associate agreement.

Employee Conduct and Disciplinary Sanctions[38] Covered entities must have disciplinary policies in place to address employee misconduct or violation of laws and regulations.

HIPAA Privacy and the Courts HIPAA Administrative Simplification does not provide a private right of action for an individual to sue for violation of privacy rights. Individuals and their lawyers must look to other federal and state statutes if they are interested in monetary or punitive damages. The case law under HIPAA privacy focuses on constitutional challenges and questions of state law preemption.

Even prior to the effective date of the HIPAA Privacy Rule, the constitutionality of the privacy regulations was contested in different courts. One of the earliest cases was *Association of American Physicians & Surgeons, Inc. v. Department of Health & Human Services*,[39] where the plaintiffs alleged that the privacy regulations violate the First, Fourth, and Tenth Amendments of the U.S. Constitution; the Regulatory Flexibility Act,[40] and the Paperwork Reduction Act.[41] The Association also alleged that DHHS exceeded the scope of its legislative authority by extending the reach of the Privacy Rule to non-electronic (i.e., paper and verbal) transmissions of patient health information. The court rejected all of the plaintiffs' claims. Of particular interest was the court's treatment of the First Amendment argument, rejecting the plaintiffs' claim that the Privacy Rule has a "chilling effect" on patient-physician communications and noting that "[a]llegations of a subjective 'chill' are not an adequate substitute for a claim of specific present harm or a threat of specific future harm." The court also found that DHHS did not go beyond HIPAA's scope by extending the Privacy Rule's coverage to information in non-electronic form. The court said, "[L]imiting the Privacy Rule to electronic information could create disincentives to comply with the Rule and to computerize medical records." (Remember the original goals of HIPAA from the beginning of this chapter.)

In *South Carolina Med. Ass'n v. Thompson*,[42] another group of doctors argued unsuccessfully that HIPAA privacy regulations were an impermissible delegation of legal authority. The plaintiff doctors also argued that DHHS impermissibly expanded the scope of HIPAA beyond the regulation of electronic records to all information held by covered entities, but the court dismissed that argument, noting that Congress had granted DHHS broad authority to regulate medical information by expressly defining "health information" "to include any information," whether oral or recorded in any form or medium." The details of agency rulemaking authority are discussed in Appendix C.

Other cases have examined whether HIPAA privacy regulations preempt state law. In *United States ex rel. Stewart v. The Louisiana Clinic*,[43] a court in Louisiana held that HIPAA preempts state law on disclosure of patient information. The court determined that HIPAA preempts contrary state law unless the state law relates to patient privacy and is "more stringent" than HIPAA's requirements. Even though the privacy regulations were not yet in effect at the time of this case, the court said that the privacy standards indicate a "strong federal policy of protection for patient medical records."

Security Rule

Like the privacy regulations, HIPAA's security regulations apply to covered entities. Key to understanding the Security Rule is the ability to distinguish it from the Privacy Rule. While the Privacy Rule has a "mini-security rule" for administrative, technical, and physical safeguards of paper and verbal communications regarding PHI, the Security Rule mandates standards for safeguarding **electronic protected health information** (referred to as e-PHI or **EPHI**) in information systems. Storage of e-PHI may be on a computer, a CD-ROM, a disk, a magnetic tape, or a network on the Internet or an intranet.

The security regulations set standards for implementation to ensure that only those persons who should have access to electronic PHI will actually have access. Some of these standards require specific implementation, necessitating policies and procedures. Others are "addressable,"[44] meaning that the covered entity must assess whether the standard is a reasonable and appropriate safeguard for its particular environment. Prior to the April 20, 2005 effective date of HIPAA security, covered entities had to conduct risk, security, and financial analyses in order to determine how to meet these general requirements.

The security standards fall into five general areas: (1) administrative safeguards, (2) physical safeguards, (3) technical safeguards, (4) organizational requirements, and (5) policies and procedures and documentation. Integration of security regulations into a covered entity's operations has required the expertise of information technology and management professionals. Below are details of the general security areas that require "tech savvy" personnel.

Administrative safeguards include

- security management process
- assignment of security responsibility
- workforce security
- information access management

ACRONYM

EPHI: electronic protected health information

- security awareness and training for the workforce
- security incident procedures
- contingency procedures
- evaluation
- business associate contracts

Physical safeguards include

- facility access controls
- workstation use
- workstation security
- device and media controls

Technical safeguards include

- access control
- audit controls
- data integrity
- authentication of person or entity
- transmission security

Of concern to health care lawyers has been the government's definition of a security incident. The federal regulations define it as ". . . the unauthorized attempted or successful access, use, disclosure, modification, or destruction of information or interference with system operations in an operations system."[45] Covered entities must be able to

- identify and respond to suspected or known security incidents
- mitigate, to the extent practicable, any harmful effects of security incidents that are known to the covered entity
- document security incidents and their outcomes

ACRONYM

CFAA: Computer Fraud and Abuse Act

For security incidents and other information technology crimes, we must look to state laws on computer crimes and to the **Computer Fraud and Abuse Act (CFAA)**.[46]

There have been few federal cases exactly on point that define "unauthorized access." Discussion of these is outside the scope of this book.

State Law Preemption

Many discussions of HIPAA lead to conflicts of authority when a state has passed a law that addresses an issue common to both (e.g., access to patient medical records). Does HIPAA **preempt** state law? According to the preemption doctrine, federal law supersedes or preempts state law when the federal law conflicts with a state law on the same subject or when the U.S. Congress intended to regulate a subject to the exclusion of state authority. Important to remember in any discussion of HIPAA regulations is that HIPAA provides the federal government's *minimum* standards for privacy and security. States may have their own laws on privacy and security that are more stringent than HIPAA's standards. But in case of conflict between the federal regulations and state laws, HIPAA preempts state law, unless the state law offers greater protections.

Enforcement and Sanctions

Enforcement of HIPAA Administrative Simplification falls to two agencies in DHHS: (1) the **Office of Civil Rights (OCR)** for privacy regulations; and (2) CMS for security regulations, national provider numbers, and transactions and code sets. In April, 2005, DHHS published a Notice of Proposed Rule for enforcement of these regulations.[47] The comment period ended June 17, 2005. Since that time, OCR has published guidance on enforcement activities and has been granted additional power to subpoena witnesses in privacy investigations.

Privacy Complaints Anyone can make a privacy complaint. Covered entities must designate a Privacy Official to receive complaints of privacy infringement. Nothing precludes a patient or other individual from making a complaint directly to DHHS's Office of Civil Rights. In fact, the source of a complaint often is a whistleblower working for the covered entity. Complaints to OCR must

- be filed in writing, either on paper or electronically (an online form is available)
- name the entity that is the subject of the complaint and describe the acts or omissions believed to violate the Privacy Rule
- be filed within 180 days of when the act or omission complained of occurred

The Office of Civil Rights has made it clear in numerous public forums that privacy infringement is a complaint-driven process. In other words, OCR does not drop in unannounced to inspect a covered entity or to quiz a CE's employees about HIPAA privacy regulations. Since the effective date of the Privacy Rule, OCR has received nearly 8,000 complaints, most of which were closed. A small number were referred to the Department of Justice for possible prosecution.[48]

In 2007, the Secretary of DHHS delegated the authority to issue subpoenas in investigations of alleged violations of the HIPAA Privacy Rule to the Director of OCR.[49]

ACRONYM

OHA: Office of HIPAA Standards

Other Administrative Simplification Complaints Although CMS is charged with enforcement of other Administrative Simplification complaints, it has been its position to provide technical assistance for implementation and compliance, rather than focusing on complaints. Nevertheless, DHHS created a new agency, the **Office of HIPAA Standards (OHA)** for enforcement of all HIPAA complaints except privacy. Complaints regarding security, national provider number, and transactions and code sets can be made online through the Administrative Simplification Enforcement Tool.[50]

Violations Violations of HIPAA Administration Simplification regulations can subject organizations and some individuals to significant civil penalties and criminal sanctions. Civil monetary and criminal penalties for any HIPAA violations are found in § 1128 of the Social Security Act.[51]

There are no penalties for incidental disclosures of PHI. However, negligent and/or intentional disclosures may subject the health care provider to civil money fines of $100 per violation per day, up to $25,000 yearly for all violations of an identical type. Negligent or intentional disclosures of PHI may subject the health care provider to exclusion from the Medicare and/or Medicaid programs. Additionally, certain public officials and corporate officers may be subject to fines and/or imprisonment for violation of any HIPAA Administration Simplification rule as follows:

- knowingly—$50,000 and/or 1 year in jail
- false pretenses—$100,000 and/or 5 years in jail
- for profit, gain, or harm—$250,000 and/or 10 years in jail

Whether individual employees of covered entities are subject to these fines and penalties has been debated by many health care lawyers and government officials. The first criminal prosecution under HIPAA involved a phlebotomist who worked at a cancer center in Washington. Richard Gibson was alleged to have stolen patients' social security numbers and then applied for credit cards in their names. He made several purchases using these fraudulent credit cards, totaling approximately nine thousand dollars. In 2004, Mr. Gibson was charged by the U.S. Attorney with "wrongful disclosure of individually identifiable health information for economic gain."[52] He pled guilty and received a sentence of 16 months' imprisonment. Many health care attorneys pointed out that Mr. Gibson could have been charged under identity theft or other criminal statutes rather than a HIPAA violation.

In June, 2005, when the **Department of Justice (DOJ)** released a copy of an internal memorandum[53] regarding the scope of criminal enforcement under 42 U.S.C. § 1320d-6, lawyers and officials again debated Mr. Gibson's case and argued whether an individual who is not a covered entity himself for HIPAA purposes can be prosecuted. In that memorandum, the DOJ limited prosecutions to

- covered entities (providers, insurance plans, clearinghouses, prescription drug plan sponsors)
- certain officers, directors, and employees of covered entities who may be criminally liable in accordance with general principles of corporate criminal liability
- certain third parties who cause, aid, abet, counsel, command, induce, procure, or conspire with covered entities to act in violation of HIPAA

Looking at these three areas, it appears that Mr. Gibson would not have been criminally charged. He was not a covered entity, nor was he an officer or director. His actions were outside the scope of his employment and clearly not authorized by the cancer center. A "wait and see" attitude might be adopted for future criminal HIPAA prosecutions.

National Provider Identifier

In May, 2005, CMS announced a system whereby all health care providers, including Medicare providers, can apply for a new single identifier, known as the **National Provider Identifier (NPI)**. This identifier must be used by HIPAA covered entities for filing and processing of

ACRONYM

DOJ: Department of Justice

ACRONYM

NPI: National Provider Identifier

electronic claims and standard transactions, effective May 2007. In order to facilitate adoption of NPI, CMS offered many "open door" forums and training for physicians prior to the 2007 deadline.

National standards of electronic data interchange encourage electronic commerce in the health care industry and ease administrative burdens. The National Provider Identifier will allow health care providers to submit transactions to any health plan in the United States for processing. With adoption of the NPI, implementation of HIPAA Administrative Simplification will be complete.

Fraud and Abuse Prevention

HIPAA authorized extension and enhancement of penalties for health care fraud and abuse.[54] In 1999, the **Healthcare Integrity and Protection Data Bank (HIPDB)** was formed pursuant to HIPAA's requirement that DHHS establish a national data collection program for health care fraud and abuse.[55] Federal and state governments and health plans are required to report certain adverse actions involving health care providers, suppliers, or other practitioners. These are

- criminal convictions that are related to health care delivery
- civil court judgments related to health care delivery
- actions by agencies responsible for licensure and certification
- exclusion from federal or state-funded health care programs
- anything else that DHHS establishes by regulation that is related to adverse actions in health care delivery

Information in this databank is not available to the general public and is subject to the confidentiality provisions of the Privacy Act of 1974.[56]

Fraud and abuse is covered in detail in Chapter 6.

TITLE III: HEALTH PROVISIONS IN INTERNAL REVENUE CODE

Health savings accounts, also known as medical savings accounts, are a popular way for individuals to save money for medical expenses by using pretax dollars deducted from paychecks or by joining certain health plan options. These accounts allow deductions for contributions and provide for disposition of unused benefits in cafeteria plans and flexible spending accounts.

Medical Savings Accounts (MSA) were included as part of HIPAA. Originally these were known as Archer MSAs and were part of a pilot program that had been established by Congress as an alternative method of providing affordable health insurance coverage for small businesses and self-employed individuals and their families. Severe limits were placed on the number of MSAs that could be established, who could own and contribute to them, and how the money in them was distributed. Employees who established MSAs with their employers had to use their contributions in a plan year or forfeit any unused contributions. This section of HIPAA had a sunset provision (a date on which it was set to expire).

The MMA re-authorized **Health Savings Accounts (HSA)** for accounts established after December 31, 2003.[57] The Internal Revenue Code was amended accordingly.[58] This new version of these savings accounts is more attractive to a greater number of individuals and businesses. Contributions are deductible, the account accumulates tax-free, and withdrawals used for medical expenses are tax-free.

ACRONYM

MSA: Medical Savings Account

ACRONYM

HSA: Health Savings Account

SUMMARY

The Health Insurance Portability and Accountability Act is a complicated piece of legislation that amended several existing laws. It is organized into different titles, with Title I providing health insurance reform and Title II addressing prevention of health care fraud and abuse and administrative simplification. Administrative simplification is further divided into sections on privacy and security protections for protected health information and electronic data interchange in insurance claims.

HIPAA spawned numerous regulations for privacy and security. DHHS and its smaller agencies, CMS and OCR, are charged with oversight of HIPAA's rules.

Although HIPAA took several years to implement, it has now become part of health care's culture.

KEY TERMS

COBRA continuation coverage: "... is coverage that is offered to you in order to satisfy the requirements of the Consolidated Omnibus Budget Reconciliation Act of 1985 (COBRA). COBRA requires employers to permit employees or family members to continue their group health coverage at their own expense, but at group rates, if they lose coverage because of a loss of employment, reduction in hours, divorce, death of the supporting spouse, or other designated events."[59]

creditable coverage: ". . . is prior health care coverage that is taken into account to determine the allowable length of preexisting condition exclusion periods (for individuals entering group health plan coverage) or to determine whether an individual is a HIPAA eligible individual (when the individual is seeking individual health insurance coverage.) Most health coverage is creditable coverage, including coverage under any of the following:

- a group health plan (related to employment)
- health insurance policy; including short-term limited duration policies
- Medicare Part A or Part B
- Medicaid
- a medical program of the Indian Health Service or tribal organization
- a State health benefits risk pool
- TRICARE (the health care program for military dependents and retirees)
- Federal Employees Health Benefit Plan
- a public health plan
- a health plan under the Peace Corps Act."[60]

designated record set: A group of records maintained by or for a covered entity that is the medical records and billing records maintained by or for a covered health care provider; the enrollment, payment, claims adjudication, and case or medical management record systems maintained by or for a health plan; or used, in whole or in part, by or for the covered entity to make decisions about individuals.[61]

electronic data interchange: Electronic data interchange refers to the exchange of routine business transactions from one computer to another in a standard format, using standard communications protocols.[62]

Employment Retirement Income Security Act: The Employee Retirement Income Security Act (ERISA) is a law that provides protections for individuals enrolled in pension, health, and other benefit plans sponsored by private-sector employers. The US Department of Labor administers ERISA.[63]

preempt: Describes the first right to do anything.

Protected Health Information (PHI): Individually identifiable health information that is written, electronic, or verbal/sign language; that reveals the state of a person's health; that identifies person in such a way that it gives reasonable basis for determining person's identity; and that is created or received by a health care provider.

REVIEW QUESTIONS AND EXERCISES

1. Many states have statutes similar to HIPAA's health insurance portability requirements. Research your state's insurance statutes to see if any comparable statutes exist. If so, compare the provisions of the state statute with HIPAA's provisions. Are there any differences? Sometimes state statutes give greater protections.

2. Most states have laws on the confidentiality of medical records and communications between patients and their doctors. Research your state statutes to find these. Were any amended after the effective date of the HIPAA Privacy Rule?

3. Who or what is considered a covered entity for HIPAA privacy and security?

4. You work in a hospital compliance department. A patient who was recently discharged from the hospital comes into the office to report that he believes his health information was disclosed without his authorization to his employer. Assume that he was not hospitalized for a work-related injury. What options can you offer to him for making a complaint? Suppose that the information was disclosed by a nurse employed by the hospital. What practices should the hospital have in place for complaint investigation and discipline?

5. A new health care clearinghouse that processes electronic Medicare information for small providers is assessing its security

risks. Assume these additional facts. Not everyone who works for the clearinghouse is involved in actual processing; there are receptionists, mailroom clerks, and a chief executive officer, for example. Not everyone has a computer or access to one. Doctors' offices often drop off envelopes of paper claims and leave these with the receptionist on duty. Claims processors work in shifts—one shift is from 7 a.m. to 3 p.m. and the other is from 3 p.m. to 11 p.m. What measures would you suggest to ensure that patient information is protected? Be sure that you address physical, technical, and administrative safeguards.

ENDNOTES

1. Publ. L. 104-191, 110 Stat. 1936 (1996).
2. "Bill Summary & Status for the 104th Congress" available at http://thomas.loc.gov, accessed July 31, 2007.
3. Publ.L. 107-105 (2001).
4. "HIPAA Insurance Reform," available at http://www.cms.hhs.gov/HealthInsReformforConsume/, accessed November 23, 2007.
5. "HIPAA Insurance Reform." available at http://www.cms.hhs.gov/HealthInsReformforConsume/, accessed November 23, 2007.
6. Pub. L 104-204 (1996), 45 C.F. R. § 146.
7. 109th Congress, H.R. 1402.
8. 109th Congress, H.R. 1946 and S. 927.
9. 109th Congress, H.R. 2133.
10. "HIPAA Administrative Simplification," available at http://www.cms.hhs.gov/HIPAAGenInfo/, accessed July 31, 2007.
11. 45 C.F.R. § 160.103.
12. Id.
13. Clymer, Adam, "Threats And Responses: Privacy; Officials Say Troops Risk Identity Theft After Burglary," New York Times, January 12, 2003.
14. Clymer, Adam, "Privacy Furor as Baby Death Goes Unsolved," New York Times, August 24, 2002.
15. Liptak, Adam, "Prozac Mailed Unsolicited To a Teenager In Florida," New York Times, July 21, 2002.

16. 45 C.F.R. §§ 160 and 164.

17. 64 Fed. Reg. 59918.

18. 65 Fed. Reg. 82462.

19. 66 Fed. Reg. 12738.

20. 65 Fed. Reg. 12433.

21. 67 Fed. Reg. 14776.

22. 45 C.F.R. § 164.524.

23. 42 C.F.R. §§ 263a and 493.3(a)(2).

24. 45 C.F.R. § 164.526.

25. 45 C.F.R. §164.522.

26. 45 C.F.R. §164.528.

27. 45 C.F.R. §154.510.

28. Id.

29. 45 C.F.R. § 164.520.

30. 45 C.F.R. § 164.530 (a).

31. 45 C.F.R. § 164.528.

32. 45 C.F.R. 164.530 (g).

33. 45 C.F.R. § 164.530 (f).

34. 45 C.F.R. § 164.530 (b)(1).

35. 45 C.F.R. § 164.530 (j).

36. 45 C.F.R. § 164.530 (c).

37. 45 C.F.R. § 160.103.

38. 45 C.F.R. § 164.530 (e) (1).

39. Civ. No. H 01-2963 (S.D. Tex., June 17, 2002).

40. 5 U.S.C. §§ 601 *et seq.*

41. 44 U.S.C. §§ 3501 *et seq.*

42. No. 02-2001 (4th Cir. Apr. 25, 2003).

43. No. 99-1767, 2002 WL 31819130 (E.D. La. Dec. 11, 2002).

44. 45 C.F.R. § 164.306 (d).

45. 45 C.F.R. § 164.304.

46. 18 U.S.C. § 1030.

47. 70 Fed. Reg. 20224.

48. WEDI SNIP Synopsis, August 12, 2004.

49. 72 Fed. Reg. 18999 (April 17, 2007).

50. Available at https://htct.hhs.gov/aset/, accessed July 31, 2007.

51. 42 U.S.C. § 1320a-7b.

52. No. CR04-0374 RSM, U.S. District Court for the Western District of Washington at Seattle.

53. "Scope of Criminal Enforcement Under 42 U.S.C. § 1320d-6, Memorandum for Alex M. Azar, II, General Counsel, DHHS and Timothy J. Coleman, Senior Counsel to the Deputy Attorney General, by Department of Justice, Office of Legal Counsel, June 1, 2005.

54. 18 U.S.C. § 1347 and 18 U.S.C. § 24(b).

55. 45 C.F.R. § 61.

56. 5 U.S.C. § 552 (a).

57. MMA § 1201.

58. I.R.C. § 223.

59. "HIPAA Insurance Reform," available at http://www.cms.hhs.gov/HealthInsReformforConsume/, accessed November 23, 2007.

60. Id.

61. 45 C.F.R. § 164.501.

62. General Glossary, available at http://www.cms.hhs.gov/apps/glossary/, accessed July 31, 2007.

63. "HIPAA Insurance Reform," available at http://www.cms.hhs.gov/HealthInsReformforConsume/, accessed November 23, 2007.

CHAPTER 9

ELECTRONIC HEALTH RECORDS

OBJECTIVES

After reading this chapter, the student should be able to

- Define the contents of an electronic health record.
- Distinguish federal and state law requirements.
- Identify Medicare and accreditation requirements.
- Incorporate legal concepts of authentication and admissibility.
- Recognize HIPAA-related issues.
- Define parameters for records retention or destruction.

INTRODUCTION

For decades, health care providers and organizations have relied on paper medical charts to document a patient's history, diagnostics, and treatment. But what happens when critical information recorded on paper is illegible, misfiled, or lost or damaged in a natural disaster like Hurricane Katrina? The risk to the patient increases if accurate, complete information about his or her medical information is not available. In the last few years, health care providers and organizations have been shifting to the use of electronic health records, stored on computers and on network infrastructures, as a more reliable method of maintaining patient health information.

Most patients do not realize how much personal health information is exposed in a vast electronic network. Computerized information helps diagnose disease, organize research data, and monitor patient conditions, while transmitting that information to health insurers, clinical research organizations, pharmaceutical benefits managers, and others.

The trend to computerize personal health information continues, with governmental initiatives aimed at improving health care quality through electronic technology. In 2004, the **Centers for Medicare & Medicaid Services (CMS)** announced a $100,000 grant to support a pilot project to provide comprehensive, standardized **electronic health record (EHR)** software to the health care community.[1] That early project represented a step toward the Bush administration's goal of improving patient quality of care through the use of electronic health records. In subsequent years, CMS has sponsored other initiatives to encourage the health care community to adopt electronic health records. An interoperable **health information technology (HIT)** infrastructure would allow fast, reliable, and secure access to patient information needed for clinical care, while still protecting patient privacy.

In 2005, the Senate passed the Wired for Health Care Quality Act,[2] a bill that provides for a paperless health records system and assists rural areas in adopting cutting-edge information technologies in electronic health records. In short, we are poised to become a fully-wired health system in the foreseeable future. In this chapter, the terms "health records," "medical records," and "patient records" are used interchangeably.

ACRONYMS

CMS: Centers for Medicare and Medicaid Services

EHR: electronic health records

HIT: health information technology

PAPER VS. ELECTRONIC MEDICAL RECORDS

Federal regulations, state licensing laws, accreditation standards, professional association guidelines, and conditions of participation in federal health care programs require that health care providers and organizations maintain medical records of the services that they provide to their patients. Traditionally, these records have been kept in paper charts. The medical record, whether paper or electronic, consists of personal, financial, social, and medical information about an individual patient. Personal information identifies the patient by name, address, birth date, sex, marital status, emergency contact, or other relevant criteria. Financial data consists of information about a patient's health insurer or other party responsible for payment. Social information may include family background and lifestyle. By necessity, medical data is the largest component of the medical record.

Definitions

Let's examine what a **legal health record** is and what goes into it.[3] A legal health record is a health care organization's business record and is the record that will be disclosed upon appropriate authorization or subpoena. The legal health record documents the health care services provided to an individual. It contains **individually identifiable patient information (IIHI)**, may be stored on any medium, and is collected and used in documenting health care, health status, and/or clinical decision-making. In layman's terms, the legal health record is the contents of the paper medical chart, along with radiology films or other imaging studies. The legal health record must meet definitions in state and federal law, as well as the standards of the CMS and health care accrediting agencies. Health care providers and organizations may also have their own polices which define the contents of the legal health record.

> **ACRONYM**
>
> IIHI: individually identifiable health information

Some examples of patient information that may be in a legal health record include

- advance directives
- anesthesia records
- care plans
- consent forms for care, treatment, and research
- consultation reports
- diagnostic images

- discharge instructions
- discharge summaries
- emergency department records
- history and physical examination records
- immunization records
- insurance information
- medication orders
- nursing assessments
- operative and procedure reports
- orders for treatment including diagnostic tests for laboratory and radiology
- pathology reports
- patient-submitted documentation
- patient education or teaching documents
- patient identifiers or medical record numbers
- photographs
- progress notes and documentation
- psychology and psychiatric assessments and summaries (excluding psychotherapy notes, as discussed in Chapter 8 on HIPAA.)
- records received from another health care provider
- research records of tests and treatments
- respiratory therapy, physical therapy, speech therapy, and occupational therapy records
- results of laboratory and radiology tests and studies
- standing orders
- telephone messages containing patient–provider or provider–provider communications regarding care or treatment of specific patients
- telephone orders by physicians
- verbal orders by physicians

This list is not exclusive. Health care providers and organizations must follow federal and state requirements as well. As you might suspect, Medicare has its own requirements for Conditions of Participation.

State laws also contain mandates governing the contents of a health record.

On the other hand, an electronic health record (EHR) is part of a HIT system that clinicians use to access a patient's health record, document care delivered to the patient, and order treatments or therapy. Like the paper health record, an EHR can contain personal, financial, social, and medical data. In general, an EHR system consists of integrated component information systems and technologies, with different data types and formats. All data and images are collected over the course of a patient's care with that provider or organization and are created, authenticated, stored, and retrieved by computer. Some health care providers have eliminated the paper chart and use EHR systems as their legal health records. For purposes of disclosure, however, a printout of the EHR is necessary.

The Joint Commission on Accreditation of Healthcare Organizations (the Joint Commission) defines electronic health information as

> a computerized format of the health care information in paper records that is used for the same range of purposes as paper records, namely to familiarize readers with the patient's status; to document care, treatment, and services; to plan for discharge; to document the need for care, treatment, and services; to assess the quality of care, treatment, and services; to determine reimbursement rates; to justify reimbursement claims; to pursue clinical or epidemiological research; and to measure outcomes of the care, treatment, and service process.[4]

Computerization of health records can enhance quality of care by making it quick and easy for health care professionals to store and retrieve relevant patient information.. A health information technology system can link the patient record to diagnostic and decision support tools. It can also increase efficiency by reducing the volume of paperwork, reporting laboratory results quickly, assisting with patient scheduling, and managing utilization of services.

SPOTLIGHT ON...

The **American Health Information Management Association** was founded in 1928 and is dedicated to the effective management of personal health information. The **AHIMA** has been in the forefront of promoting the use of EHR.

ACRONYM

AHIMA: American Health Information Management Association

Federal Preemption

Both federal and state law include regulations regarding the content and treatment of patient health records. Two federal laws that **preempt** or supersede state law on health records are **HIPAA**[5] and E-SIGN.[6]

As part of Administrative Simplification, HIPAA established that any statutory provisions and regulations

> [. . .] shall supersede any contrary provision of State law, including a provision of State law that requires medical or health plan records (including billing information) to be maintained or trans-mitted in written rather than electronic form."[7]

HIPAA explicitly enables electronic health records and preempts any state laws that require written health records.

E-SIGN legislation put electronic records and signatures on equal legal parity with their traditional ink-on-paper counterparts. Under E-SIGN, an electronic record is "a contract or other record created, gen-erated, sent, communicated, received, or stored by electronic means."[8] E-SIGN defines an electronic signature as

> an electronic sound, symbol, or process, attached to or logically associated with a contract or other record and executed or adopted by a person with the intent to sign the record."[9]

E-SIGN specifically authorized electronic contracting (with elec-tronic signatures) and record-keeping and thus enhanced the legal viability of electronic health records. E-SIGN preempts state laws that require handwritten records or signatures or retention of paper-based records, thus easing the burdens of storage and expense on health care providers and organizations. A state may either have a version of E-SIGN from which it derives its electronic health records authority or a specific statute on point.

State Licensure Requirements

All states have statutes on medical records. Each state usually includes descriptions of the required content of medical records in its licensing laws for different health care providers and organizations. For example, Louisiana law provides that

> [A] 'Hospital record' or 'hospital chart' means a compilation of the reports of the various clinical departments within a hospital, as

well as reports from health care providers, as are customarily catalogued and maintained by the hospital medical records department. Hospital records include reports of procedures such as X-rays and electrocardiograms, buy they do not include the image or graphic matter produced by such procedures.[10]

Since state laws on medical record content vary by provider, the required contents of a hospital record may differ from those of a substance-abuse clinic record or a dental record.

In addition to general content requirements, states may have specific laws on EHR. For example, in 2005, the Illinois Legislature established a task force to study implementation of electronic health records.[11] Part of the task force's duty was to consider an EHR plan that included

(1) key components of and standards for comprehensive EHR systems for recording, storing, analyzing and accessing patient health information, assisting with health care decision-making and quality assurance, and providing for online health care;

(2) consistent data elements, definitions, and formats that should be incorporated in EHR systems;

(3) analysis of costs and benefits in implementing EHR by various types and sizes of health care providers;

(4) survey of equipment, technical assistance, and resources that would be necessary to assist smaller health care providers with EHR implementation and utilization;

(5) standards, technology platforms, and issues related to patient access to their individual medical and health data;

(6) a potential phase-in plan for implementing EHR by health care providers throughout Illinois; and

(7) patient privacy, security, and compliance with applicable rules set forth in the federal Health Insurance Portability and Accountability Act of 1996 (HIPAA).[12]

Accreditation Issues

Health care providers who maintain electronic health records must also take into account the standards set by voluntary accreditation agencies such as the Joint Commission (for hospitals) and the **NCQA**

ACRONYM

NCQA: National Committee on Quality Assurance

(for managed-care plans). These accreditation standards may impact their business operations and internal practices as well as their budgets. Both the Joint Commission and the NCQA have incorporated HIPAA privacy and security regulations into their standards for electronic health records.

The NCQA and the Joint Commission set standards for patient rights that include the right of access to medical records, the right to confidentiality, and the right to accurate, complete records. Other standards apply to information management or HIT systems. Data security and integrity, as well as employee access levels to patient records, are covered in these standards.

For large hospitals and health care organizations, an integrated EHR system may be more effective than a paper-based system. It would be a lengthy task to assemble a patient record if all the needed information was located in different departments and had to be located and copied.

You might be asking yourself why a paralegal needs to be familiar with the accreditation standards for the management of health information. Usually that job falls to a person with a job title such as Health Information Manager or Registered Health Information Technologist. Lawyers advising their health care organization clients and ensuring regulatory compliance simply cannot ignore the interaction between statutes, regulations, and accreditation standards. Having the "seal of approval" from an accreditation agency is a sign of organizational excellence in the health care industry that no one wants to lose.

Medicare Requirements

In general, Medicare requires that providers and organizations maintain accurate and confidential health records and give patients access to their own medical records. These requirements are set out in the Conditions of Participation agreement that we discussed in Chapter 5. The Medicare Interpretative Guidelines (found in the CMS Operations Manual) extends the patient's right of confidentiality to computer-stored information. The Interpretative Guidelines provide that

> . . . the right to confidentiality means safeguarding the content of the information, including patient paper records, video, audio, and/or computer stored information from unauthorized disclosures without the specific informed consent of the individual, parent of a minor child, or legal guardian.[13]

The Medicare Interpretative Guidelines also state that patients have the right of access to their health records in a reasonable timeframe, meaning that

> . . . the hospital must not frustrate the legitimate efforts of individuals to gain access to their own medical records and must actively seek to meet these requests as quickly as its record keeping system permits.[14]

The Conditions of Participation mandate a standard for content of medical records that includes authentication of entries by the person responsible for ordering, providing, or evaluating the service furnished to the patient. Codes for computer entry into patient records, authentication, and electronic signatures must be maintained under appropriate safeguards. Hospitals and other health care organizations usually have policies on authentication and electronic signatures, as well as disciplinary policies for unauthorized use and access.

LEGAL ISSUES

Electronic health records raise many legal concerns: who has the right to access and use patient information; confidentiality and security of information; and traditional discovery, authentication, and admissibility of medical records. For a discussion on access, confidentiality, and security, please refer to Chapter 8.

Switching from a paper-based to electronic health record system may be costly. Although some software companies, eager to do business with physicians and other providers, may offer free or discounted software, this can raise issues of potential prohibited kickbacks, which are discussed in Chapter 6.

Authentication

With paper patient records, **authentication** means that a provider documents his or her services and signs and dates each entry. At a minimum, entries of histories, physical exams, consultations, and discharge summaries must be authenticated, although state laws, accreditation standards, and an organization's policies may require authentication of other services as well. Entries in the patient's record must be legible, timely, and accurate. In the process of authentication, the clinician is attesting that the services were actually performed.

All states have laws that recognize electronic signatures on documents. Authentication by an electronic signature is similar to the process for paper medical records, although not without risks. Clinicians enter electronic signatures with a computer code and agree to review and correct transcripts of electronic health records within a specified timeframe. Two problems are inherent in this process. First, codes for signatures must be secure so that access is restricted to the clinician providing the service. Second, if the clinician fails to review the record in a timely manner, the computerized system may deem the record complete. Some accreditation agencies do not view an unreviewed record as properly authenticated, thereby impacting an organization's accreditation status. Likewise, although Medicare's Conditions of Participation require authentication of each entry in a patient's record and allows authentication by computer, any failure to obtain a physician's signature for the record in its final form is a deficiency that can lead to federal health care program exclusions and other administrative sanctions.

Admissibility

When a patient's health is at issue in a lawsuit, admission of health records as evidence can be important, especially if the clinicians who provided services are unable to appear as witnesses. A barrier to introduction of medical records is the **hearsay** rule. An out-of-court statement is excluded from evidence unless an exception to the hearsay rule applies. Since patient records are written, out-of-court statements, they are classified as hearsay. Fortunately, most medical records fit into the business records exception to the hearsay rule, an exception available in both state and federal jurisdictions. If records are kept regularly in the course of business and not prepared specifically for trial, they may be admissible. For the exception to apply, record entries must be made at or near the time of the event recorded, the identity of the person making the entry must be captured, and the person making the entry must have firsthand knowledge of the event recorded. Electronic health records should meet these requirements if clinicians have properly recorded their services.

Another evidentiary rule relevant to the admissibility of health records is the **best evidence rule**, which expresses a judicial preference for original documents if the contents are in dispute. Would a hard copy of an

EHR be considered an original document? The Federal Rules of Evidence allow that

> . . . if data are stored on a computer or similar device, any printout or other output readable by sight, shown to reflect the data accurately, is an original.[15]

Some states also recognize the hard copy of data as an original for purposes of the best evidence rule.

E-MAIL AND PROTECTED HEALTH INFORMATION

The business world thrives on e-mail; the health care industry is no exception. Personnel in health care organizations routinely use e-mail to transmit all kinds of information: resident rotation schedules, budgets, research project proposals, and even sensitive patient information or **protected health information (PHI)**. However, transmission of PHI in e-mail raises issues of confidentiality and security. As we learned in Chapter 8, that act requires administrative, physical, and technical safeguards for PHI. Health care organizations must provide these safeguards for EHR, whose contents are predominately PHI. Technological methods for ensuring security include computer firewalls and message encryption. Organizations may also have policies that outline the accepted transmission of PHI within the facility's intranet.

ACRONYM

PHI: protected health information

Transmission of e-mail is inherently insecure. Health care providers and organizations must provide their staffs with training to ensure recognition of security risks when transmitting PHI, as well as awareness of legal consequences for misuse. Both federal and state laws address protection of privacy for electronic communications. The Electronic Communications Privacy Act of 1986 (EPCA)[16] provides protection against improper interception of electronic communications, including e-mail. EPCA imposes civil and criminal liability on individuals who intentionally

- intercept any wire, oral, or electronic communication
- disclose or use the contents of such communication with the knowledge that it was unlawfully intercepted
- access without authorization an electronic communications facility and thereby obtain, alter, or prevent authorized access to stored communications

E-mail communication between providers, and between providers and their patients, is becoming more common. It is easier to e-mail a physician's order or communicate a test result than to depend on the mail or play "phone tag" with someone. However, communication of patient information by e-mail can compromise the confidentiality, security, and integrity of data in many ways. For example:

- Unencrypted e-mail can be intercepted by hackers during transmission.
- Technical problems with the HIT system may prevent transmittal of urgent e-mails.
- If an unauthorized individual gains access to a clinician's e-mail password, he or she can read, forward, alter, and respond to that person's e-mail under the guise of a health care professional. Therefore, it is important to avoid sharing passwords.

Health care providers and organizations who use e-mail to communicate patient information, whether with other providers or with the patients themselves, need to be aware of medical malpractice liability concerns, the potential discovery of privileged information, and reimbursement considerations. Transmission of an e-mail communication about a patient has both legal and medical significance. If the e-mail contains information about a patient's diagnosis or treatment, then it should be linked to the patient's EHR to ensure that the patient's medical record is complete and accurate so that further treatment is appropriate. Unanswered e-mails can also pose liability problems. If, for example, a physician order sent by e-mail is not completed, liability can attach for failure to implement that order. Physicians should also be forewarned of the possibility that they may inadvertently create a physician/patient relationship when they respond to inquiries from unknown individuals seeking medical advice or initial appointments. Physicians likewise need to be aware of state peer review statutes in order to avoid abrogation of protections for peer review information and documents.

ACRONYM

AMA: American Medical Association

SPOTLIGHT ON...

The **American Medical Association (AMA)** recommends that physicians develop policies for electronic patient communications. The AMA provides both communication and administrative guidelines for physicians who choose to use e-mail for patient and medical practice communications. These guidelines can be found at http://www.ama-assn.org/ama/pub/category/2386.html.

Satisfying HIPAA's privacy and security requirements and avoiding legal liability are challenges for any fast-paced health care organization. An organization's policies and training programs must address many different areas of concern regarding e-mail transmission of PHI. Here are a few to consider:

- verification of sender's and receiver's e-mail addresses
- monitoring of e-mail traffic by the HIT administrator
- storage of e-mail offline, on backup tapes, and in archives
- turnaround time to respond to e-mail
- any standard content in e-mails (business information, disclaimers, etc.)
- types of transactions permitted by e-mail (prescription refills, appointment reminders, etc.)
- e-mail transmissions to and from wireless handheld devices
- prohibition of transmission of HIV status, substance abuse, mental health, developmental disability, or genetic screening records by e-mail

THE ROLE OF THE PARALEGAL

Paralegals often collect and maintain individual health records in personal injury or medical malpractice cases. Being familiar with HIT systems of EHR will be a plus for any paralegal working in these areas.

RECORDS RETENTION AND DESTRUCTION

Lawyers advising health care providers and organizations must consider applicable federal and state laws and regulations along with medical and administrative policies when determining how long patient health records, paper or electronic, should be maintained. Many other factors may influence records retention and destruction, including

- statutes of limitations for possible future litigation
- standards set by accreditation agencies and professional associations

- requirements of malpractice insurers
- space limitations
- budget concerns
- research and teaching needs

Of course, Medicare has its own requirements in the Conditions of Participation. Original patient records or legally reproduced forms must be maintained for at least 5 years.[17] State statutes may also impose specific requirements for records retention. These can range from 5 years for readily retrievable medical records in Arizona[18] to 25 years for hospital record retention in Connecticut.[19] State statutes for electronic records may reference retention requirements in other statutes. For example, Louisiana law states

> If a law requires that a record be retained, the requirement is satisfied by retaining an electronic record of the information in the record which:
>
> (1) Accurately reflects the information set forth in the record after it was first generated in its final form as an electronic record or otherwise.
> (2) Remains accessible for later reference.[20]

Health care providers and organizations should adopt effective electronic document management, retention, and destruction policies and schedules as part of their corporate compliance programs. Doing so can assure accountability, lower costs associated with storage and reproduction, and aid in discovery in potential litigation. Destruction of documents can implicate criminal liability under the Sarbanes-Oxley Act of 2002.[21] Under Sarbanes-Oxley, anyone who knowingly alters, destroys, mutilates, conceals, covers up, or falsifies records with the intent to impede, obstruct, or influence a federal investigation or bankruptcy can be fined or imprisoned for a maximum of 20 years or both.[22] If an organization receives notice that an investigation is pending, having a process in place to stop destruction of records is of paramount importance.

Some elements to consider when establishing an electronic document retention and destruction program include

- coverage of paper and electronic health records
- content of electronic health records
- e-mail archives

Description	Legal Citation, if applicable	Retention Period*
Appointment books		3 years
Dental records	R.S. 37:757 and 40:1299.96	6 years
Employee training records		3 years after separation from employment
Healthcare records	R.S. 40:1299.96	6 years after date of last treatment
HIPAA documentation	45 C.F.R. §164.530(j)	6 years
Hospital records	R.S. 40:1244	10 years after patient discharge
Medical staff files (credentialing, licensing, continuing education, etc.)		Permanent
Minutes of board meetings and committees		Permanent
Operating agreement and/or by-laws		Permanent
Prescription records	R.S. 37:1299	2 years
Safety records		6 years

EXHIBIT 9–1: SAMPLE RETENTION SCHEDULE

*Not all records have legally set retention periods. If none are cited, a "business best practice" is given.

- retrieval of information
- destruction schedule according to type of information
- compliance with discovery requests
- audit procedures

Publication and distribution of a records retention and destruction timetable is a helpful tool for a health care organization's staff. See a sample of a timetable in Exhibit 9–1.

A sample policy for records retention and destruction is included in Appendix I.

SUMMARY

Electronic health records are becoming the norm for documentation of patient information, whether personal, financial, social, or medical. However, electronic health records raise issues of confidentiality, security, and integrity. Federal statutes such as HIPAA, ECPA, and E-SIGN, along with state statues on medical records and electronic records, form the statutory basis for EHR. Medicare's Conditions of Participation and accrediting agencies' standards also address requisites for electronic health records. Electronic communication of patient information by e-mail raises medical and legal issues, as well as administrative concerns. Health care providers and organizations must be prepared to include electronic health records as part of their records management and HIT system.

KEY TERMS

authentication: Any evidence that proves that a document actually is what it seems to be.

best evidence rule: A rule of evidence law that often requires that the most reliable available proof of a fact must be produced.

hearsay: A statement about what someone else said (or wrote or otherwise communicated). Hearsay evidence is evidence, concerning what someone said outside of a court proceeding, that is offered in the proceeding to prove the truth of what was said.

legal health record: A health care provider or organization's business record on a particular patient's medical history and treatment.

preempt: Describes the first right to do anything.

REVIEW QUESTIONS AND EXERCISES

1. Is there any way to distinguish a paper from an electronic health record? Explain.

2. Review your state's Code of Evidence. Is there a rule that allows for admission of electronically reproduced records?

3. Dr. Inahurry left on vacation to Bonaire before reviewing his patients' records and authenticating them. The HIT system at his hospital has now deemed his records complete. Could the hospital and Dr. Inahurry suffer any consequences? What are they?

4. Refer to the records retention and destruction schedule in Exhibit 9–1. Now research your own state's laws to replace the citations to the Louisiana statutes on Exhibit 9–1.

5. Research your state's statutes to find its electronic signature law. Does it address authentication of medical records by electronic signature?

ENDNOTES

1. "HHS Announces Grant To Help Implement Electronic Health Records In Family Practice Medicine," <u>Medicare News</u>, May 28, 2004, available at http://cms.hhs.gov/apps/media/press/release.asp, accessed August 1, 2007.

2. S. 1418, 109th Congress, amending 42 U.S.C. § 201 *et seq.*

3. See generally "Practice Brief," Journal of AHIMA, October, 2001.

4. Glossary, <u>Comprehensive Accreditation Manual for Hospitals: The Handbook</u>, Joint Commission for the Accreditation of Healthcare Organizations (2005).

5. Health Insurance Portability and Accountability Act of 1996, Pub. L. 104-191, 110 Stat. 1936 (1996).

6. Electronic Signatures in National and Global Commerce Act, Pub. L. 106-229 (2000).

7. 42 U.S.C. § 1320d.

8. 15 U.S.C. § 7006(4).

9. 15 U.S.C. § 7006(5).

10. La. Rev. Stat. 40:2144(A)(5).

11. Public Act 094-0646, Illinois General Assembly, August 22, 2005.

12. <u>Id.</u> at § 15.

13. 42 C.F.R. § 482.13(d)(1).

14. 42 C.F.R. § 482.13(d)(2).

15. Fed. R. Evid. 1001(3).

16. 18 U.S.C. § 2510 *et seq.*

17. 42 C.F.R. § 482.24.

18. A. A. C. R9-10-221(F).

19. Conn. Agencies Regs. § 19-13-D3 (d)(6).

20. La. Rev. Stat. 9:2612(A).

21. Pub. L. 107-204, 116 Stat. 745 (2002).

22. <u>Id.</u> at § 802.

CHAPTER 10

THE EMERGENCY MEDICAL TREATMENT AND LABOR ACT

CHAPTER OUTLINE

OBJECTIVES

After reading this chapter, students should be able to

- Define what constitutes a patient's emergency, screening, stabilization, and allowable transfer.
- Discuss hospitals' obligations under EMTALA.
- Identify different remedies for violations.

INTRODUCTION

Imagine that a loved one is in a car accident and is rushed by ambulance to the nearest hospital for emergency treatment. Do you know that there is a law that guarantees that a patient must be screened and stabilized at that hospital's emergency department, regardless of financial or insurance status? The **Emergency Medical Treatment and Labor Act (EMTALA)**[1] is federal legislation whose purpose is to prevent hospitals from rejecting patients, refusing to treat them, or transferring them to public or charity hospitals because they are uninsured. EMTALA is primarily, but not exclusively, a non-discrimination statute with affirmative obligations for participating hospitals.

ACRONYM

EMTALA: Emergency Medical Treatment and Labor Act

EMTALA is widely criticized by emergency-room personnel as overly burdensome and ineffective in realizing its purported purpose. Hospitals complain of exorbitant costs of compliance, along with emergency department overcrowding.

For hospital-based health care compliance professionals, in-house hospital counsel, and health care law firms representing hospitals, an understanding of EMTALA's responsibilities and liabilities is essential. EMTALA's basic duties of patient screening and stabilization are only imposed on hospitals that participate in the Medicare program and have a dedicated emergency department. However, all patients are covered under EMTALA, not just those who are eligible for Medicare. Remember from Chapter 5 that most hospitals treat Medicare patients because Medicare is the largest insurer in the United States. Although not all hospitals have emergency rooms (for example, specialty hospitals often do not), a majority of hospitals are subject to EMTALA and its regulations.

STATUTORY AND REGULATORY AUTHORITY

EMTALA was passed as part of the Consolidated Omnibus Budget Reconciliation Act of 1986. The statute and regulations provide that any patient who comes to a hospital's emergency department requesting examination or treatment for a medical condition must be provided with an appropriate medical screening examination, within the hospital's capabilities, to determine if he or she is suffering from an emergency medical condition. If so, then the hospital is obligated to either provide the patient with treatment until stable, or to transfer the patient to another appropriate hospital according to the statute's directives. However, if the patient does not have an emergency medical condition, the statute imposes no further obligation on the hospital. Pregnant women in active labor are considered to have emergency medical conditions that warrant admission until delivery is complete. Please refer to Exhibit 10–1 for an initial EMTALA inquiry.

Patients with unstabilized emergency conditions may be transferred only if: (1) the patient makes an informed request for transfer, or (2) the hospital certifies that, based on information available at the time of transfer, the medical benefits reasonably expected from provision of appropriate medical treatment at another facility outweigh the increased risks of transfer to the individual patient or unborn child.

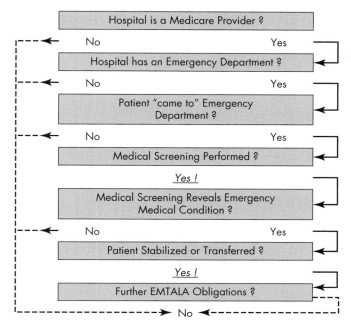

EXHIBIT 10–1: EMTALA DIAGRAM
Courtesy of R. Harold McCard, Jr., Esq.

Violations of EMTALA are treated differently for hospitals and physicians. Patients may bring civil lawsuits against hospitals under the statute, but not against a treating physician. Only the **Department of Health and Human Services (DHHS)** may bring an enforcement action against a physician for an EMTALA violation. Allowable sanctions include exclusion from Medicare programs and civil monetary penalties.[2]

Specific Requirements

The **Center for Medicare & Medicaid Services (CMS)** released the long-anticipated final regulations revising the EMTALA obligations for hospitals and physicians. These became effective in November 2003. The final regulations attempt to define more clearly to whom EMTALA applies, as well as where and when the EMTALA requirements begin and end. In addition, the final rules clarify on-call physician coverage, prior authorization requirements of insurers, and the application of EMTALA during national emergencies.

ACRONYM

DHHS: Department of Health and Human Services

ACRONYM

CMS: Centers for Medicare and Medicaid Services

Hospitals that are affected by EMTALA are those that participate in Medicare and have dedicated emergency departments. A dedicated emergency department is one that

- is licensed under applicable state law as an emergency room or department
- is held out to the public through signs, ads, name, or other means, as a place that provides emergency or urgent medical care
- provides treatment of emergencies on an urgent basis in at least one-third of all of its outpatient visits (based on a sampling of the previous year's outpatient visits)

Patients Presenting at the Emergency Department How a patient presents himself or herself at the emergency department is another important part of the statute. Patients must present at the hospital's dedicated emergency department and request treatment of an emergency medical condition. The emergency department can include labor and delivery units as well as psychiatric units. The patient must present on the hospital campus, which includes the parking lot, sidewalk, and the driveways within 250 yards of the main buildings, but not other entities on the campus that participate separately under Medicare. Also excluded from this definition are businesses such as restaurants, shops, and other nonmedical activities. The patient may also arrive at a facility or organization located off campus that is a department of the hospital and offers dedicated emergency services. "Presenting at the emergency department" also includes a patient in an ambulance owned and operated by the hospital, even if not on hospital grounds, or a patient in a non–hospital-owned ambulance that is on hospital grounds.

The final rules provide that the EMTALA obligations do not apply to an individual who has begun to receive outpatient services as part of a routine outpatient visit and then develops an emergency condition. In the event that a patient develops an emergency condition during an outpatient service, CMS states the hospital's response will be governed under the Medicare Conditions of Participation and not EMTALA, even if the patient is moved to the dedicated emergency department for follow-up examination and stabilizing treatment.

What if you are in the hospital visiting a patient at the hospital and you slip and fall? EMTALA does apply to visitors and hospital employees who are on the hospital campus for other reasons and who experience what may be an emergency medical condition.

EMTALA obligations cease once an individual is admitted for inpatient care, so long as he or she remains at least overnight and occupies a bed in the hospital.

Patient Screening The regulations require that patient screening of those presenting at the emergency department must be available to all individuals regardless of diagnosis, financial status, race, color, national origin, or handicap. However, the quality of patient screening under EMTALA has always been difficult to interpret. The patient screening must be reasonably calculated to determine whether an emergency medical condition exists. CMS states that the examination may be limited to (1) the individual's statement that he or she is not seeking emergency care, and (2) brief questioning by a qualified medical person that is sufficient to establish that there is no emergency condition. The mere log-in of a patient is insufficient as a screening. Patient **triage** is also insufficient under EMTALA. The hospital must provide screening and stabilization within its operating capabilities; depending on hospital size, type, and location, operating capabilities can vary. The patient screening must be the same one the hospital would perform on any individual coming into the emergency room with the same signs and symptoms. Lastly, the screening process must be able to reach the point at which it can be determined whether a medical emergency exists.

Definition of Emergency What constitutes an emergency? Low-income patients are often forced to use hospital emergency rooms for routine care such as flu shots. However, the regulations define an emergency as one with acute symptoms, including pain, severe enough that the absence of immediate medical attention could reasonably be expected to result in

- serious jeopardy to the health of the individual or to the unborn child of a pregnant woman
- serious impairment to bodily functions
- serious dysfunction of any bodily organ or part

An emergency for pregnant women who are having labor contractions is one in which

- there is inadequate time to effect a safe transfer to another hospital before delivery
- transfer to another hospital could pose a health or safety threat to the woman or her unborn child

---

SPOTLIGHT ON...

During Hurricane Katrina, many displaced patients from the Gulf Coast sought refills of their prescriptions at emergency rooms in other states. CMS opined that EMTALA did not require a full medical screening examination for those patients.

> CMS's EMTALA regulations make it clear that individuals seeking only prescription refills need not be given a complete medical screening examination, but rather, one that is appropriate for the request that they make. Hospitals may wish to develop specific protocols that include a streamlined screening examination for patients seeking prescription refills, consistent with the regulation cited above.[3]

Patient Transfer   Treating physicians determine whether a patient is stable enough to be transferred after the initial screening is completed. The physician must

- determine that the patient is expected to leave the hospital and be received at the second facility with no material deterioration in his or her condition
- reasonably believe that the receiving facility has the capability to manage the patient's condition and any reasonably foreseeable complication of that condition

This requirement prohibits **patient dumping** or the practice of transferring a patient from one hospital to another for admission, presumably because of a patient's lack of insurance.

Patients who are stabilized and sent to other hospitals must meet criteria for appropriate transfers. The transferring hospital must have provided medical treatment within its capacity that minimizes risks to the individual's health or the health of an unborn child. The receiving facility must have space and qualified personnel available to treat the patient and must agree to accept the patient. The transferring hospital must send the receiving facility

- all relevant medical records available at the time of transfer
- the patient's informed written consent to transfer or a required medical certification that transfer is necessary

- the name and address of any on-call physician who has refused or failed to appear within a reasonable time to provide necessary stabilizing treatment
- qualified personnel and transportation equipment, as required, and any necessary and medically appropriate life support measures

Hospitals with specialties such as burn, shock trauma, or neonatal intensive care units, and regional referral centers identified by the Centers for Medicare and Medicaid Services (CMS) for rural areas, cannot refuse to accept an appropriately transferred patient who requires care within their area of specialization.

Miscellaneous Requirements The statute and regulations impose numerous other obligations on hospitals and qualified outpatient emergency departments. These include

- maintaining a listing of physicians who are on call for duty after an initial exam to provide stabilizing treatment
- posting signs specifying rights of patients under EMTALA for emergency conditions and for women in labor
- keeping a central log on each emergency room patient with information on treatment refused by the patient or provider, admission, transfer, stabilization and transfer, and/or discharge
- having a compliance policy for EMTALA
- maintaining medical records for 5 years for any patient transferred to or from another hospital

Hospitals, as well as doctors, have expressed concerns regarding the requirements of on-call coverage for specialists such as psychiatrists, neurologists, and cardiac surgeons. In September, 2004, the American College of Emergency Physicians published a survey of 1,400 hospitals to determine the extent to which specialty coverage requirements under EMTALA have affected the willingness of specialists to participate in call schedules. Two-thirds of the respondents reported that they had less than adequate on-call coverage, citing a decrease in the number of medical specialists willing to be on call to emergency departments.[4] The CMS Interpretative Guidelines state that ultimate responsibility for ensuring adequate on-call coverage rests with hospitals.[5] Hospitals must set their own policies and/or medical staff bylaws with regard to on-call coverage and appropriate response times.

ACRONYM

MCO: managed care
organization

The final regulations also codify what had been a CMS Special Advisory Bulletin on EMTALA and **managed care organizations** or insurers. These regulations prohibit a hospital from seeking prior **authorization** from the **MCO** for screening or stabilizing an MCO-insured patient until after the hospital has actually provided the screening necessary to determine if further examination and treatment are required for stabilizing the emergency medical condition. CMS clarified that the prior authorization prohibition does not prevent the treating physician from seeking advice on the patient's medical history from others involved in his or her care.

ACRONYM

MMA: Medicare Modernization
Act of 2003

The **Medicare Modernization Act of 2003 (MMA)**[6] imposes an additional EMTALA requirement for those treating Medicare beneficiaries: an assessment of reasonableness and necessity for emergency room services in order to claim Medicare reimbursement. However, CMS may not consider the frequency with which the item or service was provided to the patient before or after the time of admission or visit.

AGENCY OVERSIGHT

The Centers for Medicare and Medicaid Services, part of DHHS, is the agency charged with promulgation of interpretative guidelines regarding EMTALA to regional offices and state survey agencies. In 2004, CMS released its revised Responsibilities of Medicare Participating Hospitals in Emergency Cases.[7] In 2005, CMS established a technical advisory group to review EMTALA regulations and seek comments from physicians and hospitals.[8] CMS is also the agency charged with reporting requirements under EMTALA. Receiving hospitals have a duty to report an inappropriate transfer. Failure to do so could result in Medicare exclusion, although not in civil monetary penalties. Sending hospitals must report the name and address of any on-call physician who has refused or failed to appear within a reasonable time to provide necessary stabilizing treatment. This, in turn, then leads to the receiving hospital's being required to report this information to CMS as an inappropriate transfer.

The enforcement of EMTALA is a complaint-driven process. Congress created a bifurcated enforcement mechanism for EMTALA within the Department of Health and Human Services. CMS authorizes investigations of dumping complaints by state survey agencies or regional offices, determines if a violation occurred, and, if appropriate, terminates a hospital's provider agreement. The **Office of the Inspector General (OIG)** in DHHS is the agency charged with administration of the sanction process for hospitals and physicians who violate EMTALA. A **civil monetary penalty (CMP)** of up to $50,000 per violation may be imposed against an offending hospital; the fine is reduced to up to $25,000 for hospitals with fewer than 100 beds. Physicians who negligently violate an EMTALA requirement, such as a refusal to respond to an on-call request, may also face CMPs of up to $50,000 per violation. As you might expect, exclusion from Medicare participation is possible if an EMTALA violation is considered an immediate, serious threat to a patient's safety and health.

In 2005, the OIG issued Supplemental Compliance Program Guidance for Hospitals,[9] which recommended that hospitals review their policies and procedures for adherence to the EMTALA statute. The OIG pointed out some particular concerns: physician understanding of on-call status, the obligation to accept emergencies even if hospital is on diversionary status, and the necessity of not delaying patient screening to ascertain insurance or financial status. In 2006, the OIG Work Plan[10] identified EMTALA compliance as a continuing area of scrutiny. The OIG reviewed and, when appropriate evidence existed, continued the negotiation, settlement, and litigation of cases involving violations of EMTALA, the patient anti-dumping statute.

> **ACRONYMS**
>
> CMP: civil monetary penalty
> OIG: Office of the Inspector General

SPOTLIGHT ON...

In July, 2005, the OIG reported that Lakeside Hospital in Louisiana agreed to pay $20,000 to resolve its liability for CMPs under EMTALA. The allegations were that

> [The] hospital failed to provide an appropriate medical screening examination for two patients who presented at its emergency department. The first incident involved a 64-year-old woman who came to the emergency room via ambulance with a complaint of being raped and experiencing chest pains. A nurse on duty allegedly directed the EMS attendant to take the patient to another facility. The second incident involved a two-month-old infant who was taken to Lakeside's Urgent Care Center for evaluation of her breathing and breathing apparatus. A physician on duty allegedly directed the parents to take the child to another facility without performing a medical screening examination.[11]

In 2001, the Office of Evaluations and Inspections within the OIG issued a report that concluded EMTALA enforcement was spotty at best. Its findings included the following statements:

- The EMTALA enforcement process is compromised by long delays and inadequate feedback from CMS to the state survey agencies and regional offices.
- The number of EMTALA investigations and their ultimate disposition vary widely among CMS regions.
- Poor tracking of EMTALA cases, omission of key information, and differences in data collection methods impedes oversight.
- Peer medical review is not always obtained before CMS considers terminating a hospital for medical reasons.[12]

THE ROLE OF THE PARALEGAL

In EMTALA cases, health care lawyers may represent either plaintiffs (such as individuals who have sought emergency department care) or defendants (such as hospital emergency departments and physicians). Paralegals may assume a traditional role in preparing for litigation of EMTALA cases (discovery, research, interviewing witnesses, preparing trial notebooks, etc.).

CASE LAW

Private litigants can choose to make EMTALA complaints to the hospitals where they were denied their EMTALA-related rights or they may decide to file lawsuits. Most cases involve interpretation of "presenting at the emergency department," what comprises an adequate medical screening, failure to stabilize, and appropriate vs. inappropriate transfers. Here are two sample cases to consider.

What constitutes an emergency department for EMTALA purposes was at issue in *Rodriguez v. American Int'l Ins. Co. of Puerto Rico.*[13] Plaintiffs' daughter, who suffered from a combination of congenital cardiovascular defects that made her prone to cyanosis, was taken to the emergency ward at Centro de Diagnóstico y Tratamiento, a diagnostic treatment center in Corozal, Puerto Rico, for respiratory difficulties. The emergency ward physician inserted an endotracheal tube in the child and decided to transfer the child the next morning to the

Pediatric Hospital at the Puerto Rico Medical Center. She died sometime after arriving there.

Plaintiffs sued the diagnostic treatment center and its insurer for damages in the U.S. District Court for the District of Puerto Rico. Plaintiffs alleged that defendants violated EMTALA by failing to provide their child with an appropriate medical screening examination so as to detect her emergency condition, and by failing to stabilize the child's condition properly before transferring her. The defendants contended that EMTALA did not apply because the diagnostic treatment center in Corozal was not a "hospital" within the meaning of EMTALA. The district court denied the defendants' summary judgment motion, concluding that the provisions of EMTALA do apply to diagnostic treatment centers in Puerto Rico that offer 24-hour emergency room services. On appeal, the First Circuit reversed. The appeals court framed the question of law posed by this case as whether a regional diagnostic and treatment center that treats only ambulatory patients and has an emergency room independent of a hospital is subject to the requirements of EMTALA. In concluding that the provisions of EMTALA did not apply to the facility, the appeals court found that the diagnostic treatment center was not primarily engaged in providing diagnostic and therapeutic or rehabilitation services to in-patients, but was engaged entirely in outpatient, ambulatory care. Furthermore, Puerto Rico law did not license or characterize diagnostic treatment centers as hospitals, but rather clearly distinguished them from hospitals. Even if a diagnostic treatment center provided emergency services, that fact did not make it an emergency room of a participating hospital.

An Alabama federal court addressed the issues of screening and stabilization and when those duties end in *Morgan v. North Mississippi Med. Ctr., Inc.*[14] Plaintiff's husband, Thomas Morgan, was rushed to the emergency room at North Mississippi Medical Center after he sustained serious injuries in a fall from a tree stand during a hunting trip. He was subsequently admitted to the hospital. The plaintiff was notified by the hospital that she would need to make financial or payment arrangements for her husband's emergency care because the family had no health insurance. After several attempts to get payment, the hospital discharged Morgan without conducting an MRI. An ambulance transported Morgan back to his home, where he died 12 hours later from untreated injuries related to the fall.

Plaintiff based her claim on allegations that the hospital failed to comply with EMTALA's screening requirement by not conducting an MRI on her husband before discharging him. However, the court noted that the purpose of EMTALA's screening requirement is to ensure that the same screening is performed on both indigent and insured patients. The court found that failing to perform even a medically advisable screening test in no way implicates EMTALA *unless* the Hospital treated Mr. Morgan differently in that regard than it would have treated a similarly situated paying patient, noting that the complaint did not allege that the hospital engaged in **disparate treatment** of Morgan. In addition, the court said, even if plaintiff had alleged disparate treatment, the EMTALA screening provision would still not be implicated because it only applies to hospital emergency departments. "[T]his court declines to engraft EMTALA's screening duty to encompass a hospital's failure to perform certain desired tests more than a week after a patient is admitted for treatment," Plaintiff also alleged that the hospital violated EMTALA's stabilization requirement because it discharged her husband in an unstable condition. The hospital argued that because the discharge occurred nine days after Morgan's arrival at the emergency department, it was too distant in time to trigger EMTALA's requirements. The court here followed the Ninth Circuit's construction, finding that "[T]he EMTALA obligation to stabilize a patient ceases at the time of the patient's admission as an inpatient, *unless* the hospital fails to admit the patient in good faith or does so as a subterfuge to avert EMTALA liability." The court then went on to find that a fair reading of the complaint supported a subterfuge theory of liability. The court noted that plaintiff alleged the hospital immediately made demands for payment after Morgan's arrival at the emergency room and then announced its intention to discharge him despite the hospital's knowledge of his extensive injuries.

SUMMARY

In this chapter, we looked at the federal requirements imposed on Medicare-participating hospitals with emergency rooms. The Emergency Medical Treatment and Labor Act allows any patient, regardless of insurance or financial status, who comes to the emergency department requesting an examination to be provided with an appropriate medical screening examination to determine if he or she is suffering from an emergency medical condition. If so, then the hospital is obligated to either provide the patient with treatment until stable, or to transfer him or her to another, appropriate hospital. However, if the patient does not have an emergency medical condition, the statute imposes no further obligation on the hospital. Pregnant women in active labor are considered to have emergency medical conditions that warrant admission until delivery is complete. EMTALA imposes additional requirements on hospitals such as maintaining a list of on-call specialist physicians, posting signs specifying patient rights, maintaining a central log on each emergency room patient, having an EMTALA compliance policy, and maintaining medical records on transferred patients.

EMTALA violations are punishable by the imposition of civil monetary penalties and/or Medicare exclusion on physicians and hospitals. Patients may file lawsuits against hospitals for alleged EMTALA infractions.

KEY TERMS

authorization: MCO approval necessary prior to the receipt of care. (Generally, this is different from a referral in that an authorization can be a verbal or written approval from the MCO whereas a referral is generally a written document that must be received by a doctor before giving care to the beneficiary.)[15]

disparate treatment: Discrimination based on race, color, religion, national origin, age, or disability that results from a practice that does not seem to be discriminatory and was not intended to be so.

patient dumping: Refers to certain situations where hospitals fail to screen, treat, or appropriately transfer patients.[16]

triage: A system of prioritizing patient treatment in an emergency room according to the urgency of the patient's need for medical care.

REVIEW QUESTIONS AND EXERCISES

1. Elliot Norbert lives in a small rural community that does not have a public hospital. Indigent care is provided through state contracts with private hospitals. Mr. Norbert works at a minimum-wage job that does not provide health insurance coverage. He is not yet

eligible for Medicare and his state does not provide Medicaid assistance to people who are employed. Mr. Norbert has had difficulty with urination for several weeks and wants to have a prostate exam because his father developed prostate cancer in his early 50s. He appears at the dedicated emergency department of Good Neighbors Hospital and requests a prostate exam. The admissions staff tells him that he must have insurance or a $300 cash deposit before he can be seen and that his case is not an emergency; Mr. Norbert is turned away. Three months later, Mr. Norbert is rushed to Best Treatment Hospital after collapsing at work. He is seen in the emergency room, is admitted to the hospital, and learns that he must have his prostate removed and may require chemotherapy because cancer has spread in his body. Does Mr. Norbert have a claim against Good Neighbors Hospital? Why or why not?

2. Explain what rights EMTALA grants, to whom, when, and in what setting.

3. During Hurricane Katrina, many hospital patients were evacuated without adequate medical records. How did CMS address this problem? See if you can locate the answer on the CMS website.

4. Research case law for the federal appellate circuit in which you reside for a recent EMTALA case. Which EMTALA requirement was at issue?

5. Dr. Joan James is an orthopedic surgeon in a midsized city. She is on call for General Medical Center for the third weekend of each month. She has not received a call from General's emergency room for several months. This past Saturday, a patient was in the emergency room with a broken ankle and a protruding bone that needed immediate surgical intervention. Dr. James received a page at 9:20 p.m., in the middle of the second act of *Il Trovatore*, an opera she had long wanted to see. She thought that it would be over by 10:00 p.m., but in actuality, she was not able to get out of the theater's parking lot until 10:45 p.m., and did not arrive at the hospital until 11:30 p.m. Is this an appropriate response time? What other factors do you need to know?

ENDNOTES

1. 42 U.S.C. § 1395dd, 42 C.F.R. § 489.24(b).

2. _Id._

3. CMS Questions and Answers, Disasters & Emergencies, Hurricanes, EMTALA, ID 5695, updated 1/18/2006, available at http://questions.cms.hhs.gov/, accessed August 3, 2007.

4. "Two-Thirds of Emergency Department Directors Report On-Call Specialty Coverage Problems," press release, September 28, 2004, American College of Emergency Physicians, available at http://www.acep.org/webportal/Newsroom/NR/general/2004/ TwoThirdsofEmergencyDepartmentDirectorsReportOnCall-SpecialtyCoverageProblems.htm, accessed August 3, 2007.

5. 42 C.F.R. § 489.24(j).

6. Pub. L. No. 108-173, 117 Stat. 2066 (2003).

7. CMS State Operations Manual, Appendix V.

8. MMA § 945.

9. "Supplemental Compliance Program Guidance for Hospitals," 70 Fed. Reg. 4858, available at http://www.oig.hhs.gov/fraud/ docs/complianceguidance, accessed August 3, 2007.

10. "Office of Inspector General Work Plan, Fiscal Year 2006," available at http://www.oig.hhs.gov/publications/reading/ workplan/2006, accessed August 3, 2007.

11. Enforcement Actions for July 2005, Fraud Prevention, Office of Inspector General, Department of Health and Human Services, available at http://www.oig.hhs.gov/fraud/enforcement/ administrative/cmp/cmpitemspd.html, accessed August 3, 2007.

12. "The Emergency Medical Treatment And Labor Act: The Enforcement Process," Office of Inspector General, Department of Health and Human Services, OEI-09-98-00221, January, 2001.

13. No. 03-2256 (1st Cir. Mar. 23, 2005).

14. 458 F.Supp.2d 1341 (S.D. Ala., October 12, 2006).

15. Glossary, Centers for Medicare and Medicaid Services, available at http://cms.hhs.gov/apps/glossary, accessed August 7, 2007.

16. "Two-Thirds of Emergency Department Directors Report On-Call Specialty Coverage Problems," press release, September 28, 2004, American College of Emergency Physicians, available at http://www.acep.org/webportal/Newsroom/NR/general/2004/TwoThirdsofEmergencyDepartmentDirectorsReportOnCallSpecialtyCoverageProblems.htm, accessed August 3, 2007.

CHAPTER 11

CLINICAL RESEARCH

OBJECTIVES

After completing this chapter, students should be able to

- Discuss the ethical principles underlying human subject research.
- Identify the sources of laws on human subject research protection.
- Identify agencies involved in human subject research protection and enforcement.
- Discuss legal theories for clinical trials litigation.

REGULATION OF RESEARCH ON HUMAN SUBJECTS

In 1999, Jesse Gelsinger was a typical teenager, fond of motorcycles and wrestling, but with a unique metabolic disorder known as ornithine transcarbamylase deficiency, controlled with a low-protein diet and drugs—32 pills a day. He signed up for a gene therapy experiment at the University of Pennsylvania and died of multiple organ system failure less than two weeks later.[1]

In 2001, families of 82 patients who participated in a **clinical trial** called Protocol 126, a failed blood-cancer experiment conducted at the Fred Hutchinson Cancer Research Center ("The Hutch") filed a class action lawsuit alleging that The Hutch neither fully warned patients of the risks and alternatives nor disclosed private financial holdings in three of the eight drugs being tested. At least twenty people died from the treatment.[2]

What went wrong in these and many other cases are examples of ethical breaches, conflicts of interest, and other legal and compliance issues involving clinical research standards. The area of human subject research protection encompasses many disciplines—medical, legal, ethical, economic, and social—all involved in health care decision making. Anyone who works in-house in a hospital, university, pharmaceutical company, academic medical center, or clinic as an attorney, paralegal, or health care compliance professional must familiarize herself with the laws and regulations governing human subject research. Attorneys practicing in the medical malpractice area have also begun to gain expertise in clinical trials litigation, making this an emerging, exciting field of study.

History of Human Subject Research

The history of human subject research is not a pretty one. Nazi war crimes trials after World War II revealed the shocking experiments perpetuated by qualified scientists and physicians on concentration camp inmates. Some inmate "volunteers" were exposed to low atmospheric pressure (in order to help the German Air Force to prepare for high altitude military operations) or forced to breathe mustard gas. Others were intentionally exposed to diseases such as malaria or typhus. All suffered or died in the name of so-called medical research. Several Nazi physicians were tried, convicted, and hanged by the Nuremberg tribunal. The most famous doctor, Dr. Mengele, the "Angel of Death," conducted experiments on children in the concentration camps. He escaped to South America in 1949 and lived there until his death in 1979.

During the Nuremberg War Crimes Trials, the Nuremberg Code was drafted to provide broad concepts for the protection of human subjects and as an international code of ethics for the conduct of physicians and scientists who conducted biomedical experiments. The Code was adopted by the United Nations in 1948 and became the prototype of many later codes intended to assure that research involving human subjects would be carried out in an ethical manner. The Nuremberg Code's standards for ethical human subject research included the following

- Informed consent is required for all experiments on humans.
- Experiments must be scientifically necessary.
- Experiments must be conducted by qualified personnel.
- Human trials should be preceded by animal studies and surveys of a disease's natural history.
- Benefit to science must be weighed against the risk to, and suffering of, experimental subjects.[3]

In 1964, the World Medical Association (a consortium of national medical associations) expanded the ethical principles of the Nuremberg Code in its Declaration of Helsinki, a document that was most recently amended in 2000. It gives basic principles for all medical research involving human subjects and additional principles for medical research combined with medical care. Some key issues addressed in the Declaration of Helsinki are conflicts of interest between researchers and their funding sources, publication of negative and positive results, and access by subjects to the best proven diagnostic and therapeutic methods identified by the study protocol.

The history of human subject research in the United States has not always been honorable or humane. The most infamous American human subject research study was the Tuskegee Syphilis Study, conducted in the 1930s by the U.S. Public Health Service on poor African American men in order to learn the natural history of syphilis. African American men were chosen because of racial stereotypes that they were more sexually active and less likely to seek treatment, but physically and mentally weaker. The study continued for nearly 40 years; even after penicillin was discovered to be an effective cure for syphilis, the participants were denied access to that treatment. Participants in that study eventually successfully sued the Public Health Service for compensation.[4] Another tawdry episode in American human subject research was the injection of plutonium or uranium into unsuspecting and uninformed subjects to study the effects of radiation.

The United States drafted its own ethical guidelines for human subject research in 1979 with publication of the Belmont Report. The Belmont Report identified three basic ethical principles: respect, beneficence, and justice. Respect recognizes the autonomy of humans and requires clear, informed consent. Beneficence means that research must be shown to be beneficial and reflect the Hippocratic idea of "Do No Harm." Justice demands that the benefits to some must be balanced against the risks to subjects.[5]

Sources of Law

The "Common Rule" is the popular name given to the body of law, regulations, and federal policy regarding human subject research protection. In actuality, several sections of the U.S. Code were amended to ensure that persons participating in clinical research had the legal protections that the Nuremberg Code, Declaration of Helsinki, and Belmont Report strove to protect ethically.

The regulations of the **Department of Health and Human Services (DHHS)** incorporate the Common Rule as Subpart A of 45 C.F.R. § 46 (56 Fed. Reg. 28003). Part B addresses protections for pregnant women; Part C addresses special concerns when using prisoners in research; and Part D ensures protections for children. Pregnant women may be subjects only if the research is therapeutic and the risk to the fetus is minimal. Use of prisoners in research is permitted only to study incarceration and its consequences (e.g., sexual assault or hepatitis) that affect prisoners as a class. The regulations provide supplementary protection to children and require adequate provisions for soliciting the assent of the child personally and the permission of one parent before a child can participate in research activities. The regulations place further limitations on research involving children who are wards of the state.

Statutory authority for the regulations derives from 5 U.S.C. § 301, 42 U.S.C. § 300v-1(b), and 42 U.S.C. § 289. The Common Rule applies to all biomedical and behavioral research involving human subjects that is conducted, supported, or subject to regulation by any federal department or agency. This includes research conducted by federal civilian employees or military personnel, as well as research conducted, supported, or otherwise subject to regulation by the federal government outside of the United States. The Common Rule does not affect any state or local laws or regulations that may be applicable and that may provide additional protections for human subjects.

The **Food and Drug Administration (FDA)** also offers protections to human subjects participating in clinical research. As early as 1938, the Food and Drug Act[6] required that drugs must be shown to be safe before

ACRONYM

DHHS: Department of Health and Human Services

ACRONYM

FDA: Food and Drug Administration

they could be marketed to consumers. This led to the need for clinical trials. In 1963, the FDA required researchers to certify informed consent. FDA regulations were amended several times to conform to DHHS regulations and now can be found at 21 C.F.R. §§ 50 and 56. The FDA's governing laws and regulations require informed consent and institutional review boards, as well as enhanced protections for children. The FDA also has regulations which permit research without consent in emergency, life-threatening situations.

SPOTLIGHT ON...

ClinicalTrials.gov is a federal government website devoted to information about federally and privately supported clinical research. It provides information on the purpose of each clinical trial, including its purpose, who may participate, locations, and phone numbers one may call for more details. Principal investigators may register their trials in accordance with the International Committee of Medical Journal Editors' initiative requiring prior entry of clinical trials in a public registry as a condition for publication. Trials must approved by an IRB (or equivalent) and conform to the regulations of the appropriate national health authorities.

Informed Consent

No clinical research can take place without an individual's informed consent, which may be written or, in some cases, spoken. The ethical principle of respect requires that people be given the opportunity to choose what shall and shall not happen to them. For informed consent to be valid, it must include (1) disclosure of relevant information to prospective subjects about the research; (2) indication that the subjects comprehend the information, and (3) their voluntary agreement, free of coercion and undue influence, to participate in the research study. Informed consent is a decision-making process that includes discussion of the research study with the **principal investigator (PI)** and signature of a written **informed consent document** by the prospective subject. Principal investigators may be medical doctors, psychologists, dentists, other health care clinicians, or other scientists. Depending on the nature and duration of the research, the PI may review and discuss amendments to the informed consent documents with the subject(s) as the study progresses.

ACRONYM

PI: principal investigator

ACRONYM

NIH: National Institutes
of Health

The **National Institutes of Health (NIH)** sets requirements for informed consent and makes suggestions for writing the actual documents. Each subject must be provided with the following specific information:

- a statement that the study involves research
- an explanation of the purpose of the research and the expected duration of the subject's participation
- a description of the procedures to be followed and identification of any procedures that are experimental
- a description of any foreseeable risks or discomforts to the subject, an estimate of their likelihood, and a description of what steps will be taken to prevent or minimize them
- a description of any benefits to the subject or to others that may reasonably be expected from the research. Monetary compensation is not a benefit. If compensation is to be provided to research subjects or healthy volunteers, the amount should be stated in the consent document.
- a disclosure of any appropriate alternative procedures or courses of treatment that might be advantageous to the subject
- a statement describing to what extent records will be kept confidential, including a description of who may have access to research records
- for research involving more than minimal risk, an explanation and description of any compensation and any medical treatments that are available if research subjects are injured, where further information may be obtained, and whom to contact in the event of a research-related injury
- an explanation of whom to contact for answers to pertinent questions about the research and the research subject's rights (including the name of the clinical center's patient representative and their telephone number)
- a statement that participation is voluntary and that refusal to participate or discontinuing participation at any time will involve no penalty or loss of benefits to which the subject is otherwise entitled[7]

Institutional Review Boards

All institutions or sites, whether domestic or foreign, where research involving human subjects is conducted or supported by the federal government are required to have prospective and continuing review and approval of research activities by a committee, typically called an **institutional review board (IRB)**. Academic medical centers and hospitals are examples of the institutions and sites where research on human subjects can take place. An academic medical center may have a fully staffed research department that oversees its IRB. The primary mandate of an IRB is to protect the rights and welfare of humans who are the subjects of research. In fulfilling this mandate, federal regulations require that an IRB be composed of individuals from diverse backgrounds in order to provide expertise in and sensitivity to a broad range of scientific and ethical considerations. For example, an IRB may be composed of several researchers, a clinical nurse, a lawyer, a clergyman, and an administrator from the institution. Some IRBs meet privately, while others may admit outsiders with advance notice. For research involving prisoners, an IRB must be an entity independent of the prison and must include one prisoner or prisoner representative. Approval for prisoner research is contingent on assurance that prisoners are given no advantages because of their participation. Private, independent organizations may also provide IRB services.

An IRB meets regularly to approve research **protocols**. It must determine that all of the following requirements are satisfied:

- Risks to subjects must be minimized by using procedures that are consistent with sound research design and do not unnecessarily expose subjects to risk.

- Risks to subjects are reasonable relative to the anticipated benefits, if any, to subjects.

- The selection of subjects is equitable. The IRB must be attentive to research that involves vulnerable populations such as children, pregnant women, prisoners, mentally disabled persons, or economically or educationally disadvantaged persons.

- Informed consent will be sought from each prospective subject, or legally authorized representative, generally by means of a written consent document. The IRB will carefully review these documents

ACRONYM

IRB: Institutional Review Board

to assure that they contain the required elements of informed consent and that they are understandable to a layperson.

- The research plan must make adequate provisions for ensuring the safety of subjects.
- There are adequate provisions to protect the privacy of subjects and to maintain the confidentiality of data.[8]

The IRB also has a duty to monitor compliance with the research protocol after approval has been granted.

AGENCY OVERSIGHT

ACRONYMS

DDIR: Deputy Director for Intramural Research

OHSR: Office of Human Subjects Research

PHS: U.S. Public Health Service

Several agencies are responsible for oversight of human subject research. The **Office of Human Subjects Research (OHSR)** operates within the **Office of the Deputy Director for Intramural Research (DDIR)**, National Institutes of Health. The NIH is part of the **U.S. Public Health Service (PHS)**, which is an agency within the Department of Health and Human Services. The mission of the NIH is to improve human health through biomedical and behavioral research, through a system of research review, approval, and oversight that assists principal investigators in understanding and complying with ethical and regulatory requirements. NIH focuses on compliance with administrative, scientific, and financial requirements of research awards. The NIH supervises its own researchers (intramural researchers) and administers awards to outside researchers (extramural researchers). Some NIH research initiatives include treatment and cures for health problems of children and teens, men, minorities, and women, as well as wellness and lifestyle issues.

SPOTLIGHT ON...

The NIH is comprised of 27 institutes and centers, with 18,627 employees, and $27,887,512,000 in congressional appropriations. The NIH distributes 80% of its funding in research grants throughout the United States, its territories, and some foreign countries.[9]

ACRONYM

OHRP: Office of Human Research Protection

The **Office of Human Research Protection (OHRP)** enforces DHHS's research regulations through audits and complaint investigations. The OHRP can suspend federal funding of research if it finds that institutions are not following the regulations. Since human subject research often involves federal funding, the **Office of Inspector General (OIG)** of DHHS enforces compliance with federal law and regulations through its focus on the avoidance of fraudulent activities and criminal and civil fraud investigations in human subject research cases. The OIG is able to use the full range of administrative, civil, and criminal sanctions against principal investigators and their sponsoring institutions when fraud is discovered. For further details, please refer to Chapter 6.

In November 2005, the OIG published a Federal Register notice[10] seeking comments on draft compliance guidance for recipients of extramural research awards from the NIH and other agencies of the PHS. In this notice, the OIG outlined its views on the value and fundamental principles of compliance programs for universities and other recipients of PHS awards for biomedical and behavioral research, along with the specific elements that these award recipients should consider when developing and implementing an effective compliance program. As with other Compliance Program Guidances for health care industry segments, a final version will be published by the OIG.

The FDA enforces the Food, Drug, and Cosmetic Act[11] and several related laws on prescription drugs, medical devices, and pediatric research. Some enforcement tools include

- The Clinical Investigator Inspection List, maintained by the Center for Biologics and Evaluation Research, which contains names, addresses, and other information gathered from inspections of clinical investigators who have conducted studies with investigational new drugs or investigational devices

- The Adequate Assurances List for Clinical Investigators, which contains the names of all clinical investigators who have provided FDA with adequate assurances of their future compliance with requirements applicable to the use of investigational drugs and biologics

- The Restricted List for Clinical Investigators, which contains the names of all clinical investigators who have agreed to certain restrictions with respect to their conduct of clinical investigations

- The Disqualified/Totally Restricted List for Clinical Investigators, which contains the names of all clinical investigators who have been disqualified or "totally restricted." The FDA may disqualify a clinical investigator if he or she has repeatedly or deliberately failed to comply with all applicable regulatory requirements or the clinical investigator has repeatedly or deliberately submitted false information to the sponsor.

- The Debarment List, which contains information about firms or persons who have been debarred from federal programs.

- The Application Integrity Policy, which describes the agency's approach regarding the review of applications that may be affected by wrongful acts that raise significant questions regarding data reliability[12]

The FDA also maintains a database of **adverse event**, or reaction, reporting to support the FDA's post-marketing safety surveillance program for all approved drug and therapeutic biologic products. The FDA receives adverse drug reaction reports from manufacturers as required by regulations. Health care professionals and consumers can also send reports voluntarily through the MedWatch program.

The FDA has published a number of Guidances and Information Sheets on Good Clinical Practice in FDA-Regulated Clinical Trials to assist researchers and institutions.

CASE LAW

In the last few years, the clinical research community has seen a dramatic increase in lawsuits seeking damages from doctors, hospitals, and sponsors who engage in clinical research. Some of these actions are ordinary medical malpractice actions, although caution must be exercised in drafting complaints to distinguish between treatment and research. Others focus on theories of violation of human dignity or violation of the principles of the Nuremberg Code and the Declaration of Helsinki. Claims may include inadequate oversight of the research, lack of informed consent, or undisclosed financial interests.

Jesse Gelsinger's death during a gene therapy trial conducted by Dr. James Wilson of the University of Pennsylvania prompted a lawsuit based on misleading and deceptive informed consent documents, failure by the defendants to disclose financial interest in Genova, the therapy being tested, and violations of FDA regulations.[13] Eventually the research was halted, and Dr. Wilson stepped down as director of the University of Pennsylvania's Institute for Gene Therapy. In 2005, he reached an agreement with the Department of Justice in which he cannot serve as a sponsor for 5 years; he must complete clinical research educational programs; he can be an investigator for only one study at a time; his research must be supervised by an external monitor; and he must author a "lessons learned" article. But Dr. Wilson and the University of Pennsylvania still made millions from their investment in Genova. Jesse's case was settled out of court for an undisclosed sum.

A case involving a study named Protocol 126 at the Fred Hutchinson Cancer Center in Seattle ("the Hutch") involved claims by 82 subjects who participated in research of blood cancer treatment between 1981 and 1993.[14] Twenty subjects' deaths were attributable to treatment received during the study. Claims in that lawsuit included: inadequate notice of adverse reactions, intentional misrepresentations of risks, breach of right to dignity, products liability, and conflicts of interest. One of the principal investigators was a former Nobel Prize winner. The study's sponsor, Genetic Systems, had given stock to the researchers and to the Hutch. That lawsuit was also settled.

Research that involves vulnerable populations or minorities is subject to special protections. In *Grimes v. Krieger Institute*,[15] a research institute created a program to study lead abatement in low-income housing. Landlords received public funding to participate, though some housing chosen only received partial lead abatement modifications. Landlords then agreed to rent to families with young children. Researchers wanted to study how effective different degrees of lead abatement procedures were, through periodic blood testing of children. The court addressed whether the informed consent process constituted a contract and questioned the ability of parents to voluntarily agree to allow their children to be subjects in potentially hazardous, nontherapeutic research. The court concluded that informed consent documents can, in some cases, be interpreted as contracts and "special relationships" which give rise to duties that, if breached, may constitute negligence.

SUMMARY

Clinical research on human subjects is one of the most fascinating and complicated areas of the health care industry. Human subject research protection is an interdisciplinary process that involves input from many disciplines—medical, legal, ethical, economic, and social.

Human subject research protection derives from many sources: the Nuremberg Code, the Declaration of Helsinki, the Belmont Report, and federal laws and regulations. Both ethical and legal concerns are addressed in the protections afforded to persons who volunteer to participate in clinical research. Informed consent documents and institutional review boards are examples of administrative requirements. Several federal agencies have oversight of clinical research. Most prominent are the NIH, the OHRP, and the OIG, all within DHHS, and the FDA.

Litigation regarding clinical trials is a recent, expanding area. Lawsuits may allege medical malpractice, lack of informed consent, undisclosed financial interest, negligence, breach of contract, or other theories of liability.

KEY TERMS

adverse event (adverse reaction): An unwanted effect caused by the administration of drugs. Onset may be sudden or develop over time.[16]

clinical trial: A clinical trial is a research study to answer specific questions about vaccines or new therapies or new ways of using known treatments. Clinical trials (also called medical research and research studies) are used to determine whether new drugs or treatments are both safe and effective. Carefully conducted clinical trials are the fastest and safest way to find treatments that work in people. Trials are in four phases: Phase I tests a new drug or treatment in a small group; Phase II expands the study to a larger group of people; Phase III expands the study to an even larger group of people; and Phase IV takes place after the drug or treatment has been licensed and marketed.[17]

informed consent document: A document that describes the rights of the study participants, and includes details about the study, such as its purpose, duration, required procedures, and key contacts. Risks and potential benefits are explained in the informed consent document. The participant then decides whether or not to sign the document. Informed consent is not a contract, and the participant may withdraw from the trial at any time.[18]

Institutional Review Board: A committee of physicians, statisticians, researchers, community advocates, and others that ensures that a clinical trial is ethical and that the rights of study participants are protected. All clinical trials in the United States must be approved by an IRB before they begin. Every institution that conducts or supports biomedical or behavioral research involving human participants must, by federal regulation, have an IRB that initially approves and periodically reviews the research in order to protect the rights of human participants.[19]

protocol: A study plan on which all clinical trials are based. The plan is carefully designed to safeguard the health of the participants as well as answer specific research questions. A protocol describes what types of people may participate in the trial; the schedule of tests, procedures, medications, and dosages; and the length of the study. While in a clinical trial, participants following a protocol are seen regularly by the research staff to monitor their health and to determine the safety and effectiveness of their treatment.[20]

REVIEW QUESTIONS AND EXERCISES

1. This chapter discusses the federal statutes and regulations that apply to human subject research. But many states have their own versions of human subject research protections. Research your state's laws to find any statutes that offer additional protections to persons participating in clinical trials.

2. Go to the government's clinical trial website and see what clinical trials are going on in your area. Are any recruiting new subjects? Who is the sponsor of each trial?

3. Who should be able to profit financially when medical researchers invent new treatment drugs? Researchers or pharmaceutical companies? Why? Would your answer be any different if a researcher took human tissue from an individual and a company developed a product that was commercially available?

4. Should subjects who are injured due to their participation in clinical trials be compensated without regard to fault? Why or why not?

5. Go to the FDA or DHHS website and look up the guidance on financial relationships in clinical research. What mechanisms are suggested to manage conflicts?

6. Why do you think an IRB must include members of the community who have no ties to the sponsoring institution?

ENDNOTES

1. See generally, Gelsinger, Paul, "Jesse's Intent," available at http://www.sskrplaw.com/gene/jessieintent.html, accessed August 6, 2007.

2. "Class action suit filed against 'The Hutch'," Seattle Times, March 27, 2001.

3. "Timeline of Laws Related to the Protection of Human Subjects," Office of NIH History, available at http://history.nih.gov/01Docs/historical/2020b.htm, accessed August 6, 2007.

4. See Pollard v. United States, 384 F. Supp. 304 (D.C. Ala. 1974).

5. "Timeline of Laws Related to the Protection of Human Subjects," Office of NIH History, available at http://history.nih.gov/01Docs/historical/2020b.htm, accessed August 6, 2007.

6. 21 U.S.C. § 301 *et seq.*

7. "Guidelines for Writing Informed Consent Documents," available at http://ohsr.od.nih.gov/info/sheet6.html, accessed August 6, 2007.

8. "Criteria for Institutional Review Board (IRB) Approval of Research Involving Human Subjects," available at http://ohsr.od.nih.gov/info/sheet3.html, accessed August 6, 2007.

9. "About NIH," available at http://www.nih.gov/about/, accessed August 6, 2007.

10. 70 Fed. Reg.71312 (November 28, 2005).

11. 21 U.S.C. § 301 *et seq.*

12. "Regulatory Activities Related to Good Clinical Practice and Clinical Trials," (updated November 9, 2005), available at http://www.fda.gov/oc/gcp/clinenforce.html, accessed August 6, 2007.

13. Gelsinger vs. Trustees of University of Pennsylvania. Civil Action filed in Philadelphia County, Court of Common Pleas, Trial

Division, Term 2000, available at http://www.sskrplaw.com/
links/health care2.htm, accessed August 6, 2007.

14. _Wright et al vs. Fred Hutchinson Cancer Center, et al_, Cause
No. 01-2-008376, Kitsap County (Wash.) Superior Court, available
at http://www.sskrplaw.com/gene/wright/complaint1.html,
accessed August 6, 2007.

15. 366 Md. 29, 782 A.2d 807 (Md. App. 2001).

16. "Glossary of Clinical Trials Terms," U.S. National Institutes
of Health, available at http://clinicaltrials.gov/ct/info/glossary,
accessed August 6, 2007.

17. _Id._

18. _Id._

19. _Id._

20. _Id._

CHAPTER 12

ETHICAL DECISION MAKING IN HEALTH CARE

CHAPTER OUTLINE

FRAMEWORK FOR ETHICS

    Codes of Ethics

    Bioethics

INTERDISCIPLINARY ISSUES IN HUMAN GENETICS

    Legal Issues

INSTITUTIONAL ETHICS COMMITTEES

OBJECTIVES

After completing this chapter, students should be able to

- Describe the roles of the medical and legal communities in health care decision-making.
- Discuss interdisciplinary issues in bioethics.
- Identify legal issues in genetics.

FRAMEWORK FOR ETHICS

Dr. Jenna admitted a 28-year-old, pregnant woman to Our Samaritan Hospital following a routine check-up, in which an X-ray revealed an inoperable tumor on her lung. The woman was a cancer survivor, having previously undergone successful chemotherapy. Over the course of the next few days, Dr. Jenna and other members of the medical staff concluded that the woman's condition was terminal. However, her 25-week-old fetus was viable, though not yet able to live outside of the womb. The woman had expressed her desire to receive palliative care until her child could be delivered at 28 weeks, but then began to waver. Her condition worsened and she drifted in and out of consciousness, necessitating a decision whether to proceed with an immediate caesarean delivery.[1] What should Dr. Jenna do? Who makes such a decision? The medical staff? The woman's family? Is there any legal liability if the caesarean is postponed? What if the woman or the fetus dies during delivery? Is there any legal liability on the part of the doctor or the hospital?

Between 1925 and 1979, about 65,000 mentally retarded individuals in the United States were sterilized without their consent.[2] Does a mentally retarded person have less of a right to have children than an individual of normal intelligence? Who has a right to make such a decision? Doctors performing the procedures? Families of the individuals? Should the involuntarily sterilized individuals be entitled to monetary damages?

Situations such as these occur with alarming frequency in health care. While the law may provide remedies in some cases, ethical decision-making involves an interdisciplinary approach: law, medicine, and social welfare. Whether you work in a law firm that represents hospitals or clinics or you are a health care compliance professional, at some point in your career you will undoubtedly face a question for which there is no easy answer that you can find in a regulation or law.

What do we mean when we talk about **ethics**? Often, we use the terms "values," "morals," and "ethics" interchangeably. Philosophers treat ethics as one of its branches and use reasoning for inquiries into the nature of and justification for general principles governing right conduct. More simply, maybe we can say that good reasons in ethics equal moral justification.

Codes of Ethics

Health care professionals and organizations often must follow codes of ethics or codes of conduct. These provide guidance or rules for expected behavior and conduct, while affirming professional or organizational ideals and standards. A good example of a code of ethics is the one for physician professional conduct adopted by the American Medical Association, which details the essential principles of medical ethics and recognized responsibilities to patients, to other health care professionals, and to society.

PRINCIPLES OF MEDICAL ETHICS

I. A physician shall be dedicated to providing competent medical care, with compassion and respect for human dignity and rights.

II. A physician shall uphold the standards of professionalism, be honest in all professional interactions, and strive to report physicians deficient in character or competence, or engaging in fraud or deception, to appropriate entities.

III. A physician shall respect the law and also recognize a responsibility to seek changes in those requirements which are contrary to the best interests of the patient.

IV. A physician shall respect the rights of patients, colleagues, and other health professionals, and shall safeguard patient confidences and privacy within the constraints of the law.

V. A physician shall continue to study, apply, and advance scientific knowledge, maintain a commitment to medical education, make relevant information available to patients, colleagues, and the public, obtain consultation, and use the talents of other health professionals when indicated.

VI. A physician shall, in the provision of appropriate patient care, except in emergencies, be free to choose whom to serve, with whom to associate, and the environment in which to provide medical care.

VII. A physician shall recognize a responsibility to participate in activities contributing to the improvement of the community and the betterment of public health.

VIII. A physician shall, while caring for a patient, regard responsibility to the patient as paramount.

IX. A physician shall support access to medical care for all people.[3]

Some health care organizations place responsibility for enforcing codes of conduct or ethics within a compliance office. Employees who suspect violations of ethical principles are encouraged to report these, just as they would report violations of regulations that could result in criminal or civil sanctions.

Bioethics

Every day we hear about new breakthroughs in biomedical science: plastic chips to measure blood sugar, ceramic spinal implants, discovery of a molecule that could be used to produce drugs to curb overeating. Should patients be required to take advantage of the latest advances? While general ethical principles guide health care professionals and organizations, the study of **bioethics** is a fairly recent subcategory of ethics that espouses specific principles in biomedical decision-making. These principles are very similar to considerations made in human subject research protection and include (1) autonomy, or the choice of the individual; (2) non-malfeasance or "do no harm"; (3) beneficence, or the duty to help others; (4) confidentiality, or respect of privacy; (5) distributive justice, or the equitable distribution of resources, benefits, and burdens among all socioeconomic groups; and (6) truth-telling, or honest disclosure of relevant information. Like the diverse members of an institutional review board in human subject research protection, bioethicists use a multidisciplinary approach in decision making. Bioethics is important in resolving issues in human genetics, which we will explore in the next section.

INTERDISCIPLINARY ISSUES IN HUMAN GENETICS

Genetics provides explanations of human characteristics or conditions. In the nineteenth century, Gregor Mendel, the "Father of Genetics," observed the manipulation of physical characteristics when farmers bred domestic animals and crops to achieve heightened productivity and durability. In the twentieth century, scientists linked genetics to DNA. Between 1990 and 2003, the Human Genome Project, a multinational project, had as its goal the discovery and mapping of the 20,000 to 25,000 genes that make up the human **genome**.

Genetic screening can show inherited disorders. For would-be parents, a genetic screen can allow them to choose desirable characteristics for future children or help make difficult decisions about reproduction and conception methods, adoption, or avoidance of reproduction altogether. Genetic screens can help control health care costs through early diagnosis, treatment, and prevention of serious genetic disorders such as sickle cell anemia or cystic fibrosis. However, genetic treatment may also be experimental and costly.

Legal Issues

Human genetics, and specifically genetic screening, raises three primary legal issues: (1) privacy and confidentiality of information, (2) discrimination based on genetic traits, and (3) ownership of genetic information.

SPOTLIGHT ON...

The National Conference of State Legislatures maintains a list of state genetics laws on employment, embryonic fetal research, genetic privacy, insurance, and other affected areas.

Privacy and Confidentiality The **Health Insurance Portability and Accountability Act (HIPAA)** protects the privacy of individually identifiable health information, but does not offer enhanced protections for genetic material. Most states have laws on human genetic screening that include provisions restricting disclosure of confidential information and often offering greater privacy protections than HIPAA. But those only prompt the question: Would you want to know, or should you have the right to know, if you or a family member had a genetic trait or predisposition to a disease or condition? Cases in this area of law may turn on whether the court finds a "duty to warn." In *Safer v. Pack*,[4] Donna Safer sued the physician who treated her father for cancer when she discovered that she suffered from cancer, some 40 years later. The court said

> We see no impediment, legal or otherwise, to recognizing a physician's duty to warn those known to be at risk of avoidable harm from a genetically transmissible condition.

ACRONYM

HIPAA: Health Insurance Portability and Accountability Act

However, the court did not address any privacy or confidentiality issues. It's also important to note that this case was decided on a motion to dismiss the complaint.

SPOTLIGHT ON...

Researchers studying coffee consumption and heart disease found that two or more cups of coffee per day can increase the risk of a non-fatal heart attack for certain individuals who have a genetic variation associated with slower caffeine metabolism.[5] Would you want to know if you had that gene? Would you cut your caffeine intake regardless of whether you knew or not?

Discrimination HIPAA prevents group health plans from using an individual's health factors as a reason for disparate treatment from other similarly situated individuals in the health plan. HIPAA's nondiscrimination rules are valuable for individuals who learn that they have inherited a disease or condition. Their health insurance coverage must remain intact.

State laws also prohibit discrimination based on genetic factors in health insurance issuance. For example, Louisiana law prohibits the requirement of disclosure or testing for genetic information in order to obtain insurance. La. Rev. Stat. 22: 213.7, provides in part that

B. (1) No insurer shall, on the basis of any genetic information concerning an individual or family member or on the basis of an individual's or family member's request for or receipt of genetic services, or the refusal to submit to a genetic test or make available the results of a genetic test:

(a) Terminate, restrict, limit, or otherwise apply conditions to the coverage of an individual or family member under the policy or plan, or restrict the sale of the policy or plan to an individual or family member.

(b) Cancel or refuse to renew the coverage of an individual or family member under the policy or plan.

(c) Deny coverage or exclude an individual or family member from coverage under the policy or plan.

(d) Impose a rider that excludes coverage for certain benefits or services under the policy or plan.

(e) Establish differentials in premium rates or cost sharing for coverage under the policy or plan.

(f) Otherwise discriminate against an individual or family member in the provision of insurance.

(2) No insurer shall require an applicant for coverage under the policy or plan, or an individual or family member who is presently covered under a policy or plan, to be the subject of a genetic test or to be subjected to questions relating to genetic information.

The statute also clarifies the need for specific authorizations for the release of genetic information:

(c) (5) A general authorization for the release of medical records or medical information shall not be construed as an authorization for disclosure of genetic information. With respect to medical records that contain genetic information, the requirements for disclosure of genetic information under this Section must be complied with.[6]

State laws, federal laws such as the Americans with Disabilities Act and Title VII of the Civil Rights Act, and federal **EEOC** regulations prohibiting discrimination based on disabilities may protect employees with genetic conditions in the workplace. In its compliance manual, the EEOC considers asymptomatic genetic conditions as disabilities. For a state statute that prohibits genetic discrimination in the workplace and provides for privacy, see La. Rev. Stat. 23:368, an excerpt from which follows.

A. No otherwise qualified person shall, on the basis of protected genetic information, be subjected to discrimination in employment.

B. An employer, labor organization, or employment agency shall not engage in any of the following practices:

(1) Discharge, fail or refuse to hire, or otherwise discriminate against any employee with respect to the compensation, terms, conditions, or privileges of employment of that employee, because of protected genetic information with respect to the employee, or because of information about a request for or the receipt of genetic services by such employee.

ACRONYM

EEOC: Equal Employment Opportunity Commission

(2) Limit, segregate, or classify employees in any way that would deprive or tend to deprive any employee of employment opportunities or otherwise adversely affect that employee's status, because of protected genetic information with respect to the employee or because of information about a request for or the receipt of genetic services by such employee.

(3) Require, collect, or purchase protected genetic information with respect to an employee, or information about a request for or the receipt of genetic services by such employee.

(4) Disclose protected genetic information with respect to an employee, or information about a request for or the receipt of genetic services by an employee except:

(a) To the employee who is the subject of the information, at his or her request.

(b) To an occupational or other health researcher, if the research conducted complies with the regulations and protections provided for under Part 46 of Title 45 of the Code of Federal Regulations.

(c) If required by a federal or state statute, legislative sub-poena, or an order issued by a court of competent juris-diction, except that if the subpoena or court order was secured without the knowledge of the individual to whom the information refers, the employer shall provide the individual with adequate notice to challenge the subpoena or court order, unless the subpoena or court order also imposes confidentiality requirements.

(d) To executive branch officials investigating compliance with this order, if the information is relevant to the investigation.

(5) Maintain protected genetic information or information about a request for or the receipt of genetic services in general personnel files; such information shall be treated as confidential medical records and kept separate from personnel files.

C. Specifically, a labor organization shall not engage in any of the following practices:

(1) Exclude or expel from membership, or otherwise discriminate against, an otherwise qualified member or applicant for membership on the basis of protected genetic information.

(2) Limit, segregate, or classify membership, or applicants for membership, or classify or fail or refuse to refer for employment an otherwise qualified person in a way which would deprive or tend to deprive him of employment opportunities, or which would limit employment opportunities or otherwise adversely affect his status as an employee or as an applicant for employment, on the basis of protected genetic information.

D. An employer, labor organization, or joint labor management committee controlling apprenticeship, on-the-job training, or other training programs shall not engage in any of the following practices:

(1) Discriminate against an otherwise qualified person based on protected genetic information.

(2) Print, publish, or cause to be printed or published a notice or advertisement relating to employment, indicating a preference, limitation, specification, or discrimination, based on protected genetic information.

E. The following exceptions shall apply to the nondiscrimination requirements:

(1) An employer, labor organization, or employment agency may request or require protected genetic information with respect to an applicant who has been given a conditional offer of employment or to an employee if:

(a) The information obtained is to be used exclusively to assess whether further medical evaluation is needed to diagnose a current disease, or medical condition or disorder;

(b) Such current disease, or medical condition or disorder could prevent the applicant or employee from performing the essential functions of the position held or desired; and

(c) The information will not be disclosed to persons other than medical personnel involved in or responsible for assessing whether further medical evaluation is needed to diagnose a current disease, or medical condition or disorder.

(2) For therapeutic purposes only, an employer, labor organization, or employment agency may request, collect, or purchase protected genetic information with respect to an

employee, or any information about a request for or receipt of genetic services by such employee if:

(a) The employee uses genetic or health care services provided by the employer.

(b) The employee who uses the genetic or health care services has provided prior knowing, voluntary, and written authorization to the employer to collect protected genetic information.

(c) The person who performs the genetic or health care services does not disclose protected genetic information to anyone except to the employee who uses the services for treatment of the individual; for program evaluation or assessment; for compiling and analyzing information in anticipation of or for use in a civil or criminal legal proceeding; or for payment or accounting purposes, to verify that the service was performed, but in such cases the genetic information itself cannot be disclosed.

(d) Such information is not used in violation of Subsection B, C, or D of this Section.

(3) Genetic monitoring of biological effects of toxic substances in the workplace shall be permitted if all of the following conditions are met:

(a) The employee has provided prior knowing, voluntary, and written authorization.

(b) The employee is notified when the results of the monitoring are available and, at that time, the employer makes any protected genetic information that may have been acquired during the monitoring available to the employee and informs the employee how to obtain such information.

(c) The monitoring conforms to any genetic monitoring regulations that may be promulgated by the secretary of the Department of Labor.

(d) The employer, excluding any licensed health care professionals that are involved in the genetic monitoring program, receives results of the monitoring only in aggregate terms that do not disclose the identity of specific employees.[7]

An interesting case of genetic discrimination involved employees of Burlington Northern Santa Fe Railroad. In 2002, the EEOC alleged that Burlington discriminated against its employees by requiring a genetic test for a condition called hereditary neuropathy with liability to pressure palsies, which might manifest itself as carpal tunnel syndrome. Employees undergoing medical examinations had their blood tested without being told that they were being screened for this condition. Burlington admitted that it had required some employees who claimed that they had developed work-related carpal tunnel syndrome to undergo an extensive medical exam, including a genetic screening, with an outside health care provider. Burlington later agreed to pay 36 employees up to $2.2 million to settle the claim. The company also agreed that it would not use genetic tests in future medical exams and that it would review its medical policies and procedures.[8]

Ownership of Genetic Information Researchers have discovered the value of stored human tissue and blood samples in the development of new products such as drugs and diagnostic tests. Health care providers and organizations may have obtained tissue and blood samples years earlier for some purpose other than future research. Although DNA repositories are a rich source of material, the ownership of genetic material and who may profit from resulting products often become legal and ethical issues.

Research using stored genetic material was the subject of *Greenberg v. Miami Children's Hospital Research Institute*,[9] a lawsuit filed by several families against a physician, Dr. Matalon, and the institution with which he was affiliated. The individual plaintiffs and the Chicago chapter of the National Tay-Sachs and Allied Disease Association provided tissue samples to Dr. Matalon in order to create a database of epidemiological, medical, and other confidential information about families of Eastern European Jewish ancestry who might be carriers of the gene that causes Canavan disease, a degenerative brain disorder that is always fatal. Dr. Matalon was successful in his research and was able to isolate this gene. Thereafter, he and Miami Children's Hospital obtained a U.S. patent on the gene sequence, acquired the ability to restrict activities related to testing and treatment of Canavan disease, and were able to commercialize their success. The families who provided the original genetic material, however, received no compensation. The plaintiffs filed suit, claiming a property interest in the tissue and genetic matter, and alleged six bases for their complaint: (1) lack of informed consent, (2) breach of fiduciary duty, (3) unjust enrichment, (4) fraudulent concealment, (5) conversion, and (6) misappropriation of trade secrets. The court dismissed the claims of informed consent, breach of fiduciary duty, fraudulent concealment, and misappropriation of trade secrets and ruled that the plaintiffs had no recourse under Florida law for the claim of conversion. However, the court allowed the unjust enrichment claim to go forward, noting that the families had invested their time and resources in the research to isolate the Canavan gene. You can find this case in the Online Companion that accompanies this text.

SPOTLIGHT ON...

The U.S. Human Genome Project was a long-term project coordinated by the U.S. Department of Energy and the National Institutes of Health. Its goals were to

- identify all the approximately 20,000–25,000 genes in human DNA
- determine the sequences of the 3 billion chemical base pairs that make up human DNA
- store this information in databases
- improve tools for data analysis
- transfer related technologies to the private sector
- address the ethical, legal, and social issues that may arise from the project[10]

Other DNA repositories and databases store genetic material and information for research, forensic identification, and public health screening. Most states have laws that mandate screening of newborns for genetic conditions such as PKU and sickle cell anemia; many states retain this material for a number of years. Other agencies and organizations may also collect and store samples for future epidemiological studies.

INSTITUTIONAL ETHICS COMMITTEES

Interdisciplinary medical decision-making has led to the development of institutional ethics committees. By the 1990s, most hospitals and many nursing homes, home health agencies, and managed care organizations had instituted institutional ethics committees to resolve difficult ethical issues. Although they may seem to resemble institutional review boards in their membership structure, the functions of these institutional ethics committees are different and are not required by law. One important aspect of an institutional ethics committee is its ability to educate others or raise awareness of medical-ethical issues within the organization. Hospital staff, for example, may not understand the legal effects of a **durable power of attorney** or a **living will**. (More details on advance directives can be found in Chapter 3.)

Institutional ethics committees may participate in drafting policies and procedures for handling difficult medical situations, such as removal of life support systems or accessing alternative healing methods. The most difficult work of an institutional ethics committee may be to resolve situations in which a physician and family are uncertain about continuing treatment.

The American Medical Association encourages the use of institutional ethics committees for educational purposes. Its principles are

(1) Ethics committees in health care institutions should be educational and advisory in purpose. Generally, the function of the ethics committee should be to consider and assist in resolving unusual, complicated ethical problems involving issues that affect the care and treatment of patients within the health care institution. Recommendations of the ethics committee should impose no obligation for acceptance on the part of the institution, its governing board, medical staff, attending physician, or other persons. However, it should be expected that the recommendations of a dedicated ethics committee will receive serious consideration by decision makers.

(2) The size of the committee should be consistent with the needs of the institution but not so large as to be unwieldy. Committee members should be selected on the basis of their concern for the welfare of the sick and infirm, their interest in ethical matters, and their reputation in the community and among their peers for integrity and mature judgment. Experience as a member of hospital or medical society committees concerned with ethical conduct or quality assurance should be considered in selecting ethics committee members. Committee members should not have other responsibilities that are likely to prove incompatible with their duties as members of the ethics

committee. Preferably, a majority of the committee should consist of physicians, nurses, and other health care providers. In hospitals, medical staff bylaws should delineate the functions of the committee, general qualifications for membership, and manner of selection of members, in accordance with these guidelines.

(3) The functions of the ethics committee should be confined exclusively to ethical matters. The Code of Medical Ethics of the American Medical Association is recommended for the guidance of ethics committees in making their own recommendations. The matters to be considered by the committee should consist of ethical subjects that a majority of its members may choose to discuss on its own initiative, matters referred to it by the executive committee of the organized medical staff or by the governing board of the institution, or appropriate requests from patients, families, or health care providers.

(4) In denominational health care institutions or those operated by religious orders, the recommendations of the ethics committee may be anticipated to be consistent with published religious tenets and principles. Where particular religious beliefs are to be taken into consideration in the committee's recommendations, this fact should be publicized to physicians, patients, and others concerned with the committee's recommendations.

(5) In its deliberations and communication of recommendations, the procedures followed by the ethics committee should comply with institutional and ethical policies for preserving the confidentiality of information regarding patients.

(6) Committee members should be prepared to meet on short notice and to render their recommendations in a timely and prompt fashion in accordance with the demands of the situation and the issues involved.[11]

SUMMARY

In this chapter, we were introduced to ethics in health care. Many organizations have codes of ethics that lay out principles of conduct and professionalism for their staff. Bioethics is a subcategory of ethics for biomedical decision-making and involves considerations similar to human subject research protections and its principles of autonomy, nonmalfeasance, beneficence, confidentiality, distributive justice, and truth telling. Ethical decisions in health care involve a multidisciplinary approach.

The study of genetics raises many legal issues in health care, including privacy and confidentiality, discrimination in insurance and employment, and ownership of genetic information. Although there is no federal legislation in genetics, most states have laws prohibiting genetic discrimination and protecting genetic information.

In order to assist with decision-making in difficult cases and to educate health care staff, many organizations have institutional ethics committees.

KEY TERMS

bioethics: The formal study of ethical and moral implications of biomedical advances and new biological discoveries that can advance health care for patients.

durable power of attorney: A power of attorney that lasts as long as a person remains incapable of making decisions, usually about health care.

ethics: Standards of fair and honest conduct in general.

genome: The genetic material that makes up an organism, such as a human being.

living will: An advance directive by which an individual authorizes his or her possible future removal from an artificial life support system.

REVIEW QUESTIONS AND EXERCISES

1. It's 4:45 p.m. on the day before the 3-day Labor Day weekend. A new associate at your firm bursts into your office and begs for your help. A spokesperson for one of the hospitals that your firm represents called to ask for advice regarding treatment of a 33-year-old patient, recently admitted for a heart attack but otherwise healthy, who has refused implantation of a pacemaker. Explain what the associate must consider before responding to the hospital's request.

2. Using the charts available on the Conference of State Legislatures' website, see what types of laws your state has on genetic privacy

or genetic discrimination. Do you feel that your state has adequately addressed all of the issues in genetics?

3. Mr. Bono signed a general authorization to release his medical records to Megamillion, Inc. in his application for health insurance. Mr. Bono was recently part of a university-led research study that identified him as a carrier of the obesity gene. Megamillion denied Mr. Bono's application when it received his full medical chart. Based on the Louisiana law in this chapter (or your state's law), does Mr. Bono have a discrimination claim against Megamillion? Explain.

4. If Mr. Bono applied for a job at Megamillion and underwent a pre-employment physical that included a genetic screen for obesity, would he have a claim for discrimination if he did not get hired? Explain.

5. Should a lawyer be a member of an institutional ethics committee? Why or why not? Would the AMA's principles allow for an in-house counsel to be part of this kind of committee?

6. Research two health care organizations in your area to see if they have codes of ethics or conduct. Do they address general principles of conduct or is it specific about ethical decision-making? What are the differences and similarities?

ENDNOTES

1. Facts loosely based on *In Re A.C.*, 573 A.2d 1235 (D.C. App. 1990).

2. Many states had involuntary sterilization programs at that time.

3. "Principles of Medical Ethics," American Medical Association, available at http://www.ama-assn.org/ama/pub/category/2512.html, accessed August 6, 2007.

4. 291 N.J. Super. 619, 677 A.2d 1188 (N.J. App. 1996).

5. News Release, Journal of the American Medical Association, March 7, 2006, available at http://pubs.ama-assn.org/media/2006j/0307.dtl#coffee, accessed March 9, 2006.

6. La. Rev. Stat. 22: 213.7.

7. La. Rev. Stat. 23:368.

8. See generally, Furrow, B. et al, "Legal, Social, and Ethical Issues in Human Genetics," in <u>Bioethics: Health Care Law and Ethics</u>, 5th ed. (Thomson-West, 2004).

9. 264 F.Supp.2d 1064 (S.D. Fl. 2003).

10. "What is the Human Genome Project?" available at <u>http://www.ornl.gov/sci/techresources/Human_Genome/project/about.shtml</u>, accessed March 13, 2006.

11. "Guidelines for Ethics Committees in Health Care Institutions," American Medical Association (1994).

Appendix A
ACRONYMS

ABN:	Advance Beneficiary Notice
AHA:	American Hospital Association
AHIMA:	American Health Information Management Association
AKS:	Anti-Kickback Statute
ALJ:	Administrative law judge
AMA:	American Medical Association
AMC:	Academic medical center
ASC:	Ambulatory surgical center
ASCA:	Administrative Simplification Compliance Act
BBA:	Balanced Budget Act
BIPA:	Benefits Improvement and Protection Act of 2000
CE:	Covered entity
CFAA:	Computer Fraud and Abuse Act
CFR:	Code of Federal Regulations
CHAMPVA:	Civilian Health and Medical Program of the Department of Veteran Affairs
CIA:	Corporate integrity agreement
CMP:	Civil monetary penalty
CMS:	Centers for Medicare and Medicaid Services
COBRA:	Consolidated Omnibus Budget Reconciliation Act
CON:	Certificate of Need

CoP:	Conditions of Participation
CPG:	Compliance Program Guidance
CPT:	Current Procedural Terminology
DDIR:	Deputy Director for Intramural Research
DHHS:	Department of Health and Human Services
DHS:	Designated health services
DME:	Durable medical equipment
DOJ:	Department of Justice
DRG:	Diagnostic-Related Groups
DSH:	Disproportionate Share Hospital
EEOC:	Equal Employment Opportunity Commission
EHR:	Electronic Health Records
EMTALA:	Emergency Medical Treatment and Labor Act
ECPA:	Electronic Communications Privacy Act of 1986
EPHI:	Electronic protected health information
ERISA:	Employment Retirement Income Security Act
ESRD:	End-stage renal disease
FCA:	False Claims Act
FDA:	Food and Drug Administration
FDLP:	Federal Depository Library Program
FI:	Fiscal Intermediary
FR:	Final Rule
GLB:	Gramm-Leach-Bliley Act
GPO:	Government Printing Office
HCPCS:	Health Care Financing Administration Common Procedural Coding System
HCQIA:	Health Care Quality Improvement Act
HHA:	Home health agency
HIPDB:	Healthcare Integrity and Protection Data Bank
HIPAA:	Health Insurance Portability and Accountability Act

HIT:	Health information technology
HMO:	Health maintenance organization
HSA:	Health savings account
ICD:	International Classification of Diseases
IDS:	Integrated Delivery System
IIHI:	Individually identifiable health information
IPA:	Independent practice (or physician) association
IRB:	Institutional review board
IRE:	Independent review entity
IRS:	Internal Revenue Service
LCD:	Local Coverage Decision
LEIE:	List of Excluded Individuals/Entities
MA:	Medicare Advantage
MCO:	Managed care organization
MHPA:	Mental Health Parity Act
MMA:	Medicare Prescription Drug, Improvement, and Modernization Act of 2003, commonly referred to as the Medicare Modernization Act of 2003
MSA:	Medical savings account
NAIC:	National Association of Insurance Commissioners
NCD:	National Coverage Decision
NCQA:	National Committee on Quality Assurance
NIH:	National Institutes of Health
NPDB:	National Practitioner Data Bank
NPI:	National Provider Identifier
NPRM:	Notice of Proposed Rulemaking
OCR:	Office of Civil Rights
OHA:	Office of HIPAA Standards
OHRP:	Office of Human Research Protection
OHSR:	Office of Human Subjects Research

OIG:	Office of the Inspector General
PCP:	Primary care physician
PDP:	Prescription drug provider
PHI:	Protected health information
PHO:	Physician–hospital organization
PHS:	U.S. Public Health Service
PI:	Principal investigator
POS:	Point of service
PPO:	Preferred provider organization
PPS:	Prospective payment system
PRRB:	Provider Reimbursement Review Board
QIC:	Qualified Independent Contractor
RBRVS:	Resource-based relative value scale
SNF:	Skilled nursing facility
SSA:	Social Security Administration
SSB:	Social Security Board
TCS:	Transactions and Code Sets
TEFRA:	Tax Equity and Fiscal Responsibility Act
VHA:	Veterans Health Administration

USEFUL WEBSITES FOR HEALTH CARE AND HEALTH LAW*

Government Resources

Centers for Disease Control and Prevention
http://www.cdc.gov

Clinical trials
http://clinicaltrials.gov

CMS regulations
http://www.cms.hhs.gov/

Code of Federal Regulations/Federal Register
http://www.gpoaccess.gov

Congressional resources
http://thomas.loc.gov/

DHHS administrative rules and regulations
http://aspe.hhs.gov/admnsimp/index.shtml

Office of Civil Rights
http://www.hhs.gov/ocr

DHHS Office of Inspector General
http://www.oig.hhs.gov/

Penalties for HIPAA violations
http://www.hhs.gov/ocr/moneypenalties.html

*Many of these sites have member-restricted areas.**

National Committee on Vital and Health Statistics (NCVHS)
http://www.ncvhs.hhs.gov

Laws enforced by the FDA and related statutes
http://www.fda.gov/opacom/laws

MedWatch
http://www.fda.gov/medwatch/index.html

FDA manuals and publications
http://www.fda.gov/opacom/7pubs.html

Reporting of adverse events and product problems to the FDA
http://www.fda.gov/cdrh/mdr/frmdr.html

Health Law Resources

Attorney Alan Goldberg's Law, Technology, and Change Home Page
http://www.healthlawyer.com/

American Health Lawyers Association
http://www.ahla.org

American Journal of Bioethics
http://www.bioethics.net

Emergency Medical Treatment and Active Labor Act (EMTALA)
http://www.emtala.com

FindLaw
http://www.findlaw.com

Health Care Organizations

American Accreditation HealthCare Commission, Inc. (URAC)
http://www.urac.org

American Association of Medical Colleges
http://www.aamc.org

American Hospital Association
http://www.aha.org

American Health Information Management Association
http://www.ahima.org

American Medical Association
http://www.ama-assn.org

Health Care Compliance Association
http://www.hcca-info.org

The Joint Commission (formerly Joint Commission on Accreditation of Health Care Organizations)
http://www.jointcommission.org

Kaiser Family Foundation
http://www.kff.org

National Commission on Quality Assurance
http://www.ncqa.org

National Health Policy Forum
http://www.nhpf.org

Appendix C

ADMINISTRATIVE LAW AND FEDERAL REGULATORY RESEARCH

OBJECTIVES

After reviewing this appendix, students should be able to

- Discuss the concept of administrative law.
- Describe the process of federal law into federal regulations.
- Demonstrate proficiency in researching federal regulations and administrative agency decisions and policies.

FEDERAL SOURCES OF ADMINISTRATIVE LAW

Most U.S. citizens may never see the inside of a courthouse, sue or be sued, or experience life as a criminal defendant. However, **administrative law** touches our lives everyday. When you obtain a social security card, when you agonize over your federal income tax return, or when you qualify for Medicare, you enter the maze of administrative law and regulations.

Before we enter this labyrinth, however, a quick review of what some of us learned long ago in civics class might prove helpful. This section provides a basic outline of the numerous steps of our federal lawmaking process, from introduction of a bill in Congress through eventual publication as a statute, and then on to the federal regulations that emanate from those statutes. Federal statutes often confer rule-making ability on administrative agencies and their subagencies, such as the Center for Medicare and Medicaid Services within the Department of Health and Human Services. In health care law and regulatory compliance, it is these regulations that govern an organization's daily operations.

How a Bill Becomes a Law[1]

Sources of ideas for legislation are limited only by one's imagination; proposed drafts of bills originate in different ways. A member of Congress may propose a new law because of a promise he or she made to constituents. For example, recent political campaigns have focused on medical malpractice and class action lawsuit reform. Some constituents may have particular needs that our laws may not address adequately, such as funding of orphan drugs (drugs needed by a small group of people). Another way that bills are introduced is through the amendment process, when a representative becomes aware of the need for modification to or repeal of an existing law.

Drafting of new bills for enactment by Congress may come at the behest of the executive departments and independent agencies that employ legislative counsels. The President of the United States often has an agenda for specific legislation that he would like to see passed as part of his legacy. Because the president cannot introduce legislation directly, he may buttonhole a member of his party to sponsor the bill's introduction in Congress.

SPOTLIGHT ON...

THOMAS, a service sponsored by the Library of Congress, provides legislative information on the Internet. THOMAS offers many databases for searching the *Congressional Record:* bill text, summary, and status; committee reports; and public laws.

Roles of Congress and the President Bills may originate in either the House of Representatives or the Senate and may be either public or private. A public bill affects the public generally. A private bill affects only a specified individual or a private entity rather than the population at large. In this text, we are concerned with public bills.

A bill originating in the House of Representatives is designated by the letters "H.R." followed by a number; a bill originating in the Senate is designated by "S.," followed by its number. A "companion bill" describes a bill introduced in one house of Congress that is similar or identical to a bill introduced in the other house. Most bills are assigned to committees for study and discussion before they are voted on by the full membership. The purpose of committee review is to determine whether the proposed law and any programs that it would create are necessary and desirable and what impact, economic or otherwise, the new law will have. Many proposed bills do not make it out of the committee process and thus are never voted on by the full membership.

A bill must be voted on by both the House of Representatives and the Senate before it becomes the law of the land. However, the process is not complete until one of the following takes place

- The President approves and signs the bill.
- The President fails to return the bill, with his objections, to the House in which it originated within 10 days (except Sundays) while Congress is in session.
- The President vetoes the bill, and the veto is then overridden by a two-thirds vote in each House.

Assignment of Public Law After enactment of a valid law, it must be made known to the people who are to be bound by it. In practice, a new law is published immediately by the Archivist of the United States. It is then assigned a public law number, and paginated for the *Statutes at Large* volume covering that session of Congress. The public and private law numbers run in numerical order and are prefixed for ready identification by the number of the Congress. For example, the first public law of the 108th Congress is designated Public Law 108-1. Subsequent laws of the 108th Congress would be numbered 108-2, etc.

Notations in the Federal Register, National Archives and Records Administration The first official publication of the law is in a pamphlet known as a "slip law." The heading of a slip law for a public law also indicates the United States Statutes at Large citation. The *United States Statutes at*

Large, prepared by the Office of the Federal Register, National Archives and Records Administration, comprises bound volumes of the laws of each session of Congress.

The Office of the Federal Register, National Archives and Records Administration, prepares the slip laws, providing marginal editorial notes and citations to laws mentioned in the text and other explanatory details. The notes also give the U.S. Code classifications, enabling the reader to quickly determine where the statute will appear in the U.S. Code (discussed below). Each slip law also includes an informative guide to the legislative history of the law.

U.S. Code Classification The *U.S. Code* is a consolidation of the general and permanent federal laws of the United States, arranged alphabetically and according to subject matter, in numerous volumes. It sets out the current status of the laws, as amended. The *U.S. Code* is **prima facie** evidence of those laws. Its purpose is to present the laws in a concise and usable form, without requiring recourse to the many volumes of the *Statutes at Large* or to the individual slip laws of each Congressional session.

New editions of the *U.S. Code* are published every 6 years in hard copy and cumulative paperback supplements are published after the conclusion of each regular session of the Congress. The *U.S. Code* can also be accessed via the Internet through various free resources.

SEARCHING FOR FEDERAL REGULATIONS

Where there are federal laws that are to be administered by federal agencies, federal regulations soon follow. There is a specific procedure by which a regulation is proposed, commented on, and eventually adopted. Federal regulations are the details of the general statutes that are in the *U.S. Code*. Anyone working in health care law or in the health care industry is affected by federal regulations for his or her segment of the industry.

Federal Register[2]

Regulations must be written, published, commented on, and rewritten before final adoption. All of these steps take place in the pages of the *Federal Register*, which is the government's official "newspaper," published daily except for weekends and federal holidays. In it you will find proposed and final rules and notices of federal agencies and organizations, as well as executive orders and other presidential documents. Anyone can access the *Federal Register* online through the government website maintained as "GPO Access." Volumes from 1994 to the present are available online. Health care lawyers and other professionals in the industry often review the *Federal Register* daily to see what their favorite government agencies are up to.

Searching the *Federal Register* is not easy. In order to find a regulation, you must have a fairly good idea of when it was published. Volumes are arranged in reverse chronological order by year and pages in each volume can number in the thousands. Word searches using Boolean connectors are allowed, but, again, you must identify the volume number(s) prior to beginning your search.

A notice that an agency invites suggestions or comments within a specified time period regarding a particular area of law with which it is charged is an early part of the process of making a regulation. Alternatively, an agency may write a preliminary draft of regulations and publish them as a **Notice of Proposed Rulemaking (NPRM)**, allowing a specific length of time for comments by the public. When the period has expired, the **Final Rule** (abbreviated **FR**) is to be published. Care must be taken when researching the *Federal Register* since word searches can lead to recovery of general notices, NPRMs, and FRs on a single subject.

Code of Federal Regulations[3]

Once a final regulation is published and adopted, it is assigned a number in the *Code of Federal Regulations.* The ***Code of Federal Regulations* (CFR)** is the codification of the general and permanent rules published in the *Federal Register* by the executive departments and agencies of the federal government. It is divided into 50 "titles" or categories that represent broad areas subject to federal regulation. For example, Title 45 is Public Welfare, which includes health care regulations.

Each volume of the CFR is updated annually and is available at federal government depositary libraries, often housed at universities. The *Code of Federal Regulations* is the primary research tool for compliance professionals in the health care industry. However, be forewarned that there are often delays between publication of a final rule in the *Federal Register* and codification in the *Code of Federal Regulations.*

Fortunately, many commercial publications track rules daily, providing valuable assistance for health care legal professionals.

For more than 140 years, the **Government Printing Office (GPO)** has kept America informed by producing and distributing Federal government information products. GPO combines conventional technology with state-of-the-art methods to provide public access to Government information online, and produces and distributes publications that serve the information needs of the U.S. Congress, Federal agencies, and the American public. Through the Superintendent of Documents classification system, GPO disseminates the largest volume of U.S. government publications and information in the world.[4]

The **Federal Depository Library Program (FDLP)** is by far the largest and best known of the Superintendent of Documents programs. Established by Congress to ensure that the American public has access to its Government's information, this program involves the acquisition, format conversion, and distribution of depository materials and the coordination of Federal depository libraries in the 50 states, the District of Columbia, and U.S. territories.

The mission of the FDLP is to disseminate information products from all three branches of the government to nearly 1,300 libraries nationwide. Libraries that have been designated as Federal Depositories maintain these information products as part of their existing collections and are responsible for assuring that the public has free access to the material provided by the FDLP.

Like the *Federal Register*, the *Code of Federal Regulations* can be accessed online through the GPO Access page. You can search for regulations by subject, agency, or citation number. A companion publication, the *List of CFR Sections Affected*, includes a table updating the "Parallel Table of Authorities and Rules" published in the annual *CFR Index and Finding Aids.*[5]

THE ROLE OF ADMINISTRATIVE AGENCIES[6]

Administrative agencies are created by the legislature, which assigns each agency specific tasks. Despite this, administrative agencies are located in the executive branch of government. The U.S. government's executive branch has 15 cabinet-level agencies. These agencies, along with other independent agencies, governmental corporations, boards, commissions and committees, handle the daily operations of how many of our laws are carried out.

Creation of an Agency

An agency's **enabling statute** or act is the fundamental source of the agency's power. The Administrative Procedure Act of 1946[7] is the federal procedural statute for all federal agencies sharing jurisdiction. Some agencies have specific enabling statutes that establish the agency's mission and set limits on its scope of authority. For example, the original Social Security Act,[8] passed during President Franklin D. Roosevelt's tenure, originally authorized the **Social Security Board (SSB)** to run the Social Security program, then just a social insurance program. In 1946, the SSB was abolished and the **Social Security Administration (SSA)** was born.[9] Part of the SSA's mission is to make general social security policy and process applications for social security and related benefits.

The enabling act establishes the minimum requirements for an agency. An agency then has great leeway or discretion to set policies and procedures as long as it remains within the bounds of the enabling legislation.

In creating agencies, Congress decides when an agency needs to regulate a particular industry or take care of a national problem. For example, following the terrorist attacks on 9/11, Congress authorized the Office of Homeland Security. Congress can decide what the agency's structure might be and its placement in the existing system of government. The President retains plenary power over any executive branch agencies, including controlling or manipulating agency policies and budgets, as well as appointment of high-level officials. An agency is thus politically accountable to its two "heads"—Congress and the President.

Decision-Making Process

The agency decision-making process consists of three parts: rulemaking, adjudication, and informal adjudication. Rulemaking is an exercise of an agency's legislative power. As noted in the previous sections, notices and comment periods that appear in the *Federal Register* give the public a "heads up" that the agency is contemplating a rule. Final rules are promulgated after the comment period has expired.

An agency can exercise its court-like authority in the adjudication process, a proceeding that is similar to a civil bench trial with an administrative law judge hearing the case. An oral hearing on the record

ACRONYMS

SSA: Social Security Administration

SSB: Social Security Board

takes place, with direct and cross-examination, although without the formal rules of evidence or comprehensive discovery. An example of adjudication is a hearing on the denial of Social Security disability benefits for an individual claimant.

Informal adjudication is a paper review of an agency decision that affects an individual claimant. Going back to the example of a Social Security disability claimant, he or she may receive written reasons of denial of benefits that can be reconsidered if a request for review is made within the applicable time period.

The differences between the usual judicial process and the administrative agency process are explained in Exhibit C–1.

Usual Judicial Process
- Complaint/lawsuit filed in federal district court
- Discovery
- Pretrial motions
- Hearing on motions and court decisions; writs to appellate court, if necessary
- Trial by judge or jury
- Court decision
- Appellate court review (optional); oral argument allowed
- Supreme Court review (discretionary); oral argument allowed
- Time limits set by law and court rules

Administrative Agency Process
- Agency or agency contractor decision
- Complaint about decision starts review—may be by letter or phone
- Limited, informal discovery
- If adjudication is a formal review by ALJ, evidentiary and procedural rules do not apply; testimony allowed; no jury; ALJ decides case
- If adjudication is an informal review by hearing officer in agency, no testimony allowed; hearing officer decides case
- If allowed by statute and agency rules, further appeal may go to appeals board; no oral argument
- If allowed by statute, after exhaustion of all administrative remedies, case can go to U.S. District Court
- Time limits set by agency rules

EXHIBIT C–1: JUDICIAL PROCESS VS. ADMINISTRATIVE AGENCY PROCESS

Judicial Review of Agency Decision Making

The role of the courts in agency decision making is very limited. Most agency decisions are never reviewed by the courts. However, legal challenges that the court system addresses may be on the constitutionality of the creation of the agency or on the extent of the agency's rulemaking authority. For example, there are cases that challenged the Health Insurance Portability and Accountability Act's privacy regulations.

Administrative enabling statutes usually have provisions that afford some type of judicial review. However, most judicial review of individual claimants' cases takes place after the exhaustion of administrative remedies, i.e., **adjudication** and informal adjudication. Since we are primarily concerned with federal laws in this course, it is important to remember that federal courts are courts of limited jurisdiction and a specific grant of subject matter jurisdiction is required.

Researching Agency Decisions and Publications

Agency adjudications are usually published in an official reporter, which may look similar to a regular court reporter. In order to stay up to date, health care regulatory attorneys may subscribe to the agency's reporter as well as to commercial services that report decisions for particular agencies. Using reported agency adjudications as controlling authority may be of limited value since agencies are not bound by the judicial doctrine of *stare decisis*, or "Let the decision stand."[10]

Besides the official sources of the *Federal Register* and the *Code of Federal Regulations*, agencies publish a considerable amount of information helpful to health care professionals as well as the general public. Most agencies have newsletters, fact sheets, and statistical data that can prove useful in understanding an agency's organization and operations. Almost all federal agencies maintain websites where recent and some archived information may be accessed.

Agency Spotlight: Department of Health and Human Services

The cabinet-level agency most closely associated with regulation of health care is the **Department of Health and Human Services (DHHS)**. Within DHHS are a number of smaller agencies whose authority encompasses many aspects of essential health and human services for our country's citizens. Chapter 5 focuses on one of those smaller agencies, the Center for Medicare and Medicaid Services. Take a look at Exhibit C–2 to view the complexity of the agency.

ACRONYM

DHHS: Department of Health and Human Services

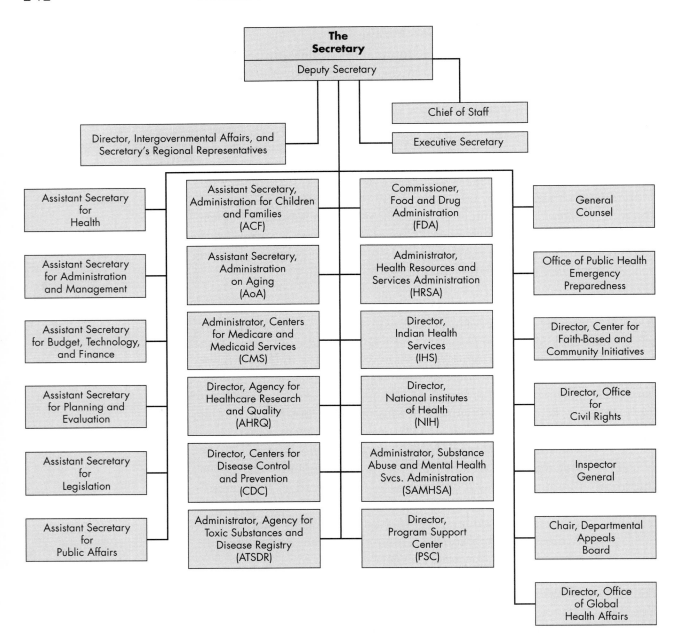

EXHIBIT C–2: DEPARTMENT OF HEALTH AND HUMAN SERVICES ORGANIZATIONAL CHART

DHHS operates more than 300 programs. Some highlights include

- Health and social science research
- Preventing disease, including immunization services
- Assuring food and drug safety
- Medicare (health insurance for elderly and disabled Americans) and Medicaid (health insurance for low-income people)
- Financial assistance and services for low-income families
- Improving maternal and infant health
- Head Start (preschool education and services)
- Preventing child abuse and domestic violence
- Substance abuse treatment and prevention
- Services for older Americans, including home-delivered meals
- Comprehensive health services for Native Americans
- Medical preparedness for emergencies, including potential terrorism[11]

DHHS accounts for a significant budgetary outlay and administers more grant dollars than any other federal agency. In 2007, its budget was $698 billion. The Centers for Medicare and Medicaid Services accounts for more than three-quarters of DHHS's expenditures: Medicare's portion of this budget was 55.5% and Medicaid's portion was 28.6%. The Office of the Secretary provides departmental leadership. The Secretary and the administrators of the agencies within DHHS are appointed by the President. Please refer to Exhibit C–2.

SUMMARY

This appendix reviewed the legislative process from bill introduction through codification of law. However, the laws that govern the health care industry take the form of regulations issued by administrative agencies. Administrative agencies are created by Congress and are located in the executive branch of federal government. Agencies are empowered under enabling acts to regulate certain areas of law. Agencies also have decision-making authority over individual claimants' cases.

Agencies publish notices, proposed rules, and final rules in the *Federal Register*. Final rules are codified in the *Code of Federal Regulations*. Agencies may also publish other materials, including decisions on claimants' cases. Because of the complexity of federal document research, many professionals rely on commercial services to keep them up-to-date.

The Department of Health and Human Services affects the operations of health care organizations. Its budget outlay and its programs are extensive.

KEY TERMS

adjudication: The formal giving, pronouncing, or recording of a judgment for one side or the other in a lawsuit.

administrative law: Laws about the duties and proper running of an administrative agency that are imposed on agencies by legislatures and courts.

enabling statute: A law that grants new powers to do something, usually to a public official, a county, or a city.

prima facie: At first sight; on the face of it; presumably. Describes something that will be considered to be true unless disproved by contrary evidence.

REVIEW QUESTIONS AND EXERCISES

1. Go to the THOMAS website. Can you determine which session of Congress we are in? Review Action Yesterday under the Legislation tab. Choose a bill that interests you and see if you can find its summary, its full text, and any committee action.

2. Go to the GPO Access website and access the *Federal Register*. Using the browse tab, see if the National Institutes of Health published any notices this year.

3. What are the three components of administrative agency decision making?

4. In what form does a new law first appear?

5. Explain the process of agency rulemaking.

6. Go to the GPO Access website again. Try accessing Title 45, Public Health, using the electronic C.F.R. data. Can you find the part that addresses human subject protection?

ENDNOTES

1. See generally, "How Our Laws Are Made," Charles W. Johnson, Parliamentarian, United States House of Representatives, http://thomas.loc.gov/home/lawsmade.toc.html, accessed August 7, 2007.

2. See generally, Federal Register Main Page, http://www.gpoaccess.gov/fr, accessed August 7, 2007.

3. See generally, Code of Federal Regulations Main Page, http://www.gpoaccess.gov/cfr, accessed August 7, 2007.

4. "About the Federal Depository Library Program," http://www.gpoaccess.gov/fdlp.html, accessed August 7, 2007.

5. "List of CFR Sections Affected (LSA): About," http://www.gpoaccess.gov/lsa/about.html, accessed August 7, 2007.

6. See generally, Fox, William F. Jr., Understanding Administrative Law, 4th ed., Matthew Bender, 2000.

7. 5 U.S.C. § 551 et seq.

8. Pub. L. 74-271 (49 Stat. 620).

9. See generally, "The History of Social Security," http://www.ssa.gov/history/history.html, accessed August 7 , 2007.

10. Id.

11. "HHS: What We Do," http://www.hhs.gov/about/whatwedo.html/, accessed August 7, 2007.

SAMPLE LIVING WILL/DECLARATION REGARDING LIFE-SUSTAINING PROCEDURES

Declaration made this _____ day of _____, 200__.

I, _____, a competent person of sound mind, willfully and voluntarily make known my desire that my dying shall not be artificially prolonged under the circumstances below. I hereby declare that:

If my doctor and another health care professional certify that I am likely to die within a short period of time and that life-sustaining procedures will only delay the moment of my death, then I do not want to have life-support treatment.

If my doctor and another health care professional certify that I am in a coma from which I am not expected to wake up or recover within a reasonable period of time, and I have brain damage, and life-sustaining procedures will only delay the moment of my death, then I do not want to have life-support treatment.

If my doctor and another health care professional certify that I have permanent and severe brain damage (e.g. I can open my eyes, but cannot speak or understand) and I am not expected to get better, and life-sustaining procedures will only delay the moment of my death, then I do not want to have life-support treatment.

If my doctor and another health care professional certify that I am in a persistent vegetative state, with no cognizance of the world around me, and I am not expected to get better, and life-sustaining procedures will only delay the moment of my death, then I do not want to have life-support treatment.

I do not want to be resuscitated if I am in a terminal, irreversible condition from which I am not expected to recover within a reasonable period of time.

If any of the above situations apply, I do not want to be kept artificially alive through the use of machines or the insertion of feeding tubes or other means.

In the absence of my ability to give directions regarding the use of life-sustaining procedures, it is my intention that this declaration will be honored by my family, friends, physicians, other health care professionals, and any religious ministers/priests/rabbis as the final expression of my legal right to refuse medical and surgical treatment.

Name _____

Address _____

City and State _____

WITNESS STATEMENT

The declarant is personally known to me. I believe that he/she is competent to make this decision and is making this decision voluntarily. I am not related to the declarant.

Witnesses:

_____   _____

TABLE OF AUTHORITIES FOR EXCLUSIONS

SOCIAL SECURITY ACT	42 USC §	Amendment
1. 1128^	1320a-7	Scope of exclusions imposed by the OIG expanded from Medicare and State health care programs to all Federal health care programs, as defined in section 1128B(f)(1).

MANDATORY EXCLUSIONS		
SOCIAL SECURITY ACT	42 USC §	Type
1. 1128(a)(1)	1320a-7(a)(1)	Conviction of program-related crimes. Minimum Period: 5 years
2. 1128(a)(2)	1320a-7(a)(2)	Conviction relating to patient abuse or neglect. Minimum Period: 5 years
3. 1128(a)(3)*	1320a-7(a)(3)	Felony conviction relating to health care fraud. Minimum Period: 5 years
4. 1128(a)(4)*	1320a-7(a)(4)	Felony conviction relating to controlled substance. Minimum Period: 5 years
5. 1128(c)(3)**(G)(i)^	1320a-7(c)(3)(G)(i)	Conviction of 2 mandatory exclusion offenses. Minimum Period: 10 years
6. 1128(c)(3)**(G)(ii)^	1320a-7(c)(3)(G)(ii)	Conviction on 3 or more occasions of mandatory exclusion offenses. Permanent Exclusion
7. 1892	1395ccc	Failure to enter an agreement to repay Health Education Assistance Loans (HEAL). Minimum Period: Until entire past due obligation is repaid.

PERMISSIVE EXCLUSIONS		
SOCIAL SECURITY ACT	**42 USC §**	**Type**
1. 1128(b)(1)(A)*	1320a-7(b)(1)(A)	Misdemeanor conviction relating to health care fraud. Minimum Period: 3 years
2. 1128(b)(1)(B)*	1320a-7(b)(1)(B)	Conviction relating to fraud in non-health care programs. Minimum Period: 3 years
3. 1128(b)(2)	1320a-7(b)(2)	Conviction relating to obstruction of an investigation. Minimum Period: 3 years
4. 1128(b)(3)*	1320a-7(b)(3)	Misdemeanor conviction relating to controlled substance. Minimum Period: 3 years
5. 1128(b)(4)	1320a-7(b)(4)	License revocation or suspension. Minimum Period: No less than the period imposed by the state licensing authority.
6. 1128(b)(5)	1320a-7(b)(5)	Exclusion or suspension under federal or state health care program. Minimum Period: No less than the period imposed by federal or state health care program.
7. 1128(b)(6)	1320a-7(b)(6)	Claims for excessive charges, unnecessary services or services which fail to meet professionally recognized standards of health care, or failure of an HMO to furnish medically necessary services. Minimum Period: 1 year
8. 1128(b)(7)	1320a-7(b)(7)	Fraud, kickbacks, and other prohibited activities. Minimum Period: None
9. 1128(b)(8)	1320a-7(b)(8)	Entities controlled by a sanctioned individual. Minimum Period: Same as length of individual's exclusion.
10. 1128(b)(8)(A)^^	1320a-7(b)(8)(A)	Entities controlled by a family or household member of an excluded individual and where there has been a transfer of ownership/control. Minimum Period: Same as length of individual's exclusion.

SOCIAL SECURITY ACT	42 USC §	Type
11. 1128(b)(9), (10), and (11)	1320a-7(b)(9), (10), and (11)	Failure to disclose required information, supply requested information on subcontractors and suppliers; or supply payment information. Minimum Period: None
12. 1128(b)(12)	1320a-7(b)(12)	Failure to grant immediate access. Minimum Period: None
13. 1128(b)(13)	1320a-7(b)(13)	Failure to take corrective action. Minimum Period: None
14. 1128(b)(14)	1320a-7(b)(14)	Default on health education loan or scholarship obligations. Minimum Period: Until default has been cured or obligations have been resolved to Public Health Service's (PHS) satisfaction.
15. 1128(b)(15)**	1320a-7(b)(15)	Individuals controlling a sanctioned entity. Minimum Period: Same period as entity.
16. 1156**	1320c-5	Failure to meet statutory obligations of practitioners and providers to provide medically necessary services meeting professionally recognized standards of health care (Peer Review Organization (PRO) findings). Minimum Period: 1 year

NOTE: All exclusions are effective prior to a hearing except those imposed under section 1128(b)(7) [42 USC 1320a-7b(b)(7)], and those imposed on rural physicians under section 1156 [42 USC 1320C-5].

FOOTNOTES

Health Insurance Portability and Accountability Act (HIPAA); Pub. L. 104-191. Enacted August 21, 1996.

*The effective date of the new provisions [sections 1128(a)(3) and 1128(a)(4)], and of the amended provisions [section 1128(b)(1)(A), (B), and section 1128(b)(3)] is August 22, 1996. These provisions apply to offenses occurring on or after that date.

**The effective date for the amendments to sections 1128(b)(15), 1128(c)(3), and 1156 is January 1, 1997.

Balanced Budget Act (BBA); Pub. L.105-33, enacted August 5, 1997.

^The effective date for the amendment to section 1128, and the new provisions section 1128(c)(3)(G)(i) and (ii) is August 5. 1997.

^^The effective date for the amendment to section 1128(b)(8)(A) is September 19, 1997 (45 days after BBA's enactment).

NOTE: Check HIPAA and BBA for effective dates concerning other new amended sections affecting exclusions. This Table of Authorities is available at http://www.oig.hhs.gov.

SAMPLE AUTHORIZATION TO RELEASE PROTECTED HEALTH INFORMATION (PHI)

Patient Name: _____ Date of Birth: _____

Address: _____

_____

Medical record or social security number: _____

Telephone: _____

Authority to Release Protected Health Information

I am the named patient or the authorized representative of the named patient and hereby authorize (name the person or entity that has the PHI) to release the information identified in this authorization from the medical records and provide such information to (name the person or entity to whom the PHI should be sent).

Information to Be Released – Covering the periods of health care
from (date) _____ to (date) _____

Please check type of information to be released:

__ Complete health record   __ Diagnosis and treatment codes
__ Discharge summary   __ History and physical exam
__ Consultation reports   __ Progress notes
__ Laboratory test results   __ X-ray reports   __ X-ray films/images
__ Photographs, videotapes   __ Complete billing record   __ Itemized bill
__ Other (specify below)

_____

Purpose of the Requested Disclosure of Protected Health Information

I am authorizing the release of my Protected Health Information for the following purposes: (Note: A purpose may be "at the request of the individual.")

_____

_____

Drug and/or Alcohol Abuse, and/or Psychiatric, and/or HIV/AIDS Records Release

I understand if my medical or billing record contains information in reference to drug and/or alcohol abuse, psychiatric care, sexually transmitted disease, hepatitis B or C testing, and/or other sensitive information, I agree to its release.
Check one: _____ Yes _____ No

I understand that if my medical or billing record contains information in reference to HIV/AIDS (Human Immunodeficiency Virus/Acquired Immunodeficiency Syndrome) testing and/or treatment, I agree to its release.
Check One: _____ Yes_____ No

Right to Revoke Authorization

Except to the extent that action has already been taken in reliance on this authorization, the authorization may be revoked at any time by submitting a written notice to [insert job title, e.g., Health Information Manager or Privacy Officer] at [insert name of person or entity providing PHI]. Unless revoked, this authorization will expire on the following date, or after the following time period or event:

_____

Re-disclosure

I understand the information disclosed by this authorization may be subject to re-disclosure by the recipient and no longer be protected by the Health Insurance Portability and Accountability Act of 1996.

Signature of Patient or Authorized Personal Representative Who May Request Disclosure

I understand that I do not have to sign this authorization, and my treatment or payment for services will not be denied if I do not sign this form. However, if health care services are being provided to me for the purpose of providing information to a third party (e.g., a fitness-for-work test), I understand that services may be denied if I do not authorize the release of information related to such health care services to the third party. I can inspect or copy the protected health information to be used or disclosed. I hereby release and discharge [insert name of person or entity providing PHI] of any liability and the undersigned will hold [insert name of person or entity providing PHI] harmless for complying with this Authorization.

Signature: _____

Date: _____

Description of authority if Authorized Personal Representative:

_____

Appendix G

SAMPLE BUSINESS ASSOCIATE CONTRACT ADDENDUM

On this _____ day of _____, 200___, the undersigned, **[Name of Covered Entity]** ("Covered Entity") and **[Name of Business Associate]** ("Business Associate") have entered into this "Business Associate Contract Addendum" ("Addendum") for the purposes herein set forth.

I. Business Associate Relationship

(a) Covered Entity and Business Associate are parties to that certain contract, denominated "[Name of underlying contract], dated _____ ("the Agreement"), and pursuant to which Business Associate is performing functions or tasks on behalf of Covered Entity.

(b) Covered Entity is bound by the regulations implementing the Health Insurance Portability and Accountability Act of 1996, P. L. 104-191 ("HIPAA"), 45 C.F.R. Parts 160 and 164 ("the Privacy Rule"). The intent and purpose of this Addendum is to comply with the requirements of the Privacy Rule, including, but not limited to, the Business Associate contract requirements at 45 C.F.R. §§ 164.502(e) and 164.504(e).

(c) In the performance of this Agreement, Business Associate is performing functions on behalf of Covered Entity which meet the definition of "Business Associate Activities" in 45 C.F.R. § 160.103, and therefore Business Associate is a "Business Associate" of Covered Entity.

(d) In order for Business Associate to perform its obligations under the Agreement, Covered Entity must disclose to Business Associate certain Protected Health Information (as defined in 45 C.F. R. §160.103) that is subject to protection under HIPAA and the Privacy Rule.

NOW, THEREFORE in consideration of the mutual promises and covenants contained herein, and in furtherance of the mutual intent of the parties to comply with the requirements of the Privacy Rule, the parties agree as follows:

II. Definitions

(a) <u>Protected Health Information</u>. "Protected Health Information" shall have the meaning found in 45 C.F.R. '160.103, limited to the information created or received by Business Associate from or on behalf of Covered Entity. "Protected Health Information" may also be referred to as "PHI".

(b) <u>Secretary</u>. "Secretary" shall mean the Secretary of the Department of Health and Human Services or his designee.

Terms used in this Addendum, but not otherwise defined herein, shall have the same meaning as in the Privacy Rule.

III. Obligations and Activities of Business Associate

(a) Business Associate agrees not to use or disclose PHI other than as stated in this Addendum or as required by law.

(b) Business Associate agrees to use appropriate safeguards to prevent use or disclosure of the PHI other than as provided for in this Addendum. Business Associate acknowledges receipt of a copy of Covered Entity's policies and procedures for safeguarding PHI, and agrees to implement substantially identical safeguards for PHI in its possession.

(c) Business Associate agrees to mitigate, to the extent practicable, any harmful effect that is known to Business Associate of a use or disclosure of PHI by Business Associate in violation of the requirements of this Addendum.

(d) Business Associate agrees to report promptly to Covered Entity any use or disclosure of the PHI not provided for by this Addendum of which it becomes aware.

(e) Business Associate agrees to ensure that any agent, including a subcontractor, to whom it provides PHI received from, or created or received by Business Associate on behalf of Covered Entity, agrees to the same restrictions and conditions that apply through this Addendum to Business Associate with respect to such information.

(f) Business Associate agrees to provide access, at the request of Covered Entity, and in a prompt and timely manner, to PHI in a Designated Record Set, to Covered Entity or, as directed by Covered Entity, to an Individual in order to meet the requirements of 45 C.F.R. § 164.524.

(g) Business Associate agrees to make any amendment(s) to PHI in a Designated Record Set that the Covered Entity directs or agrees to pursuant to 45 C.F.R. § 164.526 at the request of Covered Entity or an Individual.

(h) Business Associate agrees to make its internal practices, books, and records, including policies and procedures relating to the use and disclosure of PHI received from, or created or received by Business Associate on behalf of, Covered Entity available to the Covered Entity, or to the Secretary, in a prompt and timely manner or as designated by the Secretary, for purposes of determining Covered Entity's compliance with the Privacy Rule.

(i) Business Associate agrees to document such disclosures of PHI as would be required for Covered Entity to respond timely to a request by an Individual for an accounting of disclosures of PHI in accordance with 45 C.F.R. § 164.528.

(j) Business Associate agrees that, in requesting PHI from Covered Entity, and in using or disclosing PHI to others, only the Minimum Necessary information shall be requested, used or disclosed.

IV. HIPAA Security Requirements

Business Associate agrees to:

(1) implement and document, as set forth in 45 C.F.R. § 164.316, Administrative Safeguards, Physical Safeguards and Technical Safeguards that reasonably and appropriately protect the confidentiality, integrity, and availability of the electronic protected health information that it creates, receives, maintains, or transmits on behalf of the covered entity, as required by 45 C.F.R. Part 164, Subpart C, and specifically, but not exclusively, including the following:

    (a) Ensure the confidentiality, integrity, and availability of all electronic protected health information the Business Associate creates, receives, maintains, or transmits on behalf of LSU;

    (b) Protect against any reasonably anticipated threats or hazards to the security or integrity of such information;

    (c) Protect against any reasonably anticipated uses or disclosures of such information that are not permitted or required under the HIPAA Privacy Regulations;

    (d) Ensure compliance with this Section by its workforce;

(2) ensure that any agent, including a subcontractor, to whom it provides this information agrees to implement and document reasonable and appropriate Administrative Safeguards, Physical Safeguards and Technical Safeguards, including at least the requirements set forth in this Section for Business Associate;

(3) report to Covered Entity any security incident of which it becomes aware;

(4) make its policies and procedures, and documentation required by this Section relating to such safeguards, available to the Secretary and to Covered Entity for purposes of determining the Business Associate's compliance with this Section; and

(5) authorize termination of the contract or other relationship by Covered Entity if Covered Entity determines that the Business Associate has violated a material term of the contract or this Business Associate Addendum.

For the purposes of this Section, the following terms have the meaning assigned to them below:

Administrative Safeguards means administrative actions, and policies and procedures, to manage the selection, development, implementation, and maintenance of security measures to protect electronic protected health information and to manage the conduct of the Business Associate's workforce in relation to the protection of that information, as more particularly set forth in 45 C.F.R. § 164.308.

Physical Safeguards means physical measures, policies, and procedures to protect Business Associate's electronic information systems and related buildings and equipment, from natural and environmental hazards, and unauthorized intrusion, as more particularly set forth in 45 C.F.R. § 164.310.

Security Incident means the attempted or successful unauthorized access, use, disclosure, modification, or destruction of information or interference with system operations in an information system.

Technical Safeguards means the technology and the policy and procedures for its use that protect electronic protected health information and control access to it, as more particularly set forth in 45 C.F.R. § 164.312.

Terms used in this Section but not defined herein shall have the meaning assigned to such terms by 45 C.F.R. Part 164, Subpart C, specifically including, but without limitation, 45 C.F.R. § 164.304.

V. Permitted Uses and Disclosures by Business Associate

(a) Except as otherwise prohibited by law or limited in this Addendum, Business Associate may use or disclose PHI to perform functions, activities, or services for, or on behalf of, Covered Entity as specified in this Agreement, provided that such use or disclosure would not violate the Privacy Rule if done by Covered Entity or the minimum necessary policies and procedures of the Covered Entity or the Privacy Rule, including, but not limited to the following:

   (1) Use or disclose PHI for proper management and administration or to carry out the legal responsibilities of the Business Associate, provided that disclosures are Required By Law, or Business Associate obtains reasonable assurances from the person to whom the information is disclosed that it will remain confidential and used or further disclosed only as Required By Law or for the purpose for which it was disclosed to the person, and the person notifies the Business Associate of any instances of which it is aware in which the confidentiality of the information has been breached. Entities to which Business Associate discloses PHI for the purpose of management and administration of the Business Associate shall be deemed "agents" or "subcontractors" of Business Associate, within the meaning of Section 3(e) of this Addendum.

   (2) Use PHI to provide Data Aggregation services to Covered Entity as permitted by 45 C.F.R. § 164.504(e) (2) (i) (B).

VI. Obligations of Covered Entity

(a) Covered Entity shall notify Business Associate of any limitation(s) in its Notice of Privacy Practices in accordance with 45 C.F.R. § 164.520, to the extent that such limitation may affect Business Associate's use or disclosure of PHI. Business Associate acknowledges that it has received a copy of Covered Entity's Notice of Privacy Practices, and agrees to comply with all limitations on use and disclosure of PHI contained therein.

(b) Covered Entity shall notify Business Associate of any changes in, or revocation of, permission by an Individual to use or disclose PHI, to the extent that such changes may affect Business Associate's use or disclosure of PHI.

(c) Covered Entity shall notify Business Associate of any changes in Covered Entity's Notice of Privacy Practices.

VII. Term and Termination of Agreement

(a) <u>Term.</u> The Term of this Addendum shall be effective as of the date of execution by the last party executing same, and shall terminate when all of the Protected Health Information provided by Covered Entity to Business Associate, or created or received by Business Associate on behalf of Covered Entity, is destroyed or returned to Covered Entity, or, if it is infeasible to return or destroy Protected Health Information, protections are extended to such information, in accordance with the termination provisions in this Section.

(b) <u>Termination for Cause.</u> Notwithstanding any other provisions of this Agreement, upon Covered Entity's knowledge of a material breach by Business Associate of the terms of this Addendum, Covered Entity shall either:

    (1) Provide an opportunity for Business Associate to cure the breach. Covered Entity may terminate this Agreement if Business Associate does not cure the breach or end the violation within the time specified by Covered Entity;

    (2) Immediately terminate this Agreement if Business Associate has breached a material term of this Addendum and cure is not possible; or

    (3) If neither termination nor cure is feasible in the sole discretion of Covered Entity, Covered Entity shall report the violation to the Secretary.

(c) <u>Effect of Termination.</u>

    (1) Except as provided in paragraph (2) of this section, upon termination of this Agreement, for any reason, Business Associate shall return or destroy all PHI received from Covered Entity, or created or received by Business Associate on behalf of Covered Entity. Business Associate shall not retain copies of any PHI. This provision shall also apply to PHI that is in the possession of subcontractors or agents of Business Associate.

    (2) In the event that Business Associate determines that returning or destroying the PHI is not feasible, Business Associate shall notify Covered Entity of this determination and its reasons. If Covered Entity agrees that return or destruction of PHI is not feasible, Business Associate shall extend the protections of this Addendum to such PHI and limit further uses and disclosures, for so long as Business Associate maintains such PHI. This provision shall also apply to PHI that is in the possession of subcontractors or agents of Business Associate.

VIII. Miscellaneous

(a) <u>Regulatory References.</u> Any reference in this Addendum to a section in the Privacy Rule means the section as in effect or as amended.

(b) <u>Formal Amendment and Deemed Amendment.</u> The Parties agree to take such action as is necessary to formally amend this Addendum from time to time as is necessary for Covered Entity to comply with the requirements of the Privacy Rule and the Health Insurance Portability and Accountability Act of 1996, Pub. L. 104-191. Regardless of the execution of a formal amendment of this Addendum, the Addendum shall be deemed amended to permit the Covered Entity to comply with HIPAA and the Privacy Rule, as the same may be hereafter amended or interpreted.

(c) <u>Survival.</u> The respective rights and obligations of Business Associate under Section VI (c) of this Addendum entitled "Effect of Termination" shall survive the termination of this Addendum and/or the Agreement.

(d) <u>Interpretation.</u> Any ambiguity in this Addendum shall be resolved to permit Covered Entity to comply with the Privacy Rule.

(e) <u>Material Breach of Addendum as Breach of Agreement.</u> Any material breach of this Addendum by Business Associate shall constitute a material breach of the Agreement, and shall entitle Covered Entity to any of the remedies provided in the Agreement, in addition to the remedies provided herein.

(f) <u>Provisions of Addendum to Control.</u> In the event of any conflict between the provisions of this Addendum and any of the other provisions of the Agreement, including any renewal, extension or modification thereof, the provisions of this Addendum shall control.

(g) <u>Ownership of PHI.</u> The PHI to which Business Associate, or any agent or subcontractor of Business Associate has access under the Agreement shall be and remain the property of Covered Entity.

(h) <u>Indemnification and Contribution.</u> Each party to this Addendum shall indemnify and hold the other harmless from any and all claims, liability, damages, costs and expenses, including attorney's fees and costs of defense and attorney's fees, resulting from the action or omission of the other party. In the event that any liability, damages, costs and expenses arise as a result of the actions or omissions of both parties, each party shall bear such proportion of such liability, damages, costs and expenses as are attributable to the acts or omissions of such party.

(i) <u>Injunctive Relief.</u> Notwithstanding any rights or remedies provided for in this Agreement, Covered Entity retains all rights to seek injunctive relief to prevent or stop the inappropriate use or disclosure of PHI directly or indirectly by Business Associate, or any agent or subcontractor of Business Associate.

(j) <u>Attorney's Fees.</u> If any legal action or other proceeding is brought for the enforcement of this Addendum or in connection with any of its provisions, the prevailing party shall be entitled to an award for the attorney's fees and costs incurred therein in addition to any other right of recovery.

(k) <u>Severability.</u> If any clause or provision of this Addendum is held to be illegal, invalid or unenforceable under any present or future law, the remainder of this Addendum will not be affected thereby. It is the intention of the parties that, if any such provision is held to be illegal, invalid or unenforceable, there will be substituted in lieu thereof a provision as similar in terms to such provision as is possible which is legal, valid and enforceable.

(l) <u>Waiver of Provisions.</u> Failure by either party at any time to enforce or require the strict performance of any of the terms and conditions of this Agreement shall not constitute a waiver of such terms or conditions or modify such provision or in any manner render it unenforceable as to any other time or as to any other occurrence. Any specific waiver by either party of any of the terms and conditions of this Agreement shall be considered a one-time event and shall not constitute a continuing waiver. Neither a waiver nor any failure to enforce shall in any way affect or impair the terms or conditions of this Agreement or the right of either party to avail itself of its remedies.

(m) <u>Choice of Law.</u> To the extent not preempted by HIPAA or the Privacy Rule, the laws of the State of _____ shall govern this Addendum.

(n) <u>Notices.</u> Any notice, demand or communication required or permitted to be given by any provision of this Addendum shall be in writing and will be deemed to have been given when actually delivered (by whatever means) to the party designated to receive such notice, or on the next business day following the day sent by overnight courier, or on the third (3rd) business day after the same is sent by certified United States mail, postage and charges prepaid, directed to the addresses noted below, or to such other or additional address as any party might designate by written notice to the other party, whichever is earlier.

Notices required by this Addendum shall be sent as follows:

Covered Entity:	Business Associate:
[Name]	**[Name]**
[Institution]	**[Institution]**
[Address]	**[Address]**
[City, State Zip Code]	**[City, State Zip Code]**
Copy to:	Copy to:
[Name]	**[Name]**
[Institution]	**[Institution]**
[Address]	**[Address]**
[City, State Zip Code]	**[City, State Zip Code]**

THUS DONE AND SIGNED on the date first written above:

[Name of Covered Entity]:

_____

By:

Title:

[Name of Business Associate]:

_____

By:

Title:

SAMPLE NOTICE OF PRIVACY PRACTICES
Effective April 14, 2003

This notice describes how medical information about you may be used and disclosed, and how you can get access to this information. Please review it carefully.

We respect the confidentiality of your health information and will protect your information in a responsible and professional manner. We are required by law to maintain the privacy of your health information and to send you this notice. We maintain physical, electronic, and procedural safeguards that comply with state and federal regulations to guard non-public personal information from unauthorized access, use, and disclosure. This notice explains how we use information about you and when we can share that information with others. It also informs you of your rights with respect to your health information and how you can exercise those rights.

What is protected health information?

Protected health information is any information on a patient that reveals the state of a person's health; identifies individuals in such a way that it gives a reasonable basis for determining a person's identity; and is created or received by a health care entity such as a physician, hospital, insurer, or other health care organization.

How is health information used or shared?

- We may use the information to help pay your medical bills that have been submitted to us by doctors and hospitals for payment.
- We may share your information with your doctors or hospitals to help them provide medical care to you.
- We may use or share your information with others to help manage your health care. For example, we might talk to your doctor to suggest a disease management or wellness program that could help improve your health.
- We may share your information with our business associates who help us conduct our business operations. We will not share your information with these outside groups unless they agree in writing to keep information protected.

- We may use or share your information for public health or disaster relief efforts, as allowed by law.
- We may use or share your information to send you a reminder if you have an appointment with your doctor.
- We may use or share your information to inform you of alternative medical treatments and programs.
- We may use or share your information with an employee benefit plan's sponsor through which you receive health benefits.

There are also state and federal laws that may require us to release your health information to others. We may be required to provide information for the following reasons:

- We may report information to state and federal agencies that regulate us, such as the U.S. Department of Health and Human Services.
- We may share information for public health activities. For example, we may report information to the Food and Drug Administration for investigating or tracking of prescription drug and medical device problems.
- We may report information to public health agencies if we believe there is a serious health or safety threat.
- We may share information with a health oversight agency, such as the Centers for Medicare & Medicaid Services and the Office of Inspector General for certain oversight activities (for example, audits, inspections, licensure and disciplinary actions).
- We may provide information to a court or administrative agency (for example, pursuant to a court order, search warrant or subpoena).
- We may report information for law enforcement purposes. For example, we may give information to a law enforcement official for purposes of identifying or locating a suspect, fugitive, material witness, or missing person.
- We may report information to a government authority regarding child or elder abuse/neglect or domestic violence.
- We may share information with a coroner or medical examiner to identify a deceased person, determine a cause of death, or as authorized by law. We may also share information with funeral directors as necessary to carry out their duties.
- We may use or share information for procurement, banking or transplantation of organs, eyes, or tissue.
- We may share information relative to specialized government functions, such as military and veteran activities, national security and intelligence activities, and the protective services for the President and others.

- We may report information on job-related injuries because of requirements of your state worker compensation laws.

Other uses and disclosures of your health information may be prohibited or substantially limited by other applicable federal or state law. If one of the above reasons does not apply, we must get your written permission to use or disclose your health information. If you give us written permission and change your mind, you may revoke your written permission at any time, though that revocation will apply only to disclosures made after that date.

What Are Your Rights?

The following are your rights with respect to your health information. If you would like to exercise the following rights, please write our Privacy Officer at the address listed at the end of this statement.

You have the right to ask us to restrict how we use or disclose your information for treatment, payment, or health care operations. You also have the right to ask us to restrict information that we have been asked to give to family members or to others who are involved in your health care or payment for your health care. *However, we are not required under law to agree to these restrictions.*

You have the right to ask to receive confidential communications of information. For example, if you believe that you would be harmed if we send your information to your current mailing address (for example, in situations involving domestic disputes or violence), you can ask us to send the information by alternative means (for example, by fax) or to an alternative address. We will accommodate your reasonable requests as explained above.

You have the right to inspect and obtain a copy of information that we maintain about you in your designated record set. A "designated record set" is comprised of both your medical records and billing records, maintained by us, which are used, in whole or in part, to make decisions about your health care.

However, you **do not have** the right to access certain types of information and we may decide not to provide you with copies of the following:

- information contained in psychotherapy notes
- information compiled in reasonable anticipation of, or for use in a civil criminal or administrative action or proceeding
- any information that is subject to certain federal laws governing biological products and clinical laboratories

In certain other situations, we may deny your request to inspect or obtain a copy of your information. If we deny your request, we will notify you in writing and may provide you with a right to have the denial reviewed.

You have the right to ask us to make changes or amendments to information we maintain about you in your designated record set. Your request must be in writing and you must provide a reason for your request. We will respond to your request no later than 60 days after we receive it. If we make the amendment, we will notify you in writing that it was made. If we deny your request to amend, we will notify you in writing of the reason for the denial. The denial will explain your right to file a written statement of disagreement.

You have the right to receive an accounting of certain disclosures of your information made by us during the six years prior to your request. Please note that we are not required to provide you with an accounting of the following:

- any information collected or disclosed prior to April 14, 2003
- information disclosed or used for treatment, payment, and health care operation purposes
- information disclosed to you or pursuant to your authorization
- information that is incident to a use or disclosure otherwise permitted
- information disclosed for a facility's directory or to persons involved in your care or other notification purposes
- information disclosed for national security or intelligence purposes
- information disclosed to correctional institutions, law enforcement officials or health oversight agencies
- information that was disclosed or used as part of a limited data set for research, public health, or health care operations purposes

If you want an accounting of disclosures of your health information, your request must be in writing. We will act on your request for an accounting within 60 days. Your first accounting will be free. We will continue to provide you with one free accounting upon request every 12 months. If you request an additional accounting within 12 months of receiving your free accounting, we may charge you a fee. We will inform you in advance of the fee and provide you with an opportunity to withdraw or modify your request.

You have a right to receive a copy of this notice upon request at any time. Should any of our privacy practices change, we reserve the right to change the terms of this notice and to make the new notice effective for all protected health information we maintain. Once revised, we will provide the new notice to you by mail. If you have any questions about this notice or about how we use or share information, please contact the Privacy Officer at _____ or write us at _____.

If you believe your privacy rights have been violated, you may file a complaint with us by writing to our Privacy Officer or you may also notify the Secretary of the U.S. Department of Health and Human Services, Office of Civil Rights of your complaint. **We will not take any action against you for filing a complaint.**

SAMPLE POLICY FOR RECORDS RETENTION, MANAGEMENT, AND DESTRUCTION

PURPOSE

To establish the administration of a records management program and to ensure sound records management practices while complying with all applicable federal and state laws and regulations.

SCOPE

This policy shall apply to patient medical and dental records of (business name) maintained by/at (location(s)).

DEFINITIONS

In general, a **record** is recorded information that is generated internally or is received from external sources, and is either utilized in the transaction of business or related to the business's legal obligations. A "record" documents a transaction or verifies a receipt. All records must be tangible and retrievable. Recorded information can be comprised of various characteristics and can be found on different media. Some examples of recorded media are paper, microfiche, microfilm, audio or video recordings, computer hard drives, computer tapes and discs, and electronic messages.

Hospital records means a compilation of the reports of the various clinical departments within a hospital, as well as reports from health care providers, as are customarily catalogued and maintained by the hospital medical records department. Hospital records include reports of procedures such as X-rays and electrocardiograms, but they do not include the image or graphic matter produced by such procedures. (La. Rev. Stat. 40:2144)

Patient communication means the acquiring, recording or transmittal, of any information, in any manner whatsoever, concerning any facts, opinions or statements necessary to enable the health care provider to diagnose, treat, prescribe or to act for the patients; said communications may include, but are not limited to any and all medical records, office records, hospital records, charts, correspondence, memoranda, laboratory tests and results, X-rays, photographs, financial statements, diagnoses and prognoses. (La. Rev. Stat. 13:3734).

Research records are those related to the IRB application, approval/denial, and review process for human subject research, but that are not part of the patient's medical records; records of scientific research related to animals or food, drugs, and/or devices; any records required to be kept by funding agencies or sponsors; or records required to be maintained under federal and/or state law/regulations. (45 C.F.R. 46 *et seq*).

POLICY

It is the policy of (business name) to maintain accurate records, for the legally requisite period of time, in a manner that facilitates easy retrieval. All records are the property of (business name) and the department which originated the record; no staff has any personal or property right to such records regardless of his or her position or the fact that he or she may have developed or compiled them. The unauthorized destruction, removal, or use of any records covered by this policy is prohibited. The falsification or inappropriate alteration of any record is also prohibited.

RELATED POLICIES

(List business's other policies that may be affected)

PROCEDURE

1.0 Records Custodian
     1.1.1 (Insert name) shall designate a Records Custodian for (business name) who shall have authority over Records Retention and shall work with the departments to establish a record retention/destruction schedule.
     1.1.2 The Record Custodian shall maintain a schedule of retention and destruction of records, in accordance with federal and state laws and regulations, and which shall be available in print and on the business's website.

2.0 All Records

    2.1.1 Records which contain medical, dental, research, or other confidential and/or proprietary information shall be maintained in a secure environment to ensure no unauthorized access.

    2.1.2 When records have satisfied their required period of retention, they will be stored in a secure location until destroyed in an appropriate manner, using available resources to ensure destruction.

3.0 Electronic Records

    3.1.1 Electronic records, including but not limited to electronic medical, dental, research, or other confidential and/or proprietary information, shall be created using the business's standard software. Mainframes, servers, PCs, and other devices containing the electronic files must adhere to industry standards and procedures for data security, business continuity, and disaster recovery. All other procedures, timeliness, and requirements for records management and retention shall apply to electronic records.

    3.1.2 All electronic records of the business shall be stored on approved mainframes, servers, PCs, external drives, or other storage media. Electronic records will be backed up according to business continuity and disaster recovery plans. Backup copies of electronic records will be stored off site. (Business name) does not archive, save, or otherwise preserve e-mail transmissions or voice mail.

4.0 Paper, Media, and All Other Records

    4.1.1 All departments should strive to keep the current and previous year's records on site. The number of years for which records are maintained on site beyond that time frame is dependent upon the space constraints of the department.

REFERENCES

45 C.F.R. § 46 *et seq.*

45 C.F.R. §§ 160 and 164 *et seq.*

La. Rev. Stat. 40:1299.96.

La. Rev. Stat. 40:2144.

GLOSSARY

A

accrediting: Giving official status or recognition.

adjudication: The formal giving, pronouncing, or recording of a judgment for one side or the other in a lawsuit.

administrative law: Laws about the duties and proper running of an administrative agency that are imposed on agencies by legislatures and courts.

advance directive: A document such as a durable power of attorney, health care proxy, or living will that specifies your health care decisions and who will make decisions for you if you cannot make your own.

adverse event: (adverse reaction) An unwanted effect caused by the administration of drugs. Onset may be sudden or develop over time.

authentication: Any evidence that proves that a document actually is what it seems to be.

authorization: MCO approval necessary prior to the receipt of care. (Generally, this is different from a referral in that, an authorization can be a verbal or written approval from the MCO whereas a referral is generally a written document that must be received by a doctor before giving care to the beneficiary.)

B

beneficiary: A person to whom an insurance policy is payable.

best evidence rule: A rule of evidence law that often requires that the most reliable available proof of a fact must be produced.

bioethics: The formal study of ethical and moral implications of biomedical advances and new biological discoveries that can advance health-care for patients.

bright line: A rule or principle that is simple and straightforward; a rule that avoids or ignores ambiguity.

C

capacity: Ability to do something such as the mental ability to make a rational decision.

clinical trial: A clinical trial is a research study to answer specific questions about vaccines or new therapies or new ways of using known treatments. Clinical trials (also called medical research and research studies) are used to determine whether new drugs or treatments are both safe and effective. Carefully conducted clinical trials are the fastest and safest way to find treatments that work in people. Trials are in four phases: Phase I tests a new drug or treatment in a small group; Phase II expands the study to a larger group of people; Phase III expands the study to an even larger group of people; and Phase IV takes place after the drug or treatment has been licensed and marketed.

COBRA continuation coverage: Coverage that is offered to you in order to satisfy the requirements of the Consolidated Omnibus Budget Reconciliation Act of 1985 (COBRA). COBRA requires employers to permit employees or family members to continue their group health coverage at their own expense, but at group rates, if they lose coverage because of a loss of employment, reduction in hours, divorce, death of the supporting spouse, or other designated events.

compelling interest: A strong enough reason for a state law to make the law constitutional even though the law classifies persons on the basis of race, sex, etc. or uses the state's police powers to limit an individual's constitutional rights.

compliance: Acting in a way that does not violate a law or terms of an agreement.

consideration: The reason or main cause for a person to make a contract; something of value received or promised to induce (convince) a person to make a deal.

credentialing: Verifying and evaluating the qualifications (education, license, etc.) of a health care practitioner who provides patient care services in a hospital or other health care organization.

creditable coverage: Prior health care coverage that is taken into account to determine the allowable length of pre-existing condition exclusion periods (for individuals entering group health plan coverage) or to determine whether an individual is a HIPAA eligible individual (when the individual is seeking individual health insurance coverage.) Most health coverage is creditable coverage.

D

derivative action: A lawsuit by a stockholder of a corporation against another person (usually an officer of the company) to enforce claims the stockholder thinks the corporation has against that person.

designated record set: A group of records maintained by or for a covered entity that is the medical records and billing records maintained by or for a covered health care provider; the enrollment, payment, claims adjudication, and case or medical management record systems maintained by or for a health plan; or used, in whole or in part, by or for the covered entity to make decisions about individuals.

disenroll: End health care coverage with a health plan, including Medicare.

disparate treatment: Discrimination based on race, color, religion, national origin, age, or disability that results from a practice that does not seem to be discriminatory and was not intended to be so.

disproportionate share hospital: A hospital with a disproportionately large share of low-income patients. Under Medicaid, States augment payment to these hospitals. Medicare inpatient hospital payments are also adjusted for this added burden.

dissolution: Ending or breaking up. For example, dissolution of a contract is a mutual agreement to end it; dissolution of a corporation is ending its existence.

durable power of attorney: A power of attorney that lasts as long as a person remains incapable of making decisions, usually about health care.

E

electronic data interchange: Electronic data interchange refers to the exchange of routine business transactions from one computer to another in a standard format, using standard communications protocols.

Employment Retirement Income Security Act: The Employee Retirement Income Security Act (ERISA) is a law that provides protections for individuals enrolled in pension, health, and other benefit plans sponsored by private-sector employers. The US Department of Labor administers ERISA.

enabling statute: A law that grants new powers to do something, usually to a public official, a county, or a city.

ethics: Standards of fair and honest conduct in general.

F

fraud and abuse: *Fraud:* To purposely bill for services that were never given or to bill for a service that has a higher reimbursement than the service produced. *Abuse:* Payment for items or services that are billed by mistake by providers, but should not be paid for by Medicare. This is not the same as fraud.

G

gatekeeper: In a managed care plan, this is another name for the primary care doctor. This doctor gives you basic medical services and coordinates proper medical care and referrals.

genome: The genetic material that makes up an organism, such as a human being.

guardian: A person who has the legal right and duty to take care of another person or that person's property because that other person (for example, a child) cannot.

H

health care: Care, services, or supplies related to the health of an individual; may include diagnostic, preventative, rehabilitative, maintenance, or palliative care, and counseling, service assessment, or procedure with respect to the physical or mental condition, or functional status, of an individual, or that affects the structure or function of the body.

health care organization: A business or legal entity with a formalized structure whose primary enterprise is delivery of health care items or services. Examples include hospitals and physician networks.

health care provider: A person or organization who provides medical or health services for which payment may be billed and reimbursed. Examples include physicians and hospice facilities. Health care providers may also be health care organizations.

hearsay: A statement about what someone else said (or wrote or otherwise communicated). Hearsay evidence is evidence, concerning what someone said outside of a court proceeding, that is offered in the proceeding to prove the truth of what was said.

I

indemnify: Compensate or promise to compensate a person who has suffered a loss or may suffer a future loss.

independent contractor: A person who contracts with an "employer" to do a particular piece of work by his or her own methods and under his or her own control.

informed consent: A person's agreement to allow something to happen (such as surgery) that is based on a full disclosure or full knowledge of the facts needed to make the decision intelligently.

informed consent document: A document that describes the rights of the study participants, and includes details about the study, such as its purpose, duration, required procedures, and key contacts. Risks and potential benefits are explained in the informed consent document. The participant then decides whether or not to sign the document. Informed consent is not a contract, and the participant may withdraw from the trial at any time.

Institutional Review Board: 1. A committee of physicians, statisticians, researchers, community advocates, and others that ensures that a clinical trial is ethical and that the rights of study participants are protected. All clinical trials in the U.S. must be approved by an IRB before they begin. 2. Every institution that conducts or supports biomedical or behavioral research involving human participants must, by federal regulation, have an IRB that initially approves and periodically reviews the research in order to protect the rights of human participants.

insurable interest: The insured's financial interest in another person or in an object.

insured: The person who pays for the protection of risk; the policyholder.

insurer: The company providing protection against risk.

L

legal health record: A health care provider or organization's business record on a particular patient's medical history and treatment.

legal incompetency: The lack of legal ability to do something; the condition of persons who lack the mental ability to manage their own affairs and who have someone appointed by the state to manage their finances.

living will: An advance directive by which you authorize your possible future removal from an artificial life support system.

***locum tenens* arrangement:** A substitute physician.

M

malpractice: Professional misconduct or unreasonable lack of skill. This word usually applies to bad, incomplete, or unfaithful work done by a doctor or lawyer.

medical staff: Individual health care practitioners who are subject to the bylaws, rules, and regulations of an organized medical staff, usually in a hospital.

medicare beneficiary: A person who has health care insurance through the Medicare or Medicaid program.

O

outlier: Additions to a full episode payment in cases where costs of services delivered are estimated to exceed a fixed loss threshold. HH PPS outliers are computed as part of Medicare claims payment by Pricer Software.

P

patient dumping: Refers to certain situations where hospitals fail to screen, treat, or appropriately transfer patients.

payor or **payer:** In health care, an entity that assumes the risk of paying for medical treatments. This can be an uninsured patient, a self-insured employer, a health plan, or an HMO. The terms *payor* and *payer* are used interchangeably.

preempt: Describes the first right to do anything.

preemption: Describes the first right to do anything. For example, when the federal government pre-empts the field by passing laws in a subject area, the states must not pass conflicting laws and sometimes may not pass any laws on the subject at all.

premium: The payment to the insurer.

prima facie: At first sight; on the face of it; presumably. Describes something that will be considered to be true unless disproved by contrary evidence.

Protected Health Information (PHI): Individually identifiable health information that is written, electronic, or verbal/sign language; that reveals the state of a person's health; that identifies person in such a way that it gives reasonable basis for determining person's identity; and that is created or received by a health care provider.

protocol: A study plan on which all clinical trials are based. The plan is carefully designed to safeguard the health of the participants as well as answer specific research questions. A protocol describes what types of people may participate in the trial; the schedule of tests, procedures, medications, and dosages; and the length of the study. While in a clinical trial, participants following a protocol are seen regularly by the research staff to monitor their health and to determine the safety and effectiveness of their treatment.

provider: Any Medicare provider (e.g., hospital, skilled nursing facility, home health agency, outpatient physical therapy, comprehensive outpatient rehabilitation facility, end-stage renal disease facility, hospice, physician, non-physician provider, laboratory, supplier, etc.) providing medical services covered under Medicare Part B. Any organization, institution, or individual that provides health care services to Medicare beneficiaries. Physicians, ambulatory surgical centers, and outpatient clinics are some of the providers of services covered under Medicare Part B.

Q

qui tam: "*Who* (for himself) *as well as* (for the government)." Describes a lawsuit brought by an individual on behalf of the government, or brought by the government based on an informer's tip. If the government collects a fine or penalty from the lawsuit, the informer may get a share.

R

restrictive covenant: A clause in an employment contract that prohibits the employee from working for the employer's competitors for a certain time period after the contract ends.

S

sanctions: Administrative remedies and actions (e.g., exclusion, Civil Monetary Penalties, etc.) available to the OIG to deal with questionable, improper, or abusive behaviors of providers under the Medicare, Medicaid, or any State health programs.

supplier: Generally, any company, person, or agency that gives you a medical item or service, like a wheelchair or walker.

T

triage: A system of prioritizing patient treatment in an emergency room according to the urgency of the patient's need for medical care.

U

upcoding: Using improper billing codes to charge Medicare or Medicaid for an item or service to receive higher payments than would ordinarily be due for the treatment of a patient.

W

whistleblower: An employee who brings organizational wrongdoing to the attention of government authorities. Government laws protect some whistleblowers.

INDEX